PALESTINIANS IN THE ARAB WORLD

Palestinians in the Arab World

Institution Building and the Search for State

Laurie A. Brand

Columbia University Press
New York

Columbia University Press
New York   Guildford, Surrey
Copyright © 1988 Columbia University Press
All rights reserved
Printed in the United States of America

Library of Congress Cataloging-in-Publication Data

Brand, Laurie A.
Palestinians in the Arab world.

Bibliography: p.
Includes index.
1. Palestinian Arabs—Politics and government.
2. Palestinian Arabs—Societies, etc.—History.
3. Palestinian Arabs—Egypt. 4. Palestinian Arabs—Jordan.
5. Palestinian Arabs—Kuwait. I. Title.
DS113.6.B73   1988   909'.049275694   88-6101
ISBN 0-231-06722-4

For my parents

Contents

PART I. THE FRAMEWORK

PART II. THE CASE STUDIES

Egypt

Kuwait

Jordan

PART III. CONCLUSIONS

Tables and Figures

Preface

The 1947–1949 dispersal of the Arabs of Palestine, and the subsequent inability of their leadership to establish a Palestinian state next to the nascent Jewish state, marked the defeat of the Palestinian national movement. Most studies quickly skim over the 1949–1964 period, although a few mention the development of Fateh or the Arab Nationalist Movement. In fact, however, the seeds of later PLO and Palestinian nationalist development were planted in these early years. Some bore fruit before the establishment of the PLO. Others, frustrated by host regimes, were able to assert themselves only in the wake of the liberation organization's founding and subsequent expansion.

This study seeks to assemble and analyze a part of the previously neglected record of Palestinian political development. It focuses on the Palestinian communities in three Arab host states—Egypt, Kuwait, and Jordan—and within each examines the attempts by Palestinians to organize along corporate/sectoral lines. The emergence and differential development of the General Union of Palestine Students, the General Union of Palestine Workers, the General Union of Palestinian Women, the General Union of Palestinian Teachers, and the Palestine Red Crescent Society are discussed in the context of the three host societies. The study traces their development from just after the dispersal through the mid-1980s and suggests a new framework for understanding Palestinian institutional development in Arab host countries based on the concept of economic and political marginality.

The study of a subject so current and for which so few written materials exist could not have been accomplished without a great deal of support and assistance. I would like to thank the U.S. Department of Education for a Fulbright-Hays doctoral dissertation grant and a Fulbright Islamic civilization grant, which enabled me to conduct field research. Special thanks are due my academic adviser at Columbia University, Professor J. C. Hurewitz, for years of advice and support and for encouraging me in the very early stages of this study to attempt what at the time seemed impossible. For assistance during the course of the field research I am indebted to many, but particularly to those Palestinians who agreed to be interviewed during what was a most difficult time for them and for their national movement. Among those Palestinians and other Arabs who provided special assistance are: Mr. Fakhri Sarraj, director of the PLO office, Cairo; the staff of the American Research Center in Egypt; friends at the office of Dar al-Fata al-ʿArabi, Cairo; Dr. ʿAbd al-Munʿim ʿAbbas, Arab League Palestine Research Unit, Cairo; Dr. M. Kazem Behbehani, vice rector for research, Kuwait University; Dr. Ahmad Bishara, vice rector for academic affairs, Kuwait University; Dr. ʿAbd al-Rida al-Asiri, of the political science department, Kuwait University; Dr. Basim Sirhan of the sociology department, Kuwait University; the staff at the archives of al-Watan and al-Qabas, Kuwait; Mr. Najib al-Ahmad, director of the PLO office, Amman; friends at the American Center for Oriental Research, Amman; Dr. Asʿad ʿAbd al-Rahman of the Shoman Foundation; staff and friends at the UNRWA headquarters and the UNRWA field office in Amman; Dr. Hani al-ʿAmad, Jordan University Library; the staff and researchers at the Palestinian Studies Center, Damascus; and Mr. Hasan ʿAbd al-Rahman, director of the Palestine Information Office, Washington, D.C. Finally, I am grateful to the Institute for Palestine Studies for granting me a three-month leave of absence to gather additional material to revise the study, and to Katherine La Riviere for her invaluable assistance in the final stages of preparation of this book.

For their comments and suggestions for revising the manuscript I would like to thank (in alphabetical order): ʿAbd al-Muʿim Saʿid ʿAli, Shafeeq Ghabra, Rashid Khalidi, Fred Lawson, ʿAfaf Mahfouz, Lina Habbab al-Banna, Hasan Nafaʿa, William Quandt, Emile Sahliyeh, John Swanson, and Constantine Zurayk.

Inevitably, those who assisted me or who provided comments will differ with some aspects of my analysis. Suffice it to say that throughout the course of the study I have striven to be fair, but also to be honest, to present the facts and unfolding of events as the evidence suggested. I remain ultimately responsible for the contents of the book, for my work, and for the instances in which—wisely or not—I accepted or rejected sage advice.

A Note on Transliteration

The transliteration of Arabic names and words leaves an Arabist caught between the exigencies of clarity and the desire to remain faithful to the phonemes in question. Like most of those who have gone before me, I have chosen a middle course, which seems eminently sensible to me, but which will no doubt occasionally annoy the purist and perplex the novice. I have chosen to dispense with what I find to be cumbersome diacritical marks above and below letters to indicate long vowels or emphatic consonents. I have preserved the *'ayn* (') throughout, as well as the *hamza* (') except at the beginning of a word. I cannot, however, bring myself to use the common spellings of the names of the first president of Egypt or the present king of Jordan. The reader will therefore encounter Nasir, not Nasser; Husayn, not Hussein. On the other hand, I have given in to Arabic colloquial (as well as common English) usage in choosing to write Fateh and not Fath.

In short, I have allowed practicality to at times overwhelm my own purist instincts. I ask my readers' indulgence if the system appears byzantine. At very least I believe it is internally consistent.

Abbreviations

AHC—Arab Higher Committee
APG—All-Palestine Government
ANM—Arab Nationalist Movement
ANU—Arab Nationalist Union
AWS—Arab Women's Society
DF—Democratic Front for the Liberation of Palestine
DPO—Department of Popular Organizations
FETUW—Federation of Egyptian Trade Union Workers
FTUJ—Federation of Trade Unions in Jordan
GJWU—General Jordanian Women's Union
GUJS—General Union of Jordanian Students
GUJT—General Union of Jordanian Teachers
GUPS—General Union of Palestine Students
GUPT—General Union of Palestinian Teachers
GUPW—General Union of Palestine Workers
GUPWom—General Union of Palestinian Women
IFATU—International Federation of Arab Trade Unions
IUS—International Union of Students
JNRCS—Jordanian National Red Crescent Society
JSU—Jordanian Students Union
KSF—Kuwaiti Student Federation
KTUF—Kuwait Trade Union Federation
NUJS—National Union of Jordanian Students
PANU—Palestinian Arab Nationalist Union
PAWS—Palestine Arab Workers Society
PFLP—Popular Front for the Liberation of Palestine
PLA—Palestine Liberation Army
PLF—Palestine Liberation Front
PLO—Palestine Liberation Organization
PNC—Palestine National Council
PNF—Palestine National Fund
PRCS—Palestine Red Crescent Society
PRM—Palestinian Resistance Movement
PSU—Palestinian Students Union

SAMED—Palestine Martyrs' Works Society
SSPR—Society of Supporters of the Palestinian Revolution
UAR—United Arab Republic
UNRWA—United Nations Relief and Works Agency for Palestine
  Refugees in the Near East
USTB—Union of Students of the Two Banks
WUJ—Women's Union in Jordan

PALESTINIANS IN THE ARAB WORLD

PART I

The Framework

[1]
Diaspora, State-Building, and Arab Domestic Politics

We are a people without a state and,
therefore, a people without credentials,
without representation, without the
privileges of a nation, without the
means of self-defense, and without any
say in our fate.

Ironically, by the end of 1948, these 1945 words[1] of David Ben Gurion, the chairman of the executive committee of the Jewish Agency for Palestine, described with accuracy the condition, not of world Jewry, but of the Arabs of Palestine. The termination of the British mandate over Palestine and the war that ensued marked not the opening of a new chapter of state-building for the Palestinians, but rather the completion of the first chapter in the frustration of their national movement,[2] a chapter that also included their uprooting and dispersal.

By the time the armistice agreements were signed in 1949 concluding the hostilities, more than half of Palestine had become the new state of Israel. From the point of view of Israel's Jewish citizens, the majority of whom came from abroad, the establishment of sovereignty over the area constituted a major breakthrough in realizing Jewish national aspirations. From the point of view of the indigenous Palestinians, however, an imperial power had withdrawn only to be replaced by a settler colonial regime, with ultimately far more devastating effects for Palestinian society. State-building was initiated and successfully consolidated largely by nonindigenous forces over territory emptied of all but one-tenth of its original inhabitants.[3] The flight or expulsion of a large portion of the indigenous population was virtually a precondition for further development of the Jewish state.

Given the socioeconomic structure of Palestinian society in this period and the policies pursued by the British colonial administration, the Palestinian political leadership and institutions under the mandate were unable to develop a program capable of leading their community to self-determination. Palestinians were further pushed down the road to frustrated political aspirations and national displacement by the nature of the Arab armies' intervention in the conflict on May 15, 1948. The war, the population displacement, and the consequent renting of the sociopolitical fabric of Palestinian society destroyed any chance of consolidating a sovereign Palestinian entity in even a small part of the country. The Hashemite dynasty based in Amman gradually extended authority over, and in 1950 annexed, the territory that has come to be known as the West Bank. The remaining part of Palestine, the Gaza Strip, was occupied by the Egyptian army and kept by its Egyptian military administrators in a state of legal and political limbo—neither annexed nor granted independence. As a result, of all the mandated territories carved into separate political entities by the British and the French following World War I, Palestine alone (at least for its native Arab inhabitants) experienced a brutal interruption in the process of political development.

Transjordan and Iraq in 1932, Lebanon in 1943, and Syria in 1946—all preceded Palestine in being officially released from the colonial hold to join the community of nations as independent countries. Thus, the termination of the British mandate in Palestine in 1948 marked the end of overt colonial government in the Arab East. This is not to imply that all vestiges of the former colonial presence immediately disappeared. To cite only a few examples, Britain not only maintained its hold on the top positions in Transjordan's Arab Legion, it also retained a massive presence in the Suez Canal Zone and substantial influence in Iraq at the court of the ruling Hashemite family. Nonetheless, the task of governing the newly independent countries was at last officially turned over to the indigenous population, however closely tied to or allied with the former colonial power the new leadership remained. They then set about addressing the agenda of state consolidation. Bureaucracies were expanded and diversified to deal with the increasing administrative burdens of a modern state. Military and internal security forces—the modern state's necessary monopoly of the means of coercion[4]—were greatly strengthened, while the state's penetration into a variety of geographic regions and economic sectors grew.

Just as important, a sense of allegiance to country was carefully cultivated. The process of state consolidation in Western Europe occurred—often brutally and violently—over the course of several hundred years,[5] and a particular socioeconomic configuration was required to generate a widespread sense of identification with one's country, modern nationalism. In the Arab world, on the other hand, this process was forcibly telescoped. From a situation under the Ottomans in which primary allegiance was given to family and village or to religion, in the course of only one or two decades entire populations were regrouped in new and previously uncontemplated ways. As a result of marks on the map made by an imperial quill, Middle Easterners were forced to share "nationality" with others from outside their family, village, region, or religion. Nor was the rationale behind such a forced sharing of identity clear. A new Syrian, Iraqi, or Transjordanian identity meant little to people who had originally identified themselves as Halabis, Takritis, or Bani Sakhr. Among the countries of the Arab core only Egypt, for clear and understandable historical reasons, could claim a rather unified sense of nation that roughly corresponded to the physical boundaries of the state. Thus, one of the greatest challenges to the leaders of these countries and, indeed, to those of many others whose boundaries were determined by imperial powers, was and has continued to be the construction of economic, social, and political policies to further the extension of state control over the human and material resources that lie within their borders.

As the process of Arab state consolidation proceeded apace in the former French- and British-controlled territories, Palestinians were still recovering from the shock of dispersal. In Transjordan (which changed its name to Jordan with the incorporation of the West Bank), the state used various means—territorial annexation, extension of citizenship, and certain forms of coercion—to integrate the Palestinians. Other Palestinians, particularly those who had been bureaucrats under the mandate, left for the Gulf, where they became an important part of the nascent government bureaucracies. Others moved east later as teachers, managers, and manual laborers. Yet although they worked *for* the state, as unenfranchised guest workers, they certainly were not part *of* the state in quite the same way that their host country counterparts were. Elsewhere, in Egypt, Gaza, Syria, Lebanon, and Iraq, Palestinians found themselves in a void, lacking even the most basic element of political belonging or inclusion—a passport.

In the absence of a government to defend them, Palestinians throughout the diaspora—even some of those who had become citizens of Jordan—began shortly after the *nakbah*, as the events of 1948 are called in Arabic, to reassemble the pieces of their shattered political, economic, and social structures, rebuilding on the basis of an identity rooted in a shared dispersal, statelessness, and frustration of national aspirations. The institutions they revived or reconstructed—women's, teachers', students', and workers' organizations as well as charitable societies—were the natural heirs of pre-1948 institutions that had served similar purposes. Unconsciously at first, but later certainly purposefully (at least among the politicized), Palestinians began to lay the foundations for a national entity. The process of development that had been so brutally interrupted by the 1948 war was resumed, if under more difficult conditions. The 1950s was a critical formative period for the later development of the quasi-governmental institutions that emerged throughout the Palestinian diaspora, yet these years have been neglected in most studies of Palestinian history and politics.

Therefore, the establishment of the Palestine Liberation Organization (PLO) in 1964 should be viewed, not as the beginning of the first chapter of the reemergence of the Palestinian national movement, but as its conclusion, the natural extension of Palestinian efforts in the 1950s and early 1960s, finally adopted and bolstered by Arab regimes, to establish a national entity. The new organization had all the trappings of a government-in-exile: an executive, a cabinet, a parliament, and an army. Efforts were then undertaken to develop further and extend the sense of loyalty based on identity by mobilizing more members of the various communities and by asserting exclusivity of allegiance through expanding existing popular organizations, like worker and student groups, and through establishing new ones.[6] This represented the same process of cultivating allegiance to country that was going on throughout the Arab world, with one basic difference: the process had to be conducted without the benefit of a sovereign territorial entity to direct it.

Another process was afoot as well. The miserable performance of the Arab armies in the Palestine war had helped to discredit the traditional leadership of the front-line Arab countries. As a result of both this discrediting and the gradual emergence of new economic and political forces in the region, the region experienced a series of coups and revolutions in the 1950s and early 1960s that brought to power younger leaders, of a generally more modest class background than their predecessors. Perhaps because of Palestine's interrupted development, its parallel "revolution" did not come until later. Although the leadership under the mandate had not succeeded in realizing Palestinian national aspirations, many men of this same generation were invited to attend the first meeting of the Palestine National Council in Jerusalem in 1964 at which the establishment of the PLO was proclaimed. In the meantime, however, a younger generation and in many cases a new class of

Palestinians had, through education and hard work, succeeded in establishing itself and its influence in the region, particularly in the Gulf. It was in these countries that the Palestine National Liberation Movement (Fateh), the most prominent among the Palestinian resistance groups, garnered its earliest support, both human and financial.

Fateh officially launched the Palestinian revolution on January 1, 1965, but the real revolution in Palestinian leadership did not come until after the 1967 war, when the second major defeat of the Arab front-line countries claimed PLO chairman Ahmad al-Shuqayri among its victims. A new Palestinian leadership, many of whose members were products of the Palestinian student movement in Egypt who had gone on to found Fateh, was waiting in the wings. Within a short time these individuals had taken control of the PLO and the national movement more generally.

With more representative and popular quasi-governmental institutions developing, the struggle for Palestinian self-determination continued. In a very short time the various commando organizations often called the Palestinian resistance movement (PRM), constructed an extensive civilian and military infrastructure on the East Bank of the Jordan River, intended to lead a "people's war" against Israel. The movement's swift expansion was viewed by the Hashemite regime as a serious challenge to its own authority and legitimacy. Military confrontation was precipitated, and after bloody battles in September 1970 and July 1971, the Palestinian political and military leadership was driven from the country and the movement's infrastructure was destroyed.

To the Palestinians' good fortune regional conditions at the time were conducive to the reestablishment of the movement, this time in Lebanon. And it was in Lebanon that, as the Lebanese state gradually disintegrated, the Palestinians, through swift expansion in the political, military, social, educational, economic, and health fields, came closest to exercising effective, if not internationally recognized, sovereignty over territory and institutions. Despite the fluctuations in the security situation in the country, development continued until 1982, when it was brought to a sudden and brutal halt by the Israeli invasion, as the Arab regimes collectively looked on in silence.

Yet even worse times lay ahead. The destruction of the Palestinian infrastructure and the renewed scattering of the PLO's military and civilian personnel were followed by a rebellion within Fateh. Although the mutiny first erupted as a reform movement, with the goal of checking corruption and other irregularities in the organization, it was soon adopted by Syria as a means of destroying what remained of the PLO's autonomy in order to rein in the organization completely, once and for all. The rebellion ultimately failed, but not before the PLO as a whole had been paralyzed and internecine fighting had claimed many additional lives.

Palestinian national unity in the form of a unified PLO was restored at the April 1987 meeting of the Palestine National Council in Algiers. But the Palestinian quest for national self-determination continues. The PLO's leadership remains in Tunis, while it continues to hold out hope for the reestablishment of a strong Palestinian politico-military presence in Lebanon reminiscent of that of the 1976–1982 era. While such a revival appears unlikely, the prospects for a peace settlement that will fulfill Palestinian national aspirations seem equally if not more remote. As this study will demonstrate, the Palestinian search for state has been and will certainly continue to be an integral part of the larger ongoing process of state consolidation in the Middle East. The lack of a sovereign territorial base means that the fate of Palestinian efforts toward political mobilization and nation-building are, to a far greater degree than those of state actors, inextricably tied, not only to developments in one or two countries, but to conflicts and contradictions throughout the region as a whole.

To understand fully the degree to which Palestinian national aspirations are tied to developments in the Arab countries in which Palestinians reside, it is necessary first to discuss the characteristics of the diaspora, the bases of Palestinian identity, and the nature of Arab–Palestinian relations. It is to these issues that the discussion now turns.

THE BEGINNINGS OF DIASPORA

In November 1947, at the time of the UN resolution to partition Palestine, the Palestinian population totalled 1.3 million. The hostilities and war that followed uprooted and dispersed more than 700,000 of the country's native inhabitants. By the end of the war, only 150,000 Arabs remained in the territory that had become the state of Israel.[7] Some fled or were expelled[8] to the parts of Palestine that did not fall to Jewish forces, areas that subsequently came to be known as the Gaza Strip and the West Bank. Others sought refuge in Palestine's Arab neighbors—Egypt, Transjordan, Lebanon, and Syria. The destruction and displacement caused by the Arab-Zionist conflict rent the political and social fabric of Arab Palestinian society.

Families were uprooted or separated. Agricultural land, homes, and often entire villages were abandoned out of fear, proximity to fighting, or direct intimidation. Many of the villages were then occupied by new Jewish immigrants; others less fortunate were bulldozed and fated to survive only in the memories of their former inhabitants.[9] Those Palestinians who were able took with them a few possessions: money, which at the time must have seemed sufficient for what they assumed would be brief absences; and, certain of return, keys to their homes. Some of the wealthy succeeded in transferring money to accounts outside the country. But the hostilities continued, and the entry of Arab armies into the conflict, ostensibly to defend Palestine, brought further disasters—not the salvation the intervention had promised. For those families divided by the 1949 armistice lines that shaped the young Jewish state the only chances for communication were occasional radio programs that featured refugee messages intended to inform lost family members of their whereabouts and news.

The population movement did not end with the conclusion of the armistice. From the regions of first refuge, many Palestinians headed to other Arab countries, primarily the peninsular states of the Gulf, but later to Europe and points far beyond for both economic and political reasons. Indeed, the post-1948 history of the Palestinians reads like a series of migrations and expulsions: 1950s, movement out of Jordan and Lebanon to the Gulf; mid-1950s, expulsions of Palestinian oil industry workers from the Gulf; early and mid-1960s, increasing movement from the West Bank of Jordan to the East Bank, and from Jordan in general to the Gulf; 1967, flight and expulsion of large numbers, many of them second-time refugees, from both the West Bank and Gaza to Jordan and Egypt; post-1967, migration from the newly occupied territories to the Gulf and to Jordan; 1970–71, the expulsion of the Palestinian resistance from Jordan to Lebanon; 1982, the massive destruction caused by the Israeli invasion of Lebanon, the exodus of Palestinian fighters by boat to all corners of the Arab world, and the intimidation and massacre of thousands by local Lebanese militias. Given such a history, Palestinians' feelings of insecurity and transcience are easily understood.

In addition to these major population movements, there has been constant migration between communities, either for work, study, or marriage, just as there have been periodic expulsions of Palestinians from Israel and the occupied territories and from Arab countries, depending upon the prevailing political climate. The resulting configuration of Palestinian society (or societies), that of a series of scattered and diverse communities, has been called by some the Palestinian diaspora (see table 1.1).

The term "diaspora" has most often been used to refer to the dispersed condition of world Jewry, but has also been applied to other ethnic communities such as the Armenians and Palestinians. In Arabic the most common word for diaspora is *shatat* (dispersal). However, the word *ghurbah* (exile), the root of which carries the meaning of stranger or outsider, is also used.[10] Indeed, from full citizens of Palestine under the British mandate and Ottoman citizens before that, many Palestinians suddenly found themselves stateless, without passports, and subject to the political and economic vagaries of the countries that "hosted" them. As Palestinian writer Fawaz Turki has recounted:

> If I was not a Palestinian when I left Haifa as a child, I am one now. Living in Beirut as a stateless person for most of my growing up years, many of them in a refugee camp, I did not feel I was living among my "Arab brothers." I did not feel I was an Arab, a Lebanese or, as some wretchedly pious writers claimed, a "southern Syrian." I was a Palestinian. And that meant I was an outsider, an alien, a refugee, burden. To be that, for us, for my generation, meant to look inward, to draw closer, to be part of a minority that had its own way of doing and seeing and feeling and reacting."

THE BASES OF PALESTINIAN IDENTITY

According to the criteria most often used to define an ethnic group— culture, language, religion, race, or region[12]—Palestinians in the post-1948 period are an enigma. They have come to live throughout the Middle East and beyond, and thus are no longer residents of a single region. Palestinians may be Sunni Muslims, Druze, or Christians of a variety of sects. (According to the PLO charter, they also include some Jews, but for reasons which will be discussed later, Jewish Palestinians do not figure in this study.) Although dialect may automatically identify them, in many cases they have adapted to the dialect of the country of their residence or have at least been influenced by it and, for all practical purposes, such distinctions are minor. Culturally, they do not differ significantly from other communities of the Arab East, either in clothing, food, or custom. None of this is meant to imply that regional differences do not exist; indeed, the rural/urban distinctions and not

Table 1.1: Palestinian Population Distribution

	1949[a]	1970[b]	1975[c]	1981[d]	1982[e]
Israel	133,000	363,600	436,100	550,800	574,800
West Bank (org.)[f]	440,000	683,700	785,400	833,000	871,600
West Bank (ref.)[g]	280,000				
Gaza (org.)	88,520	345,600	390,300	451,000	476,300
Gaza (ref.)	190,000				
Lebanon	100,000	247,000	288,000	358,207	492,240
Syria	75,000	155,700	183,000	222,525	229,868
Egypt	7,000	33,000	39,000	45,605	35,436
Iraq	4,000	30,000	35,000	20,604	21,284
East Bank	70,000	591,000	644,200	1,148,334	1,189,600
Kuwait		140,300	194,000	299,710	308,177
Saudi Arabia		31,000	59,000	136,779	147,549
Rest of Gulf		15,000	29,000	113,643	64,037
Libya		5,000	10,000	23,759	23,759
U.S.		25,000	28,000	104,856	108,045
Other countries				140,116	143,780
Other Arab countries					52,683
Totals	1,387,520	2,665,900	3,121,000	4,446,938	4,739,158

[a]Figures for 1949 are taken from *United Nations: Report of the Economic Survey Mission of the Middle East* (New York, 1949), p. 22. However, the report lists the original population of the West Bank and Gaza as one figure, 529,000. The figures presented here were derived from taking the figure 88,520 as the original figure for Gaza. See Muhammad 'Ali Khulusi, *Al-Tanmiyyah al-Iqtisadiyyah fi-Qita' Ghaz-zah, Filastin, 1948–1966* [Economic Growth in the Gaza Strip, Palestine] (Cairo: United Commercial Press, 1967), p. 51. This figure was then subtracted from 529,000 and rounded to give an original West Bank population of 440,000.

[b]From Nakhleh and Zureik, *The Sociology of the Palestinians*, table 1.4, p. 31.

[c]*Ibid.*, chart 2, p. 27.

[d]From the *Palestinian Statistical Abstract for 1981* (Damascus: Palestinian Central Bureau of Statistics, 1982). The figures for Saudi Arabia and the rest of the Gulf appear high.

[e]From the *Palestinian Statistical Abstract for 1983* (Damascus: Palestinian Central Bureau of Statistics, 1984). There has been no statistical abstract published since 1984. In 1987, estimates of the total population had reached five million.

[f]Original population.

[g]Refugee population added as a result of the 1947–49 war.

the so-called national ones consecrated by European-imposed borders are often the more salient. However, such regionalisms are viewed as subcultural variations and not as bases of ethnically distinctive communities.

Arab nationalism first emerged in Syria after the Young Turks, the group that deposed Sultan Abdulhamit in 1909, instituted a policy of Turkification, which disturbed many of the Ottoman Empire's Arab subjects.[13] Small groups of Arab nationalists—primarily young urbanites from traditionally wealthy and powerful families—began to advocate Arab unity as a defense against the new discriminatory Ottoman policies. The nascent ideology's basic tenet was that the Arab nation (qawm) extended across state or imperially drawn boundaries and constituted an integral and separate unit on the basis of shared history, culture, and language.

Thus, according to the definition of the qawm, Palestinians are Arabs. Yet, concomitantly, another identity, the sense of belonging to a smaller unit, the watan (homeland), operates. The emergence of a Palestinian identity separate from or in addition to an Arab identity derived in part from the experience of some young Arab nationalists from Palestine who served in Faysal's Damascus-based Arab government (1918–1920).[14] Perhaps more important to the further development of a separate national identity (wataniyyah) among Palestinians, however, was the threat to the Arab character of Palestine posed by Zionism and its program of encouraging Jewish immigration and settlement, especially after the imposition of the British mandate over Palestine, which included support for the principle of a Jewish National Home in Palestine. Since the 1947 UN resolution to partition Palestine and the dispersal that followed, several factors have converged to bind Palestinians more firmly together as distinct from other Arabs: the shared loss of homeland; the fact of having been unable to exercise the right to self-determination; the struggle to preserve and assert traditions and history despite the disruption of scattered exile; and the desire to return.

However, analyses of Palestinian or other Arab actions on the basis of whether identification is proclaimed with the qawm or the watan produce distortions. In effect, such analyses view developments from above, from the ideological level, and therefore tend to overlook the ground-level political and economic context that is in fact responsible for activating one identity or another. Therefore, discussions of the fate or treatment of the Palestinian refugees that focus on qawmiyyah (adherence of loyalty to the qawm) or its absence fail to produce adequate explanations of Arab or Palestinian behavior. Indeed, they obscure rather than elucidate.

In this light it is significant that Palestinians have generally not sought assimilation, nor were they seeking assimilation after the 1947–49 war. The preoccupation during the immediate postwar years was physical survival. With the exception of those living within the boundaries of historical Palestine—currently Israel and the occupied West Bank and Gaza Strip—they seek self-determination *outside* the countries in which they reside. In general, then, Palestinians in the diaspora seek separate rights as a means and not as an end. For example, the PRM, insofar as it sought during the 1969–1970 period to overthrow the Hashemite regime in Jordan (and not all groups called for this), aimed, not to establish a Palestinian government, but rather to replace the regime with a government more accommodating to Palestinian demands in order to secure for itself a base from which to launch military operations against Israeli targets without Jordanian government interference. The ultimate goal remained the liberation of the homeland, not the establishment of a Palestinian state in Jordan as an alternative to self-determination in Palestine.

Given this background, it is useful to view individuals as Dov Ronen does, as "bundles of identities." According to Ronen, the fact that people choose to group together on the basis of language, religion, race, and the like results from their interaction with other groups.[15] Another analyst, Jeffrey Ross, contends that outside factors actually impose a group's identity upon it.[16] More likely, both processes—personal choice and imposition from outside—activate a given identity, with the degree of input from each source variable and depending upon the individual and his or her situation. Furthermore, the identity a person or group will choose or have chosen for it is not predetermined or fixed. While religion may prove salient in one period, language, class, or region may take on greater significance in another, depending upon the configuration of economic and political forces in society and how they affect the individual.

Therefore, the historical experience of direct and continuing confrontation with Zionism and the resulting dispossession and statelessness have been the most basic factors that have shaped—not created— a Palestinian identity and nationalism as distinct and separate from other Arab nationalisms. It was the Arab Palestinians, the "non-Jewish residents of Palestine" as they were called in the mandate instrument, who collectively, and for no reason other than that they resided in the territory carved out by the British and designated to be the site of a

Jewish National Home, experienced loss of homes, land, and life. It also explains why the native Jewish community in Palestine could activate a Jewish, as opposed to a Palestinian, identity. Moreover, had the British set aside Transjordan *and* Palestine as the site for the Jewish National Home and had Transjordan witnessed the same fighting, human displacement, and occupation as Palestine, analysts today would likely be writing of the Palestinian/Transjordanian diaspora or identity.

LIFE AND ORGANIZATION IN THE DIASPORA

For those Palestinians with relatives in Beirut, Damascus, or other major Arab urban centers, the shock of the uprooting was somewhat mitigated. Family ties often provided a source of refuge and facilitated efforts to begin anew. Generally urban themselves and often from upper-class Palestinian families, these Palestinians had the financial resources to reestablish themselves in business or the professions. A few of the wealthy were even able to purchase citizenship in Egypt and Lebanon. Some of those who rendered outstanding services to the developing oil states in the Gulf were later granted citizenship as well. Palestinian women who married host state nationals could thereby become citizens.

The lot of the Palestinian peasantry was quite different. From the early days, a large percentage of the Palestinian refugees was grouped together into camps by international relief agencies. The camps consisted of conglomerations of tents later replaced by small block structures with makeshift tin roofs, situated far from urban areas.[17] Poor, politically vulnerable, and angry, whatever the country of refuge, camp dwellers have largely remained the wards of the UN Relief and Works Agency for Palestine Refugees in the Near East (UNRWA). Opportunities for upward mobility have come primarily through vocational training, highly prized scholarships to Cairo or Beirut, or migration to the Gulf. By 1954, the refugees in Jordan had received citizenship (although, largely owing to a property ownership requirement, the camp dwellers were effectively disenfranchised until the passage of the 1986 Election Law); however, in Lebanon, Syria, and Gaza they were subject to the vagaries of political and economic currents. Egypt and Syria did eventually issue refugee travel documents (*watha'iq al-safar*), but the worth and utility of these papers rest several precarious steps below those of passports.

Nonnational status often led Palestinians to encounter severe discrimination in employment. Egypt and Syria gradually lessened restrictions and offered both education and employment to Palestinians on a par with their own nationals. Lebanon imposed the most severe work restrictions and excluded Palestinian children from government schools. Therefore, for all but the wealthy, UNRWA schools remained virtually the only avenue to higher education. For many families, particularly those with limited resources, schooling for children, especially for sons, seemed to offer the best opportunity for upward mobility and increasing economic security in a situation where political security was virtually unachievable.

Despite the obstacles, throughout the developing diaspora communities Palestinians began efforts to reconstitute their shattered society. Part of the process of reconstitution involved reviving institutions that had operated under the mandate; the other required establishing additional federations or societies to respond to new needs created by conditions in the diaspora. This study examines five of the most important of these institutions as they developed in the Palestinian communities in Egypt, Kuwait, and Jordan. Specifically, it analyzes the origins and evolution of the General Union of Palestine Students (GUPS), the General Union of Palestine Workers (GUPW), the General Union of Palestinian Women (GUPWom), the General Union of Palestinian Teachers (GUPT), and the Palestine Red Crescent Society (PRCS or Hilal). These are not the only Palestinian institutions operating in the diaspora;[18] they were selected for examination because they were among the first to emerge, served the largest sectors of the population, and had the greatest influence in the respective communities.

The study covers the period from 1948 through 1987. The year 1948 marked the mass population movement out of Palestine and hence the disruption of Palestinian society and institutions. Previous studies of the Palestinians have generally ignored or only superficially treated the years between 1948 and 1964.[19] As a result, the reorganization and mobilization of the Palestinians appear to emerge from a political and organizational void. The misperception stems from both the paucity of English source material and a common anti-Palestinian and anti-Nasir bias that lead writers to attribute the emergence of the Palestine Liberation Organization totally to the schemings of the Egyptian president rather than to any incipient trends in the Palestinian communities.

Indeed, two of the institutions examined in this study were founded before the creation of the PLO (the GUPS in 1959 and the GUPW in 1963), yet discussions of the Palestinian national movement rarely mention, much less analyze these organizations. A few studies of the post-1948 period have chronicled the activities of such organizations

Table 1.2: Palestinian Organizing and Regional Developments

Regional Developments	Palestinian Activity in Egypt	Palestinian Activity in Jordan	Palestinian Activity in Kuwait
1948–49—Palestine war 1950—Jordan annexes West Bank		1951—Palestinian Arab Workers Society (PAWS) is closed	
1952—Egyptian Free Officers' revolution	1952—Yasir 'Arafat becomes president of Palestinian Students Union	1952—PAWS reopens under Jordanian name	
		1953—UNRWA teachers form a union	
1956—Nationalist gov't elected in Jordan; Suez War 1957—Nationalist gov't in Jordan is dismissed; martial law imposed			Ongoing ANM organizing
1958—Egyptian-Syrian union 1959—Promulgation of Kuwaiti nationality law 1961—Breakup of Egyptian-Syrian union; Kuwaiti independence	1959—Founding of GUPS		
1963—Israel announces Jordan River water diversion plan 1964—PLO Founded	1962—Founding of League of Palestinian Women 1963—Founding of GUPW		1962—Fateh begins greater recruiting 1963—Founding of Palestinian Workers' Committee 1964—Founding of Palestinian Women's Committee
1967—June war; Gaza and West Bank occupied; Arab regimes discredited		1965—Fateh begins military activity; GUPWom founded 1966—Husayn closes all PLO offices 1967–1968—Fateh medical services expand to become the PRCS; UNRWA	1966—Founding of Palestinian Teachers' Chapter 1967—Major population influx follows the war

1968—Commando groups rise to power in the PLO. Military activity against Israel increases	teacher agitation leads to formation of the GUPT	
	1968—GUPS branch founded	
	1969—GUPT proclaimed	1969—PRCS branch founded; GUPT branch founded
1970—Civil war in Jordan; death of 'Abd al-Nasir	1970—Most Palestinian institutions closed or destroyed	1970—GUPWom branch founded
1970–71—Expulsion of Palestinian resistance from Jordan	1971—All remaining independent Palestinian organizations closed; [all popular organizing takes place in joint Palestinian-Jordanian framework]	
1973—October war	1974—Gradual reopening of skeletal offices	
1974—PLO designated sole representative of Palestinians by Arab League		
1975–76—Civil war in Lebanon		1976—PLO schools closed; Palestinians are reintegrated into Kuwaiti gov't schools
1977—Sadat goes to Jerusalem	1977—GUPS protests result in student expulsions	
1979—Signing of Camp David accords	1979—All PLO offices (except GUPW) are closed	1980—Islamic student league splits from GUPS
1982—Israeli invasion of Lebanon	1982–83—Palestinian offices begin to reopen	
1983—Split in Fateh; inter-Palestinian fighting		
1985—Palestinian-Jordanian cooperation formalized	1986—All Fateh offices are closed	
1986—Palestinian-Jordanian cooperation suspended		
1987—PNC unity session is held in Algiers	1987—Offices of Palestinian organizations are closed in April; reopened in November.	

Additional entries (secondary column):

1969—PRCS branch founded

1970—GUPT branch founded

as Fateh, the Ba'th, and the Arab Nationalist Movement (ANM),[20] which antedate the PLO and certainly played key roles in the development of the Palestinian national movement and its changing ideology. This study, however, concentrates not on political parties but rather on the Palestinian communities and their creation of institutions designed to respond to the changing needs of a people dispersed.

Therefore, before turning to a discussion of the theoretical framework used in this study, it is useful to review briefly the position of the Palestinian communities vis-à-vis the three host countries. A more detailed presentation of the origins and nature of the five institutions to be studied follows in chapter 2.

THE CASE STUDY COUNTRIES

The three host countries examined in detail in this study differ in size, population, regime type, economic structure, and strategic interests. Likewise, the position and treatment of Palestinians in them vary widely and so, consequently, has the development of the Palestinian communities' political and social infrastructure.

Jordan was the only Arab state to annex a part of historical Palestine and grant citizenship to its Palestinian residents en masse. King 'Abdallah had dreamed of one day ruling a large Arab kingdom and the annexation of the West Bank put him one step closer to the realization of his dream. Furthermore, the additional territory and population of the West Bank constituted important resources that the original Hashemite Kingdom had lacked. Palestinians were made citizens to legitimate the annexation and to further the Hashemite claim to their economic and human capital.

Concomitant with their enfranchisement, however, all official remnants of a separate Palestinian identity were swept or legislated away. The majority of Jordan's population has been native Palestinian or of Palestinian descent, but the regime has developed in such a way that Palestinian and Jordanian identities inside the kingdom are at best in conflict and at worst mutually exclusive. During the 1950s the Palestinians in Jordan were not so concerned with expressing an autonomous identity as they were with opposing the regime, which many viewed as inimical to Arab nationalist goals in the region. Not until the 1960s did a stronger sense of Palestinian separatism emerge.

Throughout most of Jordan's subsequent history the conflict between identities has led to periodic suppression of overt manifestations—institutional or otherwise—of a separate Palestinian identity. Only in times of political and economic siege has the Jordanian regime allowed open expressions of "Palestinianness."

Egypt, on the other hand, hosts a minuscule Palestinian presence— 7,000 in 1948 and only about 33,000 in 1970, a figure representing less than .01 percent of the population. Furthermore, although concentrated in Cairo, Palestinians have not been isolated in refugee camps as have many of their countrymen in Jordan; the community in Egypt can in no way be described as cohesive. It includes a handful of the very wealthy, but they do not wield anything resembling economic clout, periodic proclamations regarding the number of Palestinian millionaires in Egypt notwithstanding. Similarly, the small number of working-class Palestinians residing in Egypt has never posed a challenge to the interests of the Egyptian working class.

Until 1967 Egypt occupied the Gaza Strip as a buffer between itself and Israel and closely controlled Palestinian activity there. The government monitored Palestinian activity in Egypt equally carefully; however, given the small numbers and the great symbolic value involved in granting Palestinians privileges, the emergence of independent Palestinian organizations in Egypt posed no threat as long as they operated within acceptable political bounds. Cairo remained a center of Palestinian political gathering and activity into the early 1970s. However, the gradual improvement in American-Egyptian relations (first marked by the signing of Sinai II in 1975) witnessed a concomitant deterioration in Egyptian-Palestinian relations. The darkest years were 1978 (the Camp David negotiations) through 1981 (Sadat's assassination). The advent of Mubarak and, more importantly, the 1982 Israeli invasion of Lebanon opened the way for a gradual normalization of relations between Egypt and the PLO.

The third country, Kuwait, exhibits somewhat different characteristics. In the first place, it was not a country of first refuge. The monoproduct, oil-based economy of the tiny amirate—in 1957 the native Kuwaiti population stood at 113,622—drew Palestinians to its oil industry and expanding bureaucracy in small numbers in the 1950s and gradually increasing numbers in the 1960s. Palestinians moved to Kuwait by choice, although the move was generally dictated by economic necessity. Kuwait did not offer citizenship, but it is unlikely that the possibility of future naturalization was even pondered. Most Palestinians had no idea that they would stay in Kuwait long enough to raise families and see their children raise families there. They went as guest laborers and therefore had no reason to be concerned about their exclusion from participation in the political system. Ironically, as the size of the community grew to include a large number of well-educated individuals employed in teaching, the bureaucracy, the media, the liberal professions, and business, Palestinians came to exercise a marked, if unquantifiable, degree of political power.

On the military level, Kuwait has never been a confrontation state. Its distance from the Arab-Israeli battlefield has largely ensured that an armed Palestinian presence would not develop in the country. The challenge posed by the Palestinians derives from their cohesiveness and large numbers as well as the revolutionary disposition of some which, combined with domestic opposition groups, might threaten the regime if conducive regional or domestic conditions obtain. As a result, Palestinians have enjoyed relative freedom to develop separate institutions; yet the state has not hesitated to curtail Palestinian activity in times of exceptional regional tension (e.g., 1970 and 1975–76).

THE THEORETICAL FRAMEWORK

This study seeks to explain the differential development of quasi-state institutions across the Palestinian diaspora. To do so, it will make use of Charles Tilly's political mobilization model.[21] The model's most basic unit is the contender—any group that applies pooled resources to influence government policy. In this case, the contender is the Palestinian community. The model postulates three basic elements affecting mobilization: interests (the reasons for mobilizing); organization (leadership, community resources, structures already in place); and opportunity (primarily the degree of coercion or repression that may be used against the contender). From the perspective of this analysis, the most crucial of these elements is that of opportunity.

Tilly argues that opportunity is a product of the degree of repression directed against the contender's activity and the threat posed by that activity, or the degree to which the government or other groups associated with the state are vulnerable to the contender's gains. Opportunity may be viewed as having two further elements as well: the contender's marginality (degree or lack of integration into the host state) and the amount of coercive force possessed by the state.

Theorists formerly used the term "marginality" to refer either to the urban poor who lived in slums or to a particular region not fully integrated into the country's economic system.[22] However, the term has broadened in meaning. Political marginality may include the de facto or de jure limitation of political participation in decision making, voting, unionization, or work with voluntary organizations. On the socioeconomic level, structural characteristics or particular policies may generate marginality. In both cases, limits develop that preclude the absorption of the totality of the population into a country's economic and social system.[23]

According to what criteria may one determine the degree of political marginality or its opposite, integration? In the case of the Palestinians the following variables are most important: the size of the community both relatively and absolutely in a given country; the percentage of Palestinians granted citizenship; Palestinian representation in the state bureaucracy; and any indirect forms of pressure they may exercise through their presence in the media, the universities, and the like. Economic marginality is also in part determined by the size of the Palestinian community relative to the host state population. In addition it derives from the role of Palestinians in the host state labor market and, of course, the structure and nature of the host state economy.

Tilly argues that opportunity is in part a product of threat, the degree to which the government or other groups in the state are vulnerable to the contender's gains and, therefore, are likely to oppose his actions. One would expect that the less the threat posed to the host state regime by separate Palestinian institutions, the less likely the state will be to use coercive force to prevent their emergence and consolidation. Moreover, the more integral and less marginal the Palestinians are to the productive structure of a given state's economy, the greater the threat their separate organizing poses to the state and the less likely the host regime will be to permit independent Palestinian organizations from emerging. Conversely, the more marginal the Palestinian community to the productive structure of the country, the greater the chance that some freedom to mobilize on a separate basis will develop.

In considering the second factor related to opportunity, state coercive force, two elements must be examined: ability and willingness. A state's ability to use coercive force depends upon resources, tangibles like a strong army and internal security force and intangibles like regime legitimacy, which enable it to use the tangibles. Therefore, a regime may perceive a threat, but for material or ideological reasons be unable to repress it. An economic or political crisis may render a regime unable to pursue repression, or at least compel it to exercise restraint. In Jordan after the 1967 war, for example, humiliating defeat and economic disaster virtually forced the regime to allow the Palestinian *fida'iyyin* (commandos) more freedom of movement and action until the armed forces were able to regroup. When the army had recovered sufficiently from the effects of the war the Jordanian regime crushed the PRM.

On the other hand, a state's willingness to use repression is based upon its own economic and political situation, that is, the degree of threat perceived in the contender's mobilizing efforts. A regime may have the ability to suppress a Palestinian organization, but for a variety of reasons not perceive the organizing efforts as a threat and therefore see no reasons to exercise its coercive force. For example, during the Nasir period in Egypt, the Egyptian regime boasted an efficient and repressive internal security apparatus. Nevertheless, the regime chose not to exercise its ability to prevent the emergence of Palestinian students', women's, and workers' organizations. In Gaza, however, where Palestinians composed the entire population and their activity posed a clear security threat because of the shared border with Israel, the Egyptian military administration thwarted Palestinian efforts to organize.

On the basis of the argument presented here and the brief discussions of the host states that preceded it, one would expect Palestinian institutions in Egypt to be strongest, followed by those in Kuwait, with those in Jordan trailing the field. Clearly, however, other variables related to the element of resources have been decisive. The size of the Palestinian community—both absolutely and relative to the host state—and its wealth figure heavily in the equation. The quality of leadership and the cohesiveness of the community also affect the possibilities for mobilization. Finally, the degree of support—both financial and moral—supplied by the host state and the host population influence the chances for organizing.

Each of the case studies to follow examines and analyzes the socioeconomic, political, and legal structure of the host state as it relates to the Palestinian community within, to other Palestinian diaspora communities, and to the reemerging Palestinian national movement. The changing economic and regional political conditions that affected the Palestinian communities and their attempts to organize are also discussed. The chapters on the individual host states are then followed by chapters that examine five Palestinian institutions in terms of their differential organizational development in each of the case study countries. As this chapter has demonstrated, the argument throughout the individual studies will focus on the concept of "opportunity to organize" as shaped by the Palestinian communities' marginality and the host states' willingness to employ coercive force against Palestinian organizing efforts.

[2]
The Long Road Back: The Evolution of a Palestinian Entity

Although many Palestinians had already fled or been expelled from their homes when the establishment of the state of Israel was declared, May 15, 1948 did not mark the final defeat of the Palestinian national movement. The competing interests of the Arab countries bordering Palestine, played out on the post-May 15 battlefield, were in part responsible for increasing the scope of the 1948–49 debacle. While the armies of these countries were busy staking out their claims or attempting to thwart the claims of rival states, those Palestinians who sought independence for their country continued to struggle to establish a sovereign government. Their struggle was ultimately futile, but this neglected chapter of Palestinian history links the mandate period with the post-*nakbah* era, and an examination of it is necessary in order to understand subsequent Palestinian institutional development.

TRANSJORDAN, EGYPT, AND THE ALL-PALESTINE GOVERNMENT

Throughout March, April, and early May 1948 with the British mandate over Palestine drawing to an end, the Palestinian political leadership, the Arab Higher Committee (AHC), tried without success to convince the Arab League of the need to establish a Palestinian government. Internal rivalries that had divided the Palestinian national movement during the mandate persisted as the state of Israel was proclaimed and Arab armies joined the battle for Palestine. The rivalry between Egypt and Transjordan for leadership in the Arab world, combined with King 'Abdallah's territorial ambitions in Palestine, served only to exacerbate internal Palestinian factionalism. 'Abdallah was prepared to oppose any proposal for Palestinian representation or self-government. With supporters on both the East and West banks of the Jordan, Transjordan's monarch had no intention of permitting any other Arab body to extend sovereignty, whether in content or simply in name, over any part of Palestine and thus diminish his claim to the territory of the former mandate not incorporated into the state of Israel. Egypt, on the other hand, had no annexationist ambitions in Palestine, but was not prepared to watch 'Abdallah swallow up the rump of the country unopposed.[1]

On July 10, in response to the request of the AHC, but also with King 'Abdallah's objections to the formation of a Palestine government in mind, the general secretariat of the Arab League announced its agreement to the establishment of something much less than the AHC had asked for: a temporary civilian administration. Composed of ten members, its authority was to extend to all parts of Palestine in which Arab armies were deployed, and it was to be charged with handling routine services and other matters. Owing to the turmoil in the country and perhaps as well to the fact that this proposal fell far short of what the AHC had had in mind, the civil administration plan was never implemented.[2]

As the fall 1948 session of the UN General Assembly approached, and the need for a Palestine representative to attend grew, Jamal al-Husayni of the AHC set out on a tour of Arab capitals in late summer 1948 to attempt once again to garner Arab state support for the idea of establishing a Palestine government. This time, despite King 'Abdallah's opposition, on September 23 the formation of the All-Palestine Government (APG) (Hukumat 'Umum Filastin) was announced in Gaza.[3] Not to be so easily defeated, King 'Abdallah fought the new entity through an organized campaign of opposition, and Arab League mediation efforts through Lebanese Prime Minister Riyadh al-Sulh proved fruitless. Therefore, in order to affirm the legitimacy of the APG and popular Palestinian support for it, the AHC called for the convening of a Palestine National Council in Gaza.

Presided over by the mufti of Jerusalem, al-Hajj Amin al-Husayni, the council met on October 1, 1948. It was attended by more than ninety people:[4] some members of the AHC, municipality heads, leaders of local councils, former members of Palestinian delegations to Europe, tribal shaykhs, and representatives of the engineers', doctors', pharmacists', and lawyers' unions.[5] Ahmad Hilmi 'Abd al-Baqi, a prominent member of the AHC, was confirmed as president of the APG. In addition to naming a council of ministers for the government, the Gaza conference proclaimed Palestine's complete independence as a free, democratic, and sovereign state—a rather empty proclamation at a time when Palestine was in the throes of a war that left no part of the country free or sovereign.

With territorial ambitions of his own in the parts of Palestine held by the Iraqi army and the Arab Legion, ʿAbdallah called for a parallel meeting of pro-Hashemite or antimufti Palestinians in Amman to be held on the same day as the conference in Gaza. The Amman conference, as it was called, denounced the Gaza meeting and proclaimed the unity of Palestinian and Jordanian land. (Nevertheless, the APG received the recognition of all Arab states but Transjordan, and its representative, Ahmad Hilmi, was invited to the October 30, 1948 meeting of the Arab League Council.) ʿAbdallah's anti-APG campaign continued as three more conferences were convened in which pro-Hashemite West Bank Palestinians pledged their loyalty to the monarch as king of Palestine.[6] The best known of these meetings, the Jericho conference, was held on December 1, 1948, and was attended by some one thousand Palestinians. This conference was followed by the Ramallah conference on December 26, 1948. The year concluded with the final gathering in the series, the Nablus conference, attended by 400 to 500 people and convened by the municipal leaders of Nablus, Jenin, Tulkarm, Qalqiliyyah, and ʿAnabta. The message of the conferences was clear: the attendees wanted the two banks of the Jordan to be united under the leadership of King ʿAbdallah.

In the wake of these conferences, and as Transjordan set in motion a series of steps that lay the groundwork for the annexation of the West Bank in 1950, the Arab League's support for the APG gradually faded. The APG had tried to mend the rift with ʿAbdallah by sending Ahmad Hilmi and Jamal al-Husayni to Amman for discussions, but results of the trip were negligible. In a move to placate ʿAbdallah and restore Arab unity, the Arab League Council refused to invite APG representatives to attend its 1949 session.

The fact that the APG's only "sovereign" territory was occupied by the Egyptian military further hampered the activities of the abortive government. Following the conclusion of the Egyptian-Israeli armistice agreement in February 1949, the mufti, the moving force behind the APG, and several members of the National Council, were "summoned" to Cairo by the Egyptian government. Thus, even Egypt, the primary patron of the APG, began to reign in the activities of the ill-fated body. In Cairo, Amin al-Husayni was placed under surveillance and his movements were restricted. Subsequently, the APG headquarters were transferred from Gaza to Cairo—ostensibly in order to move them closer to the Arab League facilities—and an Egyptian military administration was established in Gaza.[7] Thereafter, the APG's responsibilities were limited to issuing travel documents, helping Palestinian students, and assisting in certain matters related to refugees.[8]

Effectively emasculated by the loss of Palestine, the Egyptian occupation of Gaza, Hashemite opposition, and waning Arab League support, the APG never developed into a political force of any consequence. Further, general political conditions and meager monetary resources led some of the APG's members to boycott it and others to resign.[9] An Arab League resolution of 1952 stated that

> In view of the end of activity of the All-Palestine Government because of current conditions, the president of the government shall be a representative for Palestine in the Arab League Council and 1500 LE will be provided for him to ensure the expenses of his office for 1952.[10]

Financial support from the Arab League continued until the death of APG president Ahmad Hilmi in 1963, when the APG was officially, if belatedly, laid to rest.

THE PROBLEM OF PASSPORTS

The influx into the areas surrounding Palestine of large numbers of refugees effectively rendered stateless by the developments in that country demanded some form of coordinated Arab action. However, largely owing to the fact that the refugee problem was initially viewed as only temporary, no Arab League action was taken until 1952. On September 14 of that year the league council called for the issuance of a standard passport to refugees to facilitate their travel and movement. Such a document was not to be viewed as an acceptance of the political status quo nor was it intended to diminish in any way the refugees' separate identity or rights as Palestinians. Despite the resolution, no action was taken and no documents were issued.

Almost a year and a half later, a league resolution of January 27, 1954 called upon the government of each country in which refugees lived or in whose care they were (as was the case of Egypt vis-à-vis the Palestinians of Gaza) to issue temporary travel papers according to the request of each refugee and provided the Palestinian had not obtained citizenship from another country. An October 14, 1955 resolution called for the issuance of travel documents to Palestinians living outside the Arab world. These Palestinians were to have the right to choose from which Arab country they preferred to receive the document. On April 9, 1959 the league requested that member states deal sympathetically with the refugees they hosted who sought work opportunities, but insisted at the same time that their Palestinian identity be preserved.[11]

In all cases, Arab League decisions were nonbinding and, therefore, largely ignored. No country wanted to be perceived as accepting the status quo and no country but Jordan had any desire to lay the groundwork for permanent incorporation of the Palestinians. Probably just as important, none of the people involved in the decision-making process had any firsthand experience or were concerned with what it meant in practice—in terms of travel, residence, educational and employment opportunities, and access to health care and the like on a daily basis—to be a stateless Palestinian. Consequently, despite the various resolutions adopted by the Arab League, no uniform identity paper or travel document was ever designed for or issued to the Palestinians.

ORIGINS AND DEVELOPMENT OF THE PLO

The failure of the APG to establish itself as a Palestinian government of substance and authority left the Palestinian people and their national aspirations in a political void, deprived of any form of recognized institutional expression. The decade that followed was one of reexamination, regrouping, and rebuilding. For those Palestinians inclined to political activity, transnational (and generally outlawed) political parties and organizations that covered the entire ideological spectrum beckoned: from the Communist party to the Arab Nationalist Movement and Ba'th to the Muslim Brethren. And, as the case studies will demonstrate, some Palestinian organizations—workers', women's, and students' groups—continued to operate during the 1948 war or began to regroup immediately thereafter.

The 1956 Suez War and, in particular, Gaza's first encounter with Israeli occupation appear to have been major shocks to Palestinian awareness about the imperatives of reorganizing. The experience of resisting the occupation together, regardless of political orientation, was a catalyst with long-term implications. The founding of Fateh, the timing of which can be placed at 1957 or 1959, depending upon the source consulted,[12] may even been viewed as in part a reaction to the war and occupation.

The founding of the United Arab Republic (UAR), the Egyptian-Syrian unity, in February 1958 was the first concrete manifestation on the state level of the growing Arab nationalist sentiment in the region. It therefore served as a further impetus to organizing among Palestinians.

Indeed, shortly after the union the first legislative and executive councils for Gaza were set up. While all members of the legislative council were appointed and most of the members of the executive council (selected from the legislative council) were officers drawn from the Egyptian administration, this development was the first of its kind anywhere in the Palestinian diaspora, where communities had been effectively deprived of any form of open political activity for nearly ten years.[13]

Concomitant with the establishment of the legislative council, a framework for Palestinian popular organizing was codified in the form of the Palestinian Arab Nationalist Union (PANU) (al-Ittihad al-Qawmi, al-ʿArabi al-Filastini).[14] According to Jamal al-Surani, a member of the legislative council, pressures emanating from Gazans themselves for some kind of comprehensive form of Palestinian political expression led, after discussions with one of Nasir's top men, Kamal Rifʿat, to the convening in Cairo in 1958 of a conference attended by Palestinians from the communities in Gaza, Syria, and Egypt (including al-Hajj Amin al-Husayni and Ahmad Hilmi). As a result of the conference, a preparatory committee was formed to organize Palestinians along the same lines as the Arab Nationalist Union (ANU) (al-Ittihad al-Qawmi al-ʿArabi), which had been formed in the UAR after the dissolution of all political parties. The mufti objected to the formation of the PANU on the grounds that the AHC, which he headed, was the recognized representative Palestinian body and that attempts to establish organizations like the PANU were intended to undermine and replace the AHC. His objection was apparently the reason for his departure from Egypt in 1959.[15]

The mufti's objections had no impact and a structure composed of local and regional councils and higher executive councils (all with offices and employees) provided for in the PANU's constitution was established and a budget (from the Egyptian military administration) was allotted. Elections for the union were held throughout the UAR and Gaza in 1960—the first time Palestinians had exercised the right to vote in direct elections in years. Despite its symbolic significance, however, the union had virtually no active role in Palestinian political life. The lack of effective content in the mother structure, the ANU in Egypt and Syria, was naturally reflected in the Palestinian experience, whether in Syria, Egypt, or Gaza. As a result, the activities of the PANU were limited to dealing with some of the Palestinians' daily problems with the host governments and providing services like water and electricity to the refugee camps.[16] With the dissolution of the UAR in 1961 the PANU officially ceased operations in Syria and officially ceased to function in Egypt and Gaza shortly thereafter.

The Arab League's concern with Palestine finally shifted from periodic obligatory proclamations and resolutions to a more concerted drive for Palestinian reorganization in March 1959, at the initiation of the UAR at an Arab League Council meeting. The council's call at this meeting for a study of how to reorganize the Palestinians was followed in April 1960 by a similar resolution, which also called for the establishment of a Palestinian army. Further meetings in April and June 1961 addressed the same issues. In each case, however, it was the Hashemite Kingdom of Jordan which, for one reason or another, opposed suggestions or expressed reservations. 'Abdallah was long gone, but his grandson and successor, Husayn, had the same concern that the establishment of a Palestinian government or entity would by its very nature challenge Hashemite rule over the part of Palestine annexed by the kingdom in 1950.[17]

Periodic meetings continued until January 1964, when Arab League Council summit discussions finally gave longtime Palestinian diplomat Ahmad al-Shuqayri a green light to initiate an official organizing campaign. Following the death of Ahmad Hilmi, Shuqayri had been chosen to replace the APG president as Palestine's representative in the Arab League Council. Shuqayri's efforts, bolstered by Egyptian president Nasir, finally led to the convening in Jerusalem in May 1964 of a new Palestine National Council which then proclaimed the founding of the Palestine Liberation Organization (PLO) (for more details see the discussion on the founding of the PLO in chapters 3 and 9).

Given the Palestinians' dispersal and lack of recognition internationally, it seems unlikely that the PLO or any other diasporawide Palestinian political entity could have been established and recognized without the support of the front-line Arab states, none of whom, as the case studies will later detail, sought to create the framework for independent Palestinian military initiatives. Indeed, the most important activity of the fledgling organization was expansion on the diplomatic front: the quest to open information offices and efforts to draw more of the community into some form of participation. It is therefore important to stress that the PLO has been a dynamic organization and that in the pre-1969 period the PLO was not completely synonymous with the Palestinian national movement. Nor was the PLO, at its founding, the political-institutional manifestation of a military movement. Quite the contrary, when first assembled, the PLO was largely a gathering of traditional and influential notables. Guerrilla activity was far from the minds of the PLO's conservative founders, most of whom envisioned Palestinian participation in the military struggle as that of units of a Palestine Liberation Army, under the command of and fighting alongside conventional Arab armies.

Not until 1969 did the political-commando organizations (tanzimat or fasaʾil) like Fateh come to power in the PLO. The advent of this new, younger leadership heralded a surge in the organization's activity and in national consciousness among Palestinians. In addition to the changes in generation and leadership, significant structural developments have also occurred. The PLO that was founded in 1964 in Jerusalem differed markedly from the PLO of the "people's war" of 1969–1970 Jordan, and from the organization's increasingly bureaucratized form in post–civil war, pre-1982 Lebanon. Since the loss of Lebanon as a political "capital" in 1982, diplomatic activity and maneuvering have once again assumed primacy over military activity.[18]

Particularly in Arab countries where they have large constituencies, PLO offices have gradually assumed most of the responsibilities of embassies and consulates, in addition to directing certain social welfare services. Subsidies for students, assistance with matters relating to passports, permission to take part in the hajj (the pilgrimage to Mecca), certificates for marriage, supervision of youth groups and sporting teams—all may fall under the PLO's jurisdiction, depending upon the country. The offices are also places of gathering for political discussions and celebrations marking events of national significance.

Although further articulated and often with altered or more developed roles, the basic structures of the PLO established in 1964 have remained. The Palestine National Council (PNC) is the quasi-parliament of the PLO and the Palestinians. Since 1969, its members have represented roughly the proportional strength of the tanzimat (based on their general support throughout the communities as well as their financial resources and military strength)[19] and the social and popular organizations, which are the focus of this study. In addition, prominent Palestinians from diverse backgrounds and delegates from each of the diaspora communities sit on the PNC.

The Central Council, created in 1973, comprises members of the PNC and implements its resolutions. From the ranks of the Central Council the PNC chooses the executive committee, which operates on a full-time basis and whose members carry individual portfolios, much like cabinet ministers. The Department of Popular Organizations (DPO)[20] and the Department of Social Affairs, which are responsible for the institutions examined in detail in this study, are each represented by a member of the PLO executive committee. Other departments include the military, planning, information, political, occupied homeland affairs, and education departments; the Palestine National Fund (similar to a treasury department); and so forth. The executive committee comprises a maximum of fifteen members and, like the PNC, its composition generally reflects the proportional strength of the commando organizations.

Although the commando organizations have been best known for their military operations, Fateh, the Popular Front for the Liberation of Palestine (PFLP), the Democratic Front for the Liberation of Palestine (DF), and Saʿiqah (in Syria and Lebanon) have, in addition to their military units, developed structures similar to those of political parties. Diasporawide, Fateh is the overwhelmingly preferred *tanzim*, and many who call themselves independents lean in its ideological direction. Fateh's predominance stems from its more conservative, nationalist approach to politics as compared with the leftist/Marxist orientation of the PFLP or the DF. The DF and PFLP have much smaller followings, but because many of their supporters are intellectuals, they have influence in media, educational, and professional circles. Palestinians identify with the *tanzimat* in much the same way that Americans identify with the political party of their choice.

The predominance of a particular *tanzim*, in this case Fateh, in the executive committee of the PLO derives not only from its military strength, but also from the degree to which its ideology or leadership enjoys popularity among Palestinians. Fateh's Yasir ʿArafat has been PLO chairman since 1969, managing to retain his control over the diverse and dispersed factions of the PLO even in the face of the 1983 mutiny within Fateh in Lebanon—the most serious challenge to his leadership and the unity of the organization in its history. The reunification of the PLO at the eighteenth session of the PNC in Algiers in April 1987 reaffirmed and reinforced ʿArafat's leadership role.

THE POPULAR OR MASS ORGANIZATIONS

Since its inception, the PLO has stressed the importance of popular or mass organizing. Under Shuqayri, the PLO attempted to implement a scheme of regional, as opposed to sectoral, representation whereby political offices were to be opened across the Arab world in cities in which Palestinians were concentrated. Proponents of the idea hoped that these offices would eventually serve as polling places of a sort. The program was called *al-tanzim al-sha'bi* (popular organizing). But, for internal political reasons—the democratic precedent it would have set and the fact that it would have forced the PLO to conduct censuses of Palestinians—the idea garnered no support in the Arab host states. Although offices for *al-tanzim al-sha'bi* were established, at least in Egypt, they were never permitted to carry out the task for which they had been conceived.

With regional political organizing effectively forbidden, sectoral organizing, which had begun with the GUPS in 1959 and the GUPW in 1963, probably appeared to be the only viable alternative. The fact that many Arab states had their own national sectoral organizations for students, women, writers, lawyers, and the like certainly facilitated efforts. Such federations or unions were particularly diverse and articulated in Egypt, where renewed Palestinian sectoral organizing received its first green light from President Nasir.

Despite initial attempts to establish and encourage popular organizations, the pre-1968 PLO was unable to achieve any large-scale success in attracting the interest of the Palestinian communities. A major obstacle lay in the fact that the PLO itself was too elitist to be able to attract much mass support. Moreover, Jordan's closure of the PLO headquarters in Jerusalem in 1966, and the Arab defeat and loss of the West Bank and Gaza in 1967, certainly further inhibited the PLO's efforts to expand. Indeed, not until after the rise of the commando organizations in the PLO did the organization inject new life into sectoral organizing.

Whereas the original PLO leadership envisioned that Palestinian regular units would fight alongside conventional Arab armies, for the Palestinian *fida'iyyin* armed struggle meant military operations initiated independently of Arab regimes. In their view, popular organization was meant both to complement and to prepare Palestinians for a more active role in the armed struggle. Organizing along sectoral lines developed as the means by which each individual Palestinian could participate in the national movement according to interest or occupation. Of course, participation on the basis of political ideology was also an option that those who joined one of the *tanzimat* exercised. Members of the *tanzimat* usually played dual roles as they also constituted the core of the leadership and active membership of the mass organizations—student, women, worker, and similar groups—which drew others who were not as politically or ideologically committed. Palestinian resistance movement (PRM) theorists argued that in the mass organizations the more politically mobilized would serve to politicize and recruit others. In this way, these institutions were to serve as the link between the resistance's leadership and the population at large.[21]

THE INSTITUTION CASE STUDIES

Let us now turn to the organizations to be covered in the case studies. Although two of the institutions under review were established before the PLO—the GUPS in 1959 and the GUPW in 1963—since the PLO's founding they have all come to consider themselves bases of the PLO. The Department of Popular Organizations, under whose jurisdiction these institutions fall, has a staff that includes representatives from each. Assistance from the department to the organizations ranges from financial support to occasional intercession with Arab governments on behalf of the union or individual members.

Although each of the institutions serves a particular sector of the Palestinian population, their goals are quite similar.[22] The four mass organizations stress a commitment to popular organizing as the most effective means of raising political consciousness and preparing Palestinians to participate in the national movement. Each claims exclusivity in representing its constituency, within Palestinian as well as international circles. The GUPW, in particular, emphasizes its military role, although the others also consider armed struggle central to the liberation movement. In addition to political concerns and goals, the unions are aware of their duty to defend their members' rights and privileges as workers, women, teachers, and students.

As a social institution, the PRCS (Hilal) focuses on somewhat different issues.[23] The primary thrust of PRCS activity has been the provision of humanitarian and health services to all those in need—military and civilian, Palestinian and non-Palestinian—in time of war or peace. The Hilal also trains medical personnel and monitors cases of families separated by war as well as cases of Palestinians imprisoned in Israeli jails or detention centers.

Figures 2.1, 2.2, 2.3, and 2.4 depict the relatively uniform internal structures of the unions. The lowest level, the chapter, is usually city based. Officials at this level sit on regional committees which elect an administrative committee to choose delegates to the biennial branch (countrywide) conference. The branch conferences send representatives to a general meeting to designate the union's administrative council

Figure 2.1. Organizational Structure of the GUPS

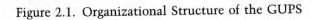

Figure 2.1. Organizational Structure of the GUPS

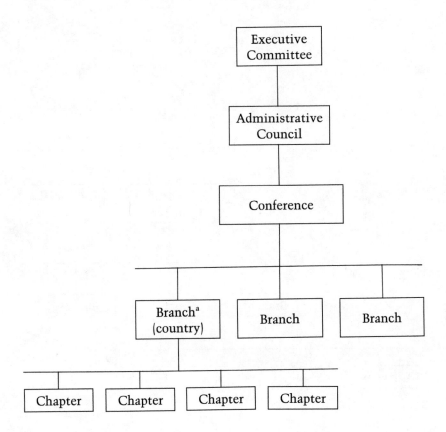

[a]The organizational structure on the branch level closely resembles that of the general union.

Figure 2.2. Organizational Structure of the GUPW

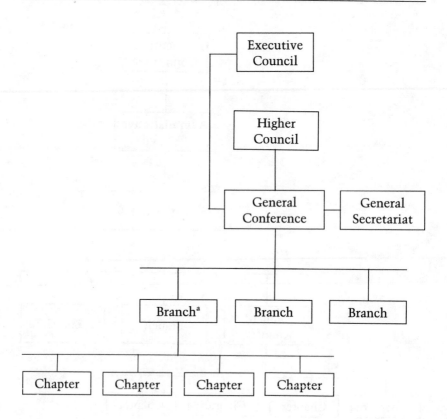

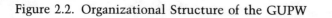

^aThe organizational structure on the branch level closely resembles that of the general union.

Figure 2.3. Organizational Structure of the GUPWom

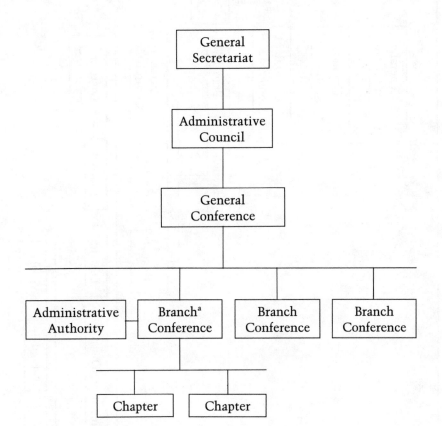

[a]The organizational structure on the branch level closely resembles that of the general union.

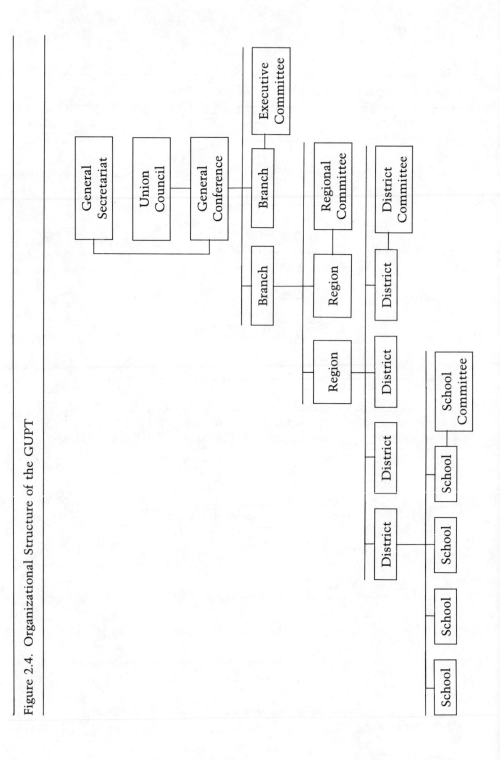

Figure 2.4. Organizational Structure of the GUPT

which in turn selects the executive committee—the highest level of the union.[24]

The degree to which these organizations have been active has varied from institution to institution, country to country, and period to period. The reasons for their successes or failures in mobilization and leadership form the core of the case studies. The skeletal histories presented below are intended as brief introductions to the development, functions, and range of activities of each. Detailed presentations follow in subsequent chapters.

The General Union of Palestine Students (GUPS)

This group took the lead in reorganizing the Palestinians. In 1959, members of organizations of Palestinian students in Cairo, Alexandria, Asyut, Beirut, and Damascus met in Cairo to form a Palestinian student federation. This federation, the GUPS, gradually proceeded to establish new branches in other parts of the Arab world and beyond. Initially opposed to the composition of the nascent PLO in 1964, former GUPS members gradually rose to top leadership positions in the organization after 1967. The GUPS distinguished itself as the first purely Palestinian organization to regroup after the 1948 dispersal, the first to call for a Palestinian entity, and the first to demand mandatory conscription for Palestinians. It has remained the most influential of the mass organizations and has continued to serve as a major vehicle for politicizing and mobilizing young Palestinians.

The General Union of Palestine Workers (GUPW)

The GUPW was an offspring of the Palestinian Arab Workers' Society, which had organized and rallied labor in Palestine under the mandate. Launched from Cairo in 1963 by a group of former Palestinian trade unionists who fled Jordan in 1957, the GUPW proceeded to open branches throughout the Arab world. During the 1960s it was strongly influenced by the political orientation of its patron regime, Egypt. In the 1970s, however, its headquarters was transferred to Damascus where the leadership passed to former ANM members who came to constitute the core of the PFLP. In keeping with the GUPW contention that the workers are the most natural proponents of the Palestinian struggle, large numbers of *fida'iyyin* have traditionally been recruited from its ranks.

The General Union of Palestinian Women (GUPWom)

Like the workers' union, the GUPWom was heir to a rich pre-1948 tradition. From its inception in 1919, the women's movement combined dedication to the national cause with humanitarian concerns. After the 1948 war, some members of the Palestinian Arab Women's Society took refuge in Beirut, the only place where the society continued to operate under its original name. Work also continued in small, diverse organizations on the West Bank. In the meantime, groupings of Palestinian women outside historical Palestine began to form. Calls for reorganization from Beirut, Jerusalem, and the PLO itself finally resulted in the convening in 1965 of a large conference which established the GUPWom.

The operation of the union's leadership was disrupted first by Jordan's closure of all PLO offices in 1966 and later by the occupation of Jerusalem by the Israelis in 1967. The headquarters moved temporarily to Cairo and then to Amman. Despite organizational disarray, on the ground level the union's work expanded between 1965 and 1970, as women entered activities as diverse as literacy classes and military training. A conference held in 1974 in Beirut reorganized and reinvigorated the upper-level structure. The union then proceeded to develop its most articulated infrastructure in Lebanon in the 1975–1982 period. The union has always stressed the need to improve Palestinian women's economic, legal, and social status, and the obligation to prepare women for a more active part in the liberation movement.

The General Union of Palestinian Teachers (GUPT)

After the 1967 war, UNRWA attempted to introduce into its rules and curriculum changes to which its Palestinian teachers objected. Teachers' committees in existence in Jordan since 1953 joined younger groups in Lebanon and Syria to fight the new regulations, which they viewed as unfair to teachers and students. Strikes erupted throughout the areas of UNRWA operations in the spring of 1968, but not until the fall did a month-long strike finally force the agency to meet the teachers' demands. After the successful strike, the PLO's DPO approached the UNRWA teachers to convince them to form a general union. The ground-level organization had developed during the process of mobilizing against UNRWA. The PLO oversaw the drafting of a constitution and selected the top leaders. The GUPT's president since its founding, Jamil Shihadah, is also vice-president of the international teachers' federation, thus giving the GUPT an important voice in international teachers' gatherings.

The Palestine Red Crescent Society (PRCS or Hilal)

Young Palestinian doctors and medical personnel who were members of Fateh and recognized the inadequacy of medical services available to refugee camp residents through UNRWA founded organized medical services in Salt, Jordan in 1967. Expanded facilities, mobile and underground, were gradually created in response to the multiplying *fida'i* attacks on Israeli targets and Israeli preemptive and retaliatory raids. Contributions from Palestinians, as well as from sympathetic foreign governments, began to pour in, thus enabling the organization to widen its range of services. The organization changed its name from Fateh Medical Services to the PRCS, and in 1969 the PNC declared the PRCS the official health organization of the PLO. The Hilal's first and most developed base of operations was Jordan; after the 1970–71 expulsion of the PRM from Jordan and the destruction of the PRCS facilities there, the Hilal moved on to Lebanon and Syria, where it began to enlarge and expand its volume and range of medical services.

As they have developed, the mass organizations have engaged primarily in organizing and informational work. They have stressed activities to promote and preserve traditional Palestinian culture and to address the material concerns of their members and the Palestinian community as a whole. Even the PRCS, effectively the PLO's ministry of health, has played a political role insofar as it has emphasized Palestinian traditional culture and heritage and used its participation in international conferences to bring the Palestinian people and their cause to the fore.

The institutions' achievements most often noted by Palestinians include the reorganization of the Palestinians into independent, representative institutions according to occupation or sector; the development of political consciousness; the establishment of social welfare institutions; and the representation of Palestinians in international forums, which has enabled them to gain wider political recognition and to disseminate information concerning their struggle.

Despite the conditions of political insecurity and uncertainty in which the PLO and its constituent institutions function, they are by no means fragile. Recurrent wars and expulsions have taught Palestinians how to regroup and reorganize swiftly: the 1967 war served as an organizing catalyst; after the civil war in Jordan in 1970–71 Palestinians moved to Lebanon where they developed a highly diversified political and socioeconomic infrastructure; since the destruction of the 1982 invasion they have moved headquarters to Tunis, while expanding operations on Cyprus and resurrecting facilities in Egypt, as well as other parts of the Arab world such as Algeria, Iraq, and the Yemens. Indeed, resilience in the face of major losses and setbacks has characterized these organizations in particular and the movement as a whole.

The case studies that follow discuss in greater historical and organizational detail the evolution of the five institutions as part of diasporawide attempts to revive, redefine, and give concrete structure to the Palestinian national movement. As noted in chapter 1, the differential development of the organizations both transnationally and chronologically will be examined with particular emphasis on the socioeconomic order (as most visibly embodied in the legal structure) of the host countries. Within that framework the discussion will focus on the economic integration or marginality of resident Palestinian communities vis-à-vis the economic and political structure of three Arab host states.

PART II
The Case Studies

[3]
The Powerful Patron

By the late 1940s in Egypt, growing economic problems and popular dissatisfaction with, among other things, the continued British presence in the Suez Canal Zone had produced a number of opposition movements, some of which advocated and engaged in antiregime violence. The humiliating defeat suffered by the Egyptian army in the Palestine war only added to the ranks of the opposition in the country. When a handful of young, nationalist officers carried out a bloodless coup in July 1952, none could predict with certainty what direction the new republic might take. Despite an initial flirtation with the West, by 1956 Egypt's dynamic new president, Gamal 'Abd al-Nasir, had become the champion of Arab nationalism, the most powerful and influential leader in the Arab world.

For domestic political reasons Nasir's predecessors had formulated policies that had kept the 1948 influx of refugees from Palestine to a minimum and that severely restricted immigation to Egypt from the most likely provenance, Gaza, an area that came under Egyptian military administration after the creation of the Arab-Israeli armistice regime in 1949. The tiny, fragmented Palestinian community resident in Egypt posed no internal political threat and Nasir continued his predecessors' restrictive policies on immigration from Gaza. However, the Egyptian leader's admission of large numbers of Palestinian (many of them Gazan) students to Egyptian universities and his support, both financial and political, for "the Palestine cause" earned him wide support among the Arab masses. A politicized core of Palestinians had been champing at the bit, awaiting any political opening to reorganize more freely. Nasir gave them their chance.

THE POLITICAL BACKGROUND

The Muslim Brethren (al-Ikhwan al-Muslimun), an Islamic society that emerged in Egypt in the 1930s, was the first Egyptian political faction to take an active part in the events preceding the Palestine war. Although the Brethren had actively opposed the continuing British presence in the country, it was the Palestine issue that provided it with its first opportunity for effective involvement in politics. In 1935 ʿAbd al-Rahman al-Banna, brother of the Ikhwan leader Hasan al-Banna, visited Palestine and met with al-Hajj Amin al-Husayni, the mufti of Jerusalem and the acknowledged leader of the Palestinian national movement.[1] The following year the Brethren collected contributions and engaged in demonstrating, pamphleteering, and speechmaking in support of the Arab general strike in Palestine. In October 1947, before the UN General Assembly's adoption of the partition resolution Hasan al-Banna ordered the branches of the society to prepare for a jihad in defense of Palestine. Composed of trained members of roving guerrilla groups and a secret apparatus, the Brethren's battalions were able to mobilize quickly.[2]

The participation of the Egyptian army in the 1948 war, on the other hand, derived from factors more complex than a shared concern for fellow Arabs or Muslims. The Egyptian monarch, Faruq, sought through Egyptian involvement in the war to assert his leadership in the Arab world over other contenders, especially his primary rival, King ʿAbdallah of Transjordan. The general feeling in the country in support of Palestine as expressed through the political parties and organizations was also clearly a factor.[3] Just as important was the attitude of Egypt's ruling class which, after World War II and the independence of some of the former mandated territories, had the opportunity to expand economically into the Arab East. The establishment of a Jewish state threatened to create a geographic barrier to Egypt's access to the Arab East and to squeeze Egypt out of its markets.[4] When the war failed to uproot the Jewish state, Egypt led the Arab states in interdicting all relations with Israel, a policy it maintained until the Camp David accords in 1979.

The years immediately following the Arab military defeat in Palestine witnessed mounting political discontent and instability in Egypt. Population problems had first begun to plague the country in the 1930s. In 1937, the population of the country was approaching 16 million and was growing at a rate of 1.15 percent per year. By 1947, the population exceeded 19 million and was climbing at a rate of 1.78 percent per year.[5] The population pressure created a steadily increasing labor supply at a time when the urban sector was expanding slowly. Land rents rose sharply while real wages remained constant or declined.[6] The economic difficulties were reflected on the political level in frequent cabinet reshuffles and political violence.

The Egyptian Free Officers' revolution of July 1952 is generally viewed as stemming, at least in part, from the 1948 defeat. Yet, as Nasir wrote in his *Philosophy of the Revolution,* even as cells of the Free Officers gathered during the Palestine war to discuss what was happening, the preoccupation was not with Palestine, but with Egypt. They understood the war and its significance in far broader terms, convinced that the developments in Palestine could just as easily take place in Egypt (or elsewhere) "as long as it resigned itself to the domination of the present factors, elements, and powers."[7]

THE PALESTINIAN REFUGEES IN EGYPT

When the Irgun attacked Jaffa on April 25, 1948, some 3,000 of the city's Arab residents set out for Port Sa'id and Alexandria by boat; another 10,000 to 15,000 went to Gaza. After the first and second ceasefires, additional numbers crossed the Sinai: some accompanied Egyptian army units in their withdrawal; others sought refuge with relatives already living in Egypt.

On the day of the Irgun attack, the Egyptian Ministry of Social Affairs was requested to make preparations to receive Palestinians fleeing from the hostilities in Palestine.[8] The first camp to shelter refugees was established in Cairo in al-'Abbasiyyah, where Palestinians were grouped together in British wartime barracks. However, the refugees soon came in such numbers that in early May, the ministry was forced to set up another camp in al-Qantarah Sharq (on the Sinai side of the Suez Canal). To coordinate relief efforts, on May 9, 1948, the prime minister ordered the establishment of a Higher Committee for Palestian Immigrant Affairs under the presidency of a deputy of the minister of the interior and including representatives of the ministries of social affairs, health, defense, agriculture, and foreign affairs, as well as the director of the General Security Administration. A budget of LE (Egyptian pounds) 300,000 ($1,240,000) was set aside for the committee's relief work.

On September 3, 1948, those refugees housed in al-'Abbasiyyah were moved to al-Qantarah, which remained in operation until September 1949. After the consolidation of the two camps, al-Qantarah counted 11,000 refugees. As time passed, many of the refugees requested permission to leave the camp to reside in Egypt. A committee was formed to examine the case of each refugee. If the refugee had sufficient funds to provide for himself and his family and knew an Egyptian national willing to serve as guarantor, the Passport Office of the Ministry of the Interior issued him temporary residence in Egypt. The length of validity of the residence varied from case to case. The process itself took time and many of those with families outside the camps had to wait months to be reunited.

There were also those Palestinians who arrived before April 25 and were able from the beginning to avoid the camps. Some came and stayed with family members or with friends. Those who had money rented hotel rooms or apartments. For example, Hala Sakakini, the daughter of Palestinian writer and historian Khalil Sakakini, and her family went from Jerusalem to Cairo, where her brother Sari was studying. She wrote on May 16, 1948:

> Up till now we have been very lucky. First of all, upon arriving in Cairo we found two good rooms in a clean hotel. Other families had to live all in one room in dirty hotels. Second, if we had left Jerusalem Saturday [April 25] instead of Friday [April 24] we would have been among the thousands of Palestinian refugees who are living in different camps in Egypt in awful conditions. . . . Heliopolis, where we are living now, has become a Palestinian colony. Every other house is occupied by a Palestinian family.[9]

Despite the efforts of many to leave the camps, some 7,000 refugees remained in al-Qantarah at the war's end. Rather than settling them in Egypt, the Higher Committee decided to appropriate money to enable them to join relatives in other Arab countries. In the meantime, the Egyptian cabinet issued a decree in September 1949 to send al-Qantarah's residents to Gaza. The government concluded an agreement with the Quakers, who had been involved in early refugee relief efforts in Gaza, regarding the transfer of the refugees and that same September al-Qantarah was emptied.[10]

In May 1950, UNRWA (United Nations Relief and Works Agency for Palestine Refugees in the Near East) assumed responsibility for administering what was viewed as temporary relief assistance to the Palestinian refugees. However, when the refugees had first begun to arrive in Egypt, the government had not requested assistance from the UN. Consequently, the refugees who went to Egypt were not registered with the United Nations Relief for Palestine Refugees (the forerunner of UNRWA). UNRWA therefore contended that these Palestinians were not eligible for UNRWA assistance. Consequently relief for these refugees remained the responsibility of the Egyptian government.

The Higher Committee continued to provide funds to those who wished to join family members elsewhere, but it realized that not all refugees wanted to go to Gaza, where it had decided to send them. Moreover, to return forcibly to Gaza those who preferred to stay in Egypt—as long as they had means of support—was unjustifiable. Thus, a policy was announced whereby all those who wished to travel were asked to submit a formal request. The ʿAbbasiyyah camp was reopened as a transit station for the people whose travel requests were being processed. Beginning June 5, 1950, Egypt Air, in a series of flights, transported 516 Palestinians to Jerusalem. And in August 1950 another group was sent to Gaza.

Only a few thousand Palestinians remained in Egypt. However, by 1953, five years after their flight, their needs were no longer simply shelter and emergency relief. Forbidden to work and with their savings exhausted, the majority required more substantial assistance. In addition to the original refugees there were those who, desperately seeking aid and assistance, had slipped illegally into Egypt from Gaza. By the admission of the report of the Higher Committee, relief in the early period was carried out in a disorderly and unstudied manner.[11] As a result, there were undeserving refugees who received assistance and needy ones who went without. To respond more effectively to the problem, the Higher Committee was reorganized to serve as a regular aid agency. It assembled statistics—albeit conflicting ones—and then classified Palestinians according to economic need. For the purposes of distribution, a Palestinian refugee was defined as a person who had taken refuge in Egypt during the period between 1948 and 1950. Proof was required and could be obtained after securing from the Office of Passports and Nationality a residency card in which status as a Palestinian refugee was recorded.

On October 7, 1954, a meeting was held for representatives from several organizations involved in refugee relief. The purpose of the meeting was to find ways to obtain and distribute food and clothing to the refugees. The initial goal was to provide assistance to 5,000 refugees, although the ultimate target figure was 7,000. On February 17, 1955, the Higher Committee designated the World Council of Churches to administer the assistance program. Money as well as food and commodities were supplied through the UN and, somewhat later, through the United States Agency for International Development (USAID).[12]

Distribution centers were set up in Cairo; Alexandria and Dimyat on the Mediterranean; Port Saʿid and Ismaʿiliyyah in the Suez Canal Zone; Zaqaziq, Kafr Saqr and Mansurah in the Delta; and elsewhere.

Food assistance in the form of flour, cooking fat or oil, and powdered milk was distributed each month to needy families. In some cases, the program awarded financial assistance for specific projects that aimed at rendering a family self-sufficient. Aid through this program continued until just after the June 1967 war. Table 3.1 lists the types of assistance provided as well as the categories of aid recipients and their numbers. The largest numbers in all categories resided in the northeastern part of the country, primarily in the major urban center, Cairo-Giza; the cities of the canal zone—Port Sa'id, Isma'iliyyah, and Suez; and the eastern Delta, al-Sharqiyyah Governorate. Although economic or educational opportunities partially explain the Palestinian presence in these areas, Khadijah 'Arafat, sister of the PLO chief, contended that the gathering of Palestinians had another cause: "The proximity enables us to turn and face Palestine."[13]

In 1960, according to Egyptian statistics there were 15,493 Palestinians in the country.[14] In the early 1960s, however, the number of Gazans entering Egypt increased. Indeed, the last large wave of Palestinians moved to Egypt from Gaza during the 1967 war. Some Palestinians who had served with the police in Gaza fled the Israeli occupation and subsequently arranged to have their families join them. The members of the Palestine Liberation Army's 'Ayn Jalut Brigade, stationed in Gaza, retreated along with the Egyptian army. Furthermore, the chaos and disorder at the Egyptian-Gazan border during the war allowed others to enter.[15] By 1969, the number of Palestinians in Egypt had risen to an estimated 33,000.[16]

As of 1986, the distribution of Palestinians had not greatly changed from the picture indicated by the figures in table 3.1. The Palestinians have concentrated in Cairo, Alexandria, al-Sharqiyyah Governorate, the canal area, and the Sinai. Of those in Cairo, the wealthy tend to live in Heliopolis and al-Duqqi, while the middle class has come to live in al-'Abbasiyyah, Shubra, Madinat Nasr, and Heliopolis. The poor are concentrated in Madinat Nasr, Shubra, and 'Ayn Shams. In al-Sharqiyyah they are centered in Abu Kabir, Zaqaziq, Faqus al-Salahiyyah, and al-Khatarah. Those in the Sinai are primarily found in al-'Arish and Abu Zuwayid.[17]

THE SITUATION IN GAZA

Although Gaza and its institutions are not covered in depth in this study, an examination of the economic and political conditions in the

Table 3.1: Number of Palestinians in Egypt Classified (by Governorate) According to Their Assistance Category as of 1966

Governorate	High Income	Self-Sufficient	Receive Commodity Assistance	Receive Cash Grants	Receive Sewing Machine	Receive Monthly Stipend	Total
Cairo	318	612	1,110	165	155	1,928	4,288
Sharqiyyah	—	75	1,593	70	11	322	2,071
Port Saʿid	11	21	479	204	57	225	997
Giza	35	27	284	9	22	114	491
Alexandria	30	20	282	37	—	82	451
Daqahiliyyah	—	15	197	6	—	58	276
Dimyat	—	17	122	13	—	3	155
Qalyubiyyah	—	5	97	9	—	84	195
Ismaʿiliyyah	—	—	97	11	—	21	129
al-ʿArish	—	20	46	22	4	4	96
Gharbiyyah	5	—	20	—	—	9	34
Buhayrah	—	—	16	—	—	—	16
Kafr al-Shaykh	—	—	7	—	—	—	7
Suez	—	—	8	10	—	19	37
Total	399	812	4,358	556	239	2,869	9,243[a]

SOURCE: Al-Lajnah al-ʿUlya li-Shuʾun al-Muhajirin al-Filastiniyyin, p. 49.

[a]This figure does not represent the total number of Palestinians resident in Egypt at the time. It merely indicates the number of those registered and receiving some form of assistance.

area is necessary in order to understand Gaza's relationship with Egypt. It also provides a basis for comparing the position of Palestinians in Egypt with that of their countrymen in Gaza.

After the February 1949 signing of the Egyptian-Israeli armistice agreement and the transfer of the APG headquarters to Cairo, an Egyptian military administration was established in Gaza. From 1949 until 1962 (when a formal constitution was issued by proclamation of President Nasir) the territory was treated as a military area subject to emergency law. According to the text of its appointment in 1949, the administration had the validity of the British high commissioner in Palestine before 1948. The Egyptian governor-general (al-hakim al-ʿamm) remained the only authority and British law prevailed as it had under the mandate as the basis of organization in what were called "Palestinian lands subject to Egyptian armed forces supervision."[18] Economic control began officially on April 23, 1950 when the Egyptian government ordered the replacement of Palestine currency with Egyptian currency.[19] The name of the area was officially changed to the Gaza Strip (Qita Ghazzah) with the issuance of Law Number 255 of 1955, a law that also established a constitution of sorts and effectively legalized the governor-general's retention of most power.

Since the border with Israel was closed, Egypt was Gaza's only land opening. Yet Egypt refused to allow any large refugee immigration for residence or work. The Egyptian government did underwrite some jobs for Palestinians who graduated from the UNRWA vocational training schools in Gaza. Many taught in Egyptian village schools in areas where Egyptian teachers preferred not to work. Others, according to their skills, found work in industry or agriculture.[20]

In general, entering or leaving Egypt was problematic for Palestinians and required financial guarantees. In order to leave Gaza a Palestinian had to secure the consent of the All-Palestine and Egyptian governments. Permission from the Egyptian government cost 80 piasters ($2.30), no small sum for many Palestinians at a time when one piaster could buy an entire meal. Even if one was allowed to leave, one had then to obtain permission to go to Lebanon, Syria, or another Arab country from the consulate of the country in Cairo. That required influence. Many countries simply refused to receive anyone who carried APG travel papers because they had never recognized or had withdrawn their recognition of the government.[21]

Overcrowding and chronic unemployment have plagued Gaza since the 1948 war. In its truncated post-1948 form, Gaza lacked the primary bases required for building an independent economy. In 1950, while the total area was 325,000 dunums (1 dunum = .25 acres), the number of original residents was estimated at 88,520 and the number of refugees at 199,587. By 1960 the numbers had risen to 118,750 and 255,542 respectively.[22] Eighty percent of the original inhabitants had lost their means of livelihood as a result of the 1948 war. Of an original 22,000 dunums of citrus groves in the pre-1948 Gaza District, there were only 4,000 in the post-1948 Gaza Strip, and of approximately one million dunums of barley and grain fields, the Strip retained only 71,000.[23] Thus, Gaza's land area was small, it lacked basic resources, and it was overpopulated, although not with skilled labor.

Not surprisingly, then, Gaza was the target of several refugee resettlement plans. The best-known plan, proposed in 1951, recommended the transfer of Nile water to the Sinai to enable a limited number of poor refugee families from Gaza to farm there. The Egyptian government agreed to take 7,000 Palestinians for settlement, and in 1953 signed an agreement with UNRWA according to which it offered 230,000 feddans (1 feddan = 4,200 square meters) of desert land for experimentation, from which 50,000 feddans were to be chosen for agricultural development. Experts estimated that the land area could eventually sustain between 50,000 and 70,000 refugees. But Gazans had a different set of priorities and goals. They objected strenuously to any idea of permanent resettlement outside Palestine. Demonstrations against the proposal erupted in Gaza on February 25, 1955 and lasted three days. The 1956 Suez War finally led Egypt to drop the resettlement plan.[24]

No long-range development plan for Gaza was ever drafted and the execution of what plans were formulated was often delayed. Economic policy, such as it was, aimed at developing citrus exports, encouraging Gazans working abroad to send supplies to build up the Strip, and encouraging banks to finance projects.[25] What limited industrial production there was in Gaza was geared to the needs of the Egyptian army, the Egyptian military administration, and the employees of the UN. As an occupied territory Gaza depended heavily upon the Egyptian economy, and the average Gazan held the Egyptian administration responsible for the deteriorating economic conditions in the Strip. But popular resentment was not the only negative effect of the military administration's misplaced priorities. The policies also placed unnecessary economic burdens on Egypt, which was forced to provide basic commodities, goods which local merchants did not consider lucrative enough to import. At the same time, Gazan merchants, in cooperation with the military administration, took advantage of Gaza's open port to import luxury goods which eventually found their way to the Egyptian market.[26]

Thus, the Egyptian administration, insofar as it maintained Gaza as an administrative and economic preserve unto itself, in effect served a handful of Gazan merchants. In spite of the economic expansion of the Strip, its "development" in fact meant its transformation into a huge black market.[27] Gaza desperately needed industrial growth—something that demanded centralized supervision as well as substantial financial capabilities and commitments. Neither the Egyptian administration nor the Gazan bourgeoisie was willing to make such investments. Economic expansion would have required the establishment of new administrative relations between Gaza and Egypt, and the Egyptian government was either unprepared or unwilling to bear the political consequences of such a move.[28]

On the internal political level, the fact that the Egyptian government made no move to incorporate or annex Gaza was certainly significant for future Palestinian political developments. Although the political structures that were constructed and legislated for the Strip were designed with Egyptian interests and control in mind, they were, nonetheless, Palestinian in content. Neither legislated to be outsiders to the system as they were in Israel, nor forcibly included in the polity as they were under the Hashemites, the Palestinians in Gaza, though occupied, were able to preserve a clear Palestinian identity. Perhaps owing to the weakness of the socioeconomic structure of the Strip after the *nakbah*, perhaps owing to the immense popularity of Nasir among Palestinians, Gazan dissatisfaction with certain political and economic aspects of the Egyptian administration did not lead to calls for its ouster or to the development of any organized opposition to it.[29]

PASSPORTS FOR PALESTINIANS

Shortly after the arrival of the refugees, the Egyptian government replaced some of their Palestine passports or identity cards with Egyptian identity cards. They were subsequently issued APG travel documents, as were the Palestinian refugees in Gaza. However the value of those documents decreased as inter-Arab recognition of the APG waned.[30] Moreover, although the APG papers provided for a year's residence, they did not permit the bearer to work in Egypt: written directly on the document was the phrase "work for or without wages is forbidden."[31] Economic conditions in Egypt as a whole were difficult at the time and unemployment was common. Thus, the stipulation that work be forbidden to those holding the APG document must be understood in terms of the economic situation in the country and in terms of Palestinian and Arab perceptions of the refugees' situation: it was a problem of limited duration and, therefore, the refugees needed not find employment in the host countries because they would soon be returning home. The "no-work" restriction rendered life extremely difficult for many. Even those Palestinians who had brought money with them gradually watched their resources dwindle. Some managed to elude the Egyptian authorities and found work, especially in rural areas. Others, because businesses had to be registered in the name of an Egyptian, formed partnerships with nationals.

It was not until 1960 (Decision Number 28 of 1960)[32] that the United Arab Republic (Egypt and Syria) issued travel papers (watha'iq al-safar) for Palestinian refugees living in the UAR. In order for a Palestinian to obtain a travel document he had to present proof of refugee status and UAR residency. The travel document mentioned in which region of the UAR one resided but did not provide for travel between the two regions—during the period, Syria was known as the northern region of the UAR—nor for travel to any countries not specifically mentioned in it. Nor could the bearer of the document enter the UAR from abroad unless he or she obtained prior permission from a UAR embassy or consulate. (Travel documents issued by other Arab states did not carry the same restrictions.)[33] A 1961 amendment of the law provided for a two-year period of validity which could be extended for another two years and then an additional year.

Thus, the travel document did not offer the same privileges or protection as a regular passport (although it is worth noting here that during this period the process of getting a passport, visas, and permission to travel was quite difficult even for Egyptian nationals). Those who carry regular passports are generally oblivious to the problems a travel document may pose: uncertainty of renewal, lack of or limited access to consular officials abroad, variable acceptance of the document from country to country, travel restrictions, and the like. Although Palestinians who carried them often took pride in being able to retain their Palestinian "nationality," in fact the documents were often worth little more than identity cards.

In matters of nationality and travel documents, Palestinians residing in Egypt fit into three categories. The first comprises those who resided in Egypt prior to 1948. Their numbers were small and most were able to obtain Egyptian citizenship. The second category includes those who came to Egypt in 1948. While a few of the wealthier ones (no more than a few hundred) managed to obtain citizenship, the vast majority did not. At least officially, this policy was based on the Arab League decree that Arab states not grant citizenship to the refugees. The final group comprises those who fled to Egypt in 1967, primarily from Gaza. They generally carried Palestinian travel documents and very few acquired citizenship.[34] Throughout the period under review, the travel document continued to be the sole "passport" available to the vast majority of Palestinians in Egypt. Most of the 1948 group must renew their documents yearly; however, in some cases the document is valid for only ten or eleven months. In some cases, Palestinians must demonstrate the presence of a certain level of monetary reserves in order to renew the document.[35]

EGYPTIAN LEGISLATION REGARDING PALESTINIANS

Outside the realm of residence, the earliest legal provisions made for Palestinians in Egypt concerned the practice of the liberal professions. In 1954, a series of laws was passed that allowed Palestinians to practice professions in Egypt according to the same standards and regulations as Egyptians. The first of the laws dealt with Palestinian medical doctors and empowered the Egyptian Ministry of Health to license all refugee doctors and veterinarians (Laws 415 and 416 of 1954).[36] The next measure, Law Number 481 of 1954, empowered the Ministry of Health to license Palestinian midwives and assistants provided they held the required certificates.[37] Finally, Law Number 537 of 1954 enabled the Ministry of Health to license Palestinian dentists.[38] It should be noted that the laws were not drafted solely for Palestinians. Rather, they were general laws promulgated to regulate the professions and in each case an article dealing with Palestinians was included.

Although certainly significant for those in the professions, the series of 1954 laws did not affect many Palestinians in what was in any case a tiny community. More important was the gradual relaxation of the no-work restriction of the days of the monarchy following Nasir's rise to power. Palestinians were also permitted to obtain commercial registers and, unlike other Arabs, were accorded the right to import and export.[39] Egyptian hospitals also provided free health care to Palestinians. However, the most important law for the community was Presidential Decree Number 66 of 1962 which stated that "it is permitted to appoint Arab Palestinians to positions of state employment the same as the citizens of the UAR."[40] The timing of the issuance of the presidential decree may have been connected with the then recent breakup of the Syrian-Egyptian union and may have been a means by which Nasir sought to boost his pan-Arab credentials. Given the employment situation of Palestinians in other Arab countries, the move was certain to have substantial propaganda value.

Again, the law did not apply to large numbers of Palestinians; however, it was indicative of a general policy line of the Nasir regime which also opened Egyptian government schools to Palestinian children on the same basis as Egyptian children. Likewise, Egyptian universities accepted Palestinians in large numbers during the period. This latter privilege, however, was not the result of a specific law or decree, but rather the result of the evolution of what had been an open admissions policy under the monarchy.[41] In addition, although UNRWA did not provide services to Palestinians in Egypt, an agreement did exist between Egypt and UNRWA by which some Gazan refugee students were accepted into the government schools. UNRWA paid the Egyptian government for the educational services it provided, but the compensation did not cover all the costs. By the mid-1960s, the cost to the government had reached LE360,000 (over a million dollars) with the average cost per student LE124 ($350).[42]

In 1965–66, the government gave loans to 1,192 students with the average LE48 ($110) per student. It also awarded university scholarships of about LE100 ($230) to outstanding Palestinian students.[43] Furthermore, needy Palestinians were exempted from educational fees that would have totaled about LE20,000 ($57,000).[44] Owing to the stipends available, the scholarships offered, and the overall lower cost of living, Egyptian universities attracted large numbers of Palestinian students, especially in the fields of medicine and engineering. In a situation where many Palestinians in Egypt and Gaza were quite poor, such assistance opened lanes of upward mobility that would otherwise have remained blocked. From the mid-1950s to the mid-1960s, Egypt accepted 5,642 Palestinian university students from Gaza alone.[45] Many others came from the West Bank and beyond.

POLITICAL SUPPORT

Egyptian policy in the wake of the 1952 revolution showed no initial inclination to address the rights or claims of the Palestinians. To the contrary, in the years immediately following the revolution the new leadership's primary concern was the internal power struggle, as the Free Officers concentrated on consolidating their position within the country. The delicate internal situation convinced Egypt's new leadership not to embark upon any bold foreign policy initiatives. Given such constraints, the Palestinian problem was simply not at the top of the agenda. Indeed, the fledgling regime showed some signs of seeking peace with its new Jewish neighbor.[46]

Frustrated in his dealings with the West, once Nasir had consolidated power, Egyptian policy toward Palestine began to change. In 1955 the Egyptian government began to supervise the training of commandos that then operated out of Gaza and East Sinai. The commando groups were intended to be tactical as well as intelligence-gathering groups. Composed of both Egyptians and Palestinians and supervised and trained by Egyptian officers, they cannot really be considered part of an independent Palestinian attempt to take control of their struggle.

The Suez War of 1956, which followed Nasir's nationalization of the Suez Canal Company, elevated the Egyptian president, who was already strengthened by the 1955 transfer of Soviet arms to Egypt, to the position of champion of Arabism and anti-Westernism. The 1952 revolution had been a first jolt to Palestinian national consciousness. The 1956 Suez War was another. The Israeli occupation of Gaza from October 1956 until January 1957 convinced many of the need for armed opposition to Israel, and Palestinians began increasingly to view Nasir as a natural ally or patron in their own struggle. After the Israeli withdrawal from Gaza, new Palestinian commando groups emerged and began to launch raids against Israel.

It was not just among Palestinians that Nasir came to be viewed as a potential ally. In Syria, where internal coalition shifting had produced numerous coups since 1949, members of the Ba'th party looked to the power and stability of revolutionary Egypt to shore up their defenses against internal rivals, primarily the Communists, and Syria's external enemies, Britain and the West in the guise of the Hashemite regime in Iraq. Nasir hesitated to embrace the Syrian Ba'th's 1958 pleas for unity with Egypt, arguing that the country needed first to achieve internal cohesion before seeking integration with another country. He finally consented, and the United Arab Republic (UAR) was established; but in his terms of agreement he planted the seeds of the eventual dissolution of the merger.[47] Nasir insisted on a centralized union and on the withdrawal of the army from politics. He disbanded all political parties, including the one that had courted him, the Ba'th.[48] The seeds of discontent finally matured and on September 28, 1961 a group of Syrian army officers arrested Nasir's deputy in Syria, Marshall 'Abd al-Hakim 'Amir, sent him packing to Cairo, and declared the dissolution of the union.

The 1958 unity had been viewed as a great victory by most Arabs and certainly by the Palestians. Therefore, the 1961 dissolution of the UAR came as a severe blow, shaking the Palestinians' belief that their political salvation lay in the realization of Arab unity. Shortly thereafter, in 1962 Algeria secured its independence after a long, bloody struggle against the French. For Palestinians, both events demonstrated the importance of self-reliance rather than dependence on a future Arab unity to regain Palestine.

TOWARD A PALESTINIAN ENTITY

The 34th session of the Arab League Council (March 4, 1959) had called for the creation of a Palestinian army to be stationed in Arab countries. However, the first inter-Arab resolution on a Palestinian political entity was issued during the first summit conference of the Arab League Council in January 1964. In February 1964, Ahmad al-Shuqayri, a Palestinian with long diplomatic experience who had been appointed to represent the Palestinians at the Arab League Council meeting in September 1963 following the death of Ahmad Hilmi, called for the convening of a Palestine National Council (PNC), to be held in Jerusalem in May 1964.

The January 1964 summit had empowered Shuqayri only to study a way of arriving at sound bases for organizing the Palestinians. However, before the second Arab summit and before the convening of the first PNC in May 1964 Shuqayri, owing largely to Nasir's support, went beyond the bounds of organizing Palestinians discussed by the summit. He succeeded in convincing Nasir to open camps to train Palestinian army units and to provide equipment. Cairo also empowered Shuqayri to prepare a law for the mandatory conscription of Gazans, and ordered the authorities in Gaza to give the Palestinian representative full cooperation.[49]

Also prior to the May 1964 PNC, Shuqayri showed Nasir a copy of a draft of the Palestine National Covenant and discussed his plans for a Palestinian entity, all of which Nasir supported. Beyond considerations of Arab unity and the Palestinian cause, for Nasir such an entity could be an important reserve in the Arab game of "verbal outbidding" (*muzayidat kalamiyyah*), as well as an important political weapon in the struggle with Israel and her allies who denied the existence of a Palestinian people and who claimed that the Arabs concocted stories of border problems with their neighbor.[50] Given other developments among Palestinians in Egypt (see chapter 4 on the GUPS and chapter 5 on the GUPW) and in other parts of the diaspora, Nasir may also have sensed that such an entity was soon bound to emerge, in which case early support meant greater potential hegemony at the expense of Egypt's Arab rivals.

Acting with Egyptian support, the Palestine Liberation Organization, during the period immediately following its founding at the May 1964 PNC meeting, was able to form and expand Palestine Liberation Army (PLA) units in Gaza (the ʿAyn Jalut Brigade), Syria (the Hittin Brigade), and Iraq (the Qadisiyyah Brigade). On a diplomatic and informational level, it opened additional offices in Arab and foreign capitals. Nasir himself addressed the second PNC meeting, held in Cairo from May 31 to June 4, 1965. Nevertheless, the Egyptian president had stated during the 1964 summit that the liberation of Palestine was not an immediate issue and would have to await the solution of a number of other, more pressing, Arab problems. His view of the PLO was that of an entity that would act in concert with Arab plans, and not of a group acting with relative independence.

Numerous Palestinian factions expressed reservations about the form the new entity was taking. The major objection stemmed from the traditional nature of the PLO leadership and the control exercised over it by Arab regimes. Therefore, some Palestinians continued to act outside the bounds of the PLO through independent guerrilla organizations. The military wing of Fateh, al-ʿAsifah (then supported by Syria), began launching military operations on January 1, 1965. However, not until the June 1967 war and the discrediting of the front-line Arab leaders and their military forces did most Palestinians as well as many other Arabs decide that a new approach was needed. Arab leaders were no longer able to argue convincingly that combined, traditional, military action was the key to the liberation of Arab land.

Because of Shuqayri's personal political style and his close ties with the defeated front-line Arab regimes, after the 1967 defeat Palestinian support for the PLO leader plummeted. Conversely, throughout the Arab world the popularity of the *fidaʾiyyin* organizations soared. Before the war, Syria had been a leading proponent of the concept of a people's war and along with Algeria had been Fateh's primary sponsor. Nasir, on the other hand, remained commited to the PLO, during this period an organization primarily of information offices and political bureaus. After the March 1968 battle of Karamah, the first major guerrilla victory against Israeli forces, the Egyptian regime realized that Fateh could no longer be ignored. At the same time, Fateh was seeking to strengthen its hand within the PLO and in inter-Arab and international circles. To that end, Egypt, which at the time surpassed Syria in power and influence, had to be courted. Nasir's advisor Muhammad Heikal finally arranged for the Egyptian president to meet with Fateh's Faruq al-Qaddumi and Salah Khalaf. As a result of the meeting, Nasir agreed to provide Fateh training facilities and to supply it with arms. In this way, although he maintained his role in PLO affairs, Nasir began to garner support among those whom he must have felt would eventually take the reins of the PLO.[51]

In the meantime, at the end of 1967 Shuqayri was ousted as PLO chief and replaced by Yahya Hammudah. Fateh's Yasir 'Arafat finally assumed the chairmanship in 1969. The change in leadership reflected a significant change in the PLO's orientation, a shift from an emphasis on political or diplomatic activity—which was less dangerous in the view of Nasir and most other Arab leaders—to an emphasis on independent Palestinian military activity. After the disaster of 1967, however, Nasir no longer had the political reserves either domestically or abroad to oppose Palestinian commando activity. The war of attrition between Egypt and Israel in the canal zone 1969–1971 further enhanced the appeal of the idea of a Palestinian guerrilla war against Israel. Thus, although the level of political repression in Egypt after 1967 remained generally high, guerrilla activity out of Sinai was permitted and many young Egyptians volunteered to fight with the *fida'iyyin.*

Although one of Fateh's basic principles was noninterference in the internal affairs of host states, conflicts, especially with the Lebanese and Jordanian regimes, became common. Nasir struggled to keep the Jordanian and Lebanese governments from cracking down too forcefully on the PRM, while at the same time he urged 'Arafat to keep the various commando groups in check so as to avoid costly Israeli retaliatory raids.[52] Palestinians were aware that Egyptian objectives were not completely coincident with their own. When Egypt accepted the Rogers Plan (announced June 25, 1970), Beirut and Amman exploded in large anti-Nasir demonstrations. After strong Palestinian verbal attacks on the Egyptian leader, Nasir responded on July 29 by closing the PLO radio station that he had allowed to broadcast out of Cairo.

The Jordanian-Palestinian tensions that finally erupted in civil war in September 1970 were of great concern to the Egyptian president.

Although interested in the fate of the Palestinian resistance Nasir was probably more worried that the events in Jordan might lead Syria to enter the conflict on behalf of the Palestinians. This, in turn, might trigger Israeli intervention and provide an excuse for the Americans to impose a solution. The Egyptian president, therefore, took an active role in mediation. On September 28, 1970, the day after he had arranged what proved to be only a temporary reconciliation between King Husayn and 'Arafat, Nasir, who had been suffering from heart trouble, died.

Anger over the Rogers Plan vanished as news of his death drew masses of Arabs into the streets for what was an unparalleled display of mourning for a political leader. Even in the 1980s, his memory continues to command great symbolic influence among Arabs as a bold leader who dared to challenge the West. Palestinians' feelings about Nasir were perhaps most eloquently expressed by Palestinian poet Mahmud Darwish in the following excerpt from "The Man with the Green Shadow, to the Memory of Gamal 'Abd al-Nasir":[53]

> With you we live,
> With you we march forward,
> With you we hunger;
> And when you die, we try not to die with you . . .
> You promised the tribes a summer's journey out of the *jahi-liyyah*—"the days of ignorance";
> You promised those in chains that there would be a mighty firing of guns;
> And you promised the warrior a battle that brings back memories of al-Qadisiyyah.
> Your voice now resounds from all throats
> Like hurricanes, one following another . . .
> Upon your grave new wheat will grow,
> And upon it new rain will fall;
> And you will see us marching forward, forward, forward.

THE ADMINISTRATION OF PALESTINIAN AFFAIRS IN EGYPT

Before continuing the discussion of the Palestinian community in Egypt under Sadat and Mubarak, mention should be made of the respective roles of the PLO office and of the Office of the Military Governor of Gaza. From the time of the establishment of the PLO until the 1967 war, the PLO office in Cairo operated as the sole authority responsible for the Palestinians in Egypt, handling all the administrative and political matters generally dealt with by an embassy. When the 1967 war drove the Egyptian military administration from the Gaza Strip, many of its employees retreated with it to Cairo, where the office was reestablished and where it then assumed responsibility for the affairs of Gazans in Egypt. Uprooted from the territory in which it was the sole responsible authority, the Office of the Military Governor's duties were severely reduced. What ensued was an inevitable bureaucratic struggle in which the Gazan military administration tried to carve out for itself a larger realm of responsibility at the expense of the PLO office.[54]

As it has evolved, the Office of the Military Governor coordinates the services of several ministries and bureaucratic apparatus in Egypt.[55] It handles primarily routine administrative and executive matters, whereas the Egyptian Ministry of Foreign Affairs sets the general political line of the country vis-à-vis Palestinians. In Gaza the office employed thousands; the office now located in Madinat Nasr is but a fraction of the size of its predecessor in Gaza. It deals with far fewer people, and certain directorates such as that of municipalities are not needed outside Gaza. Those employees who came to Egypt in 1967 and could not be absorbed by the smaller administration, were found jobs elsewhere, but they are paid by the Office of the Military Governor. Those who remained in Gaza continue to receive salaries even though they no longer work for the office. They are known as *al-samidun*, the steadfast ones.

The Office of the Military Governor contains the following directorates: interior and general security; education; social affairs; finance and economy; and legal and civil affairs. The Interior Directorate issues government papers such as birth certificates and permission for marriage. The Education Directorate deals with all Palestinian students in Egyptian schools below the university level. The Civil Affairs Directorate primarily handles the administration's own employees, although it is also involved in such matters as the certification of work experience. The Social Affairs Directorate oversees a kind of social insurance for employees of the office and collects contributions from wealthy Palestinians for distribution to the poor on special occasions. The Financial and Economic Directorate issues commercial registers to merchants and supervises the budget of the other directorates. Other special services are available for the Gazan refugees of 1967: there are educational privileges; exemption from various government fees; and the availability of financial assistance if disaster strikes a family or if the supporter of the family dies or is disabled.

An important function of the PLO office in which the Office of the Military Governor of Gaza has not become involved is that of collecting the "liberation tax." Since October 1969, all Palestinians working in Egyptian government offices have been required to pay three percent of their salaries as a liberation tax, which goes to support the PLO. To extend the tax base, a council of Palestinians was assembled to decide how much other Palestinians—businessmen and others working in the private sector—should pay. All the money is then deposited in the Palestine National Fund, the equivalent of the PLO treasury, and its use is centrally determined. PLO officials admit that they have no means of enforcing the private sector's contribution. However, if someone comes to the PLO for help or services he may be denied assistance if he has not been paying the tax. What generally happens is that the person is asked to begin paying the tax: services would only rarely be denied.[56]

THE SADAT REGIME

Just as the 1952 Free Officers' revolution initially changed little for the Palestinians in Egypt, the advent of Anwar Sadat seemed to portend no change in Egypt's political course. Indeed, aside from the general depression which gripped the community in the wake of the bloody confrontations between Jordanian forces and the Palestinian *fida'iyyin* and their allies in September 1970, Palestinian political and organizing work in Egypt continued as it had under ʿAbd al-Nasir. While Palestinian students were among those involved in the massive protests of 1972 they did not participate in large numbers, and their antiregime activity did not damage PLO-Egyptian relations (see chapter 4 on the GUPS).

Indeed, Egypt was a cosponsor of the resolution at Rabat in October 1974 which officially proclaimed the PLO the sole, legitimate representative of the Palestinian people. However, an indication of what lay ahead may have been discernible the previous July, following a meeting in Alexandria between Sadat and King Husayn. The communiqué issued at the end of the meeting declared that the PLO was the representative of all Palestinians *except* those living in Jordan. The PLO reacted by immediately issuing a reply charging that the communiqué undermined the national rights of the Palestinian people.[57]

The signing of the Sinai II disengagement agreement in September

1975, which effectively confirmed Egypt's withdrawal from the front, led to a brief strain in PLO-Egyptian ties, but had no real effect on the community in Egypt. Despite the subtle signals that Egypt was leaning in a new direction, relations remained good until Sadat addressed a session of the People's Assembly on November 9, 1977—a session that he had expressly invited Yasir 'Arafat to attend—and announced his intention to go to Jerusalem. An embarrassment to 'Arafat and a shock to many, the announcement and the subsequent trip spurred antiregime demonstrations by Palestinian students in Egypt. Many students were subsequently expelled and the offices of the General Union of Palestine Students were closed.

The PLO and Syria then proceeded to form a united front, and at an Arab League summit held in Tripoli in the wake of the Jerusalem trip, Algeria, Libya, and South Yemen joined them in what they called the Steadfastness and Confrontation Front. As if that were not sufficient to send PLO-Egyptian relations into a tailspin, the February 1978 assassination of Egyptian journalist Yusuf al-Siba'i in Cyprus at the hands of Palestinian gunmen (an act deplored by the PLO) and the subsequent rescue attempt fiasco, which left Egyptian commandos dead on the runway at Larnaca airport, killed by Cypriot soldiers, was the symbolic last straw. The Egyptian media, certainly with government approval, if not encouragement, began what was to be a three-and-a-half-year assault on the PLO in particular and Palestinians in general.[58]

As a corollary, many of the privileges that Palestinians in Egypt had enjoyed since the 1950s and early 1960s were gradually reviewed and cancelled. Scholarships and subsidies for Palestinian students wishing to study in Egyptian universities were terminated; even Palestinian entry into Egyptian universities was restricted; and those who were accepted had to pay tuition in hard currency. The days of subsidized health care for Palestinians in Egyptian hospitals also ended: Palestinians were expected to pay for their treatment in hard currency like other foreigners. Gone were the days of the relatively free movement of members of the Palestinian resistance movement in and out of Egypt and the days of generalized feelings of solidarity and sympathy for the Palestinians among average Egyptians. The media gradually succeeded in convincing many Egyptians that it was Palestinians who were responsible for Egypt's involvement and sacrifices in four wars; that Palestinians were living in Egypt like kings; and that the resistance was corrupt. Most devastating, the Egyptian media adopted and popularized one of the favorite Zionist myths: that the Palestinians had sold their land prior to 1948 and therefore did not deserve Palestine.

As the peace "process" took form, Palestinian activity and even presence in Egypt was under siege. With the final signing of the Camp David accords in March 1979, the PLO "froze" its relations with Egypt. Only the office of the GUPW remained officially, if pitifully, open. Two PLO offices continued to handle daily Palestinian affairs—matters related to passports, personal status, and the like. But as the Israeli flag was raised over the Egyptian capital, the Palestinian flag was lowered and locked away.

The euphoria over the peace treaty that swept through much of the Egyptian population was not shared by the various professional unions—the lawyers, engineers, and journalists—nor by the country's organized or disorganized left. Their continued refusal to embrace the treaty remained an important reminder of the role Egypt had once played in the Arab world, a role withdrawn and passed on in a mutilated form to its Syrian understudy.

The July 1981 Israeli raid on the Iraqi nuclear reactor, and the subsequent massive Israeli bombing raid on the Fakahani district in Beirut, gave some Egyptians pause. But Sadat clearly had more important problems, problems that in September 1981 led several young Egyptian soldiers to jump off a truck at a military parade marking the anniversary of the 1973 war and spray the Egyptian president and the members of his entourage with bullets and hand grenades. Those who knew Egypt knew why there was no mass outpouring of grief for the slain president. While Western commentators puzzled over the phenomenon, it was, quite appropriately, the United States and Israel who donned sackcloth and ashes to mourn the passing of the most openly pliant Arab leader in recent history.

MUBARAK AND BEYOND

As of this writing the so-called "cold peace" continues. If Egyptians were startled by the Israeli raids of 1981, they were outraged by the 1982 invasion of Lebanon, for which their country's peace treaty with Israel had so conveniently paved the way. It was during the summer of 1982 that Palestinians, either sensing that the atmosphere in the country was changing or else from anger and frustration unable to remain silent, began again to work openly, but cautiously. The sphere was still limited. The real breakthrough in Palestinian-Egyptian relations came in December 1983 when, having just escaped the inter-Palestinian fighting in Tripoli, 'Arafat and his men passed through the

Suez Canal on their way to Yemen, and the PLO chairman debarked for a brief, televised meeting with President Mubarak.

Since then, PLO-Egyptian relations have continued to improve, if not without setbacks. Notably, the PLO offices in Cairo were closed in the wake of the April 1987 PNC meeting in Algiers, which restored PLO unity, but during which certain statements were made that angered Egypt. Nevertheless, the liberalization that has taken place under Mubarak—most noticeably in the development of the opposition parties and their press—has enabled the parties of the left, the Palestinians' natural Egyptian constituency, once again to begin to coordinate activities. On a popular level, however, the record since Sadat's passing has been mixed. Perhaps the most disturbing development was the passage in the summer of 1985 of a law that terminated the Palestinians' exemption from the application of another law forbidding foreigners to own agricultural land.[59] Much of the agricultural land held by Palestinians in Egypt is land that they have reclaimed; and some families rely on the land as a financial guarantee for renewing their residency each year. Although the PLO has protested the law, the Egyptian government has shown no sign of intending to repeal it.

Although a reevaluation of the exclusionary policies in education and health care implemented in the post-1977 period was hinted at in December 1987, at this writing no changes had been instituted. The activity of the mass organizations continues to be closely monitored, although the Palestine Red Crescent Society in particular has made tremendous strides in the development and delivery of services. With the exception of the GUPW, the offices of all the organizations covered in this study were closed again in April 1987 following the PNC meeting in Algiers and were not reopened until November 29, 1987.

Anwar Sadat is gone, but the Palestinian community's memories of that era remain vivid, despite the gradual improvement in Egyptian-Palestinian relations. Although the restoration of PLO unity in Algiers initially resulted in a deterioration in relations, the reunification of the PLO was the most basic and pressing problem at the time. A reunified PLO would seem to be the most basic requirement for a future reactivization of the Palestinian community in Egypt.

[4]
GUPS: The Political Training Ground

Like other sectors of Palestinian society, students became involved in the national movement and the question of the Zionist challenge to Palestine during the mandate period. Palestine had no national university, so those who were privileged enough to pursue an advanced education were usually sent to Beirut, England, or points beyond. Although sources on the pre-1948 student movement are few, it appears that a Palestinian student association in Cairo dates to as early as 1911–13 when Amin al-Husayni studied there.[1] In Palestine itself, there was no general federation of students but there were debating societies (jam'iyyat khitabah), which sponsored social, cultural, athletic, and political activities. These societies called for and convened the first Palestinian student conference in Jaffa in 1936. It was attended by representatives of various Palestinian schools and had as its theme the threat of Zionism.[2]

The heirs to these pre-1948 student societies began to emerge shortly after the nakbah, and nowhere were they stronger or of greater consequence than in Egypt. The Palestinian Students Union (PSU) had been founded in 1944,[3] but its activities were limited by the regime under the monarchy to the social and cultural realm. King Faruq's overthrow in 1952 meant a change in Palestinian student fortunes. In the 1950s, Egypt, the rising star on the Arab political horizon, boasted the oldest and most elaborate university system in the Arab Middle East. Even more important, a policy of open university admissions under the monarchy was expanded by the post-1952 Free Officers' regime to render Egyptian universities the primary educators of Palestinian youth, particularly those Palestinians from Gaza. The low cost of living, the nationalist political climate after 1955, and the availability of stipends and scholarships attracted Palestinians as well as Arabs from other countries by the hundreds and later by the thousands.

Egypt's policy of hosting and educating Arab youth must be understood in the context of Egypt's role in the Arab world at the time. Considerations of Arab unity aside, Nasir likely viewed the cost of educating the students a minor investment in comparison with the returns:

politicized cadres of professionals indebted to the Egyptian regime who, after graduation, could be expected to head to all parts of the Middle East, North Africa, and the Gulf. Moreover, the small size of the indigenous Palestinian community—those who continued to reside in Egypt after their university years—meant that, at least during the 1950s and 1960s, Nasir was in little danger of training groups of young people who might mobilize against him at home. The more highly visible and influential the students were abroad, the more Nasir stood to gain from supporting them. It was in Cairo's universities in the early 1950s that Yasir ʿArafat, Salah Khalaf, Faruq al-Qaddumi, and others met and sowed the seeds of the restoration of the national movement. These same men, fifteen years later, emerged as leaders of the largest Palestinian political-commando organization, Fateh, and by 1969, had assumed the reins of power of the PLO itself.

THE POLITICAL HISTORY OF THE PALESTINIAN STUDENTS UNION (PSU)

For Palestinians already studying in Egypt in the late 1940s, the deteriorating political situation in Palestine in 1947 and the outbreak of war in many cases led to the severance of lines of financial support. Between 1948 and 1949, the hostilities prevented the arrival of any new students and the influx of refugees monopolized student attention. Having lost most of their material possessions in the dispersal from Palestine, after 1948 many Palestinian families viewed higher education as one of only a few unassailable commodities that might serve as the basis of a more secure future. However, Gaza and the West Bank—the areas of greatest Palestinian concentration—were devoid of university facilities. Egypt, on the other hand, was not distant and its university system was the most developed and respected in the Arab world. Many of the Palestinian students who went to Egypt in the early period enrolled in al-Azhar (Cairo's thousand-year-old Islamic university and the only university at the time that subsidized needy students),[4] Cairo University (Fuʾad I University until the 1952 revolution), and the American University in Cairo. With the expansion of universities in the 1950s, students began heading for Alexandria University, ʿAyn Shams (Cairo), Asyut, and some of the higher institutes.[5] As the Palestinian student population in Egypt grew, the PSU grew with it.

In 1951, a young Palestinian named Salah Khalaf, originally from Jaffa, left a refugee camp in Gaza to go to Cairo to study. Although from a religious family, Khalaf selected Dar al-ʿUlum (a teachers' training college) rather than al-Azhar University. In the fall of 1951, an Arab League Council decision to discontinue allocations for Palestinian student subsidies triggered Khalaf's political activism.[6] Lack of money was the major problem of Palestinian students at the time, and to save money they often lived six or seven to an apartment. Thus, the discontinuation of the subsidies was a serious development. Khalaf joined other Palestinians in a demonstration at the league's headquarters in downtown Cairo to protest the decision. According to Khalaf, the students occupied the league headquarters, and ransacked the office of Ahmad al-Shuqayri, the assistant secretary-general of the league in charge of Palestinian affairs. As a result, the student subsidies were reinstated; but the preceived ringleaders (among them, Khalaf) were rewarded with an all-expenses-paid six-week stay in ʿAbdin prison.[7]

It was also in 1951 that the young activist first encountered Yasir ʿArafat, a twenty-two-year-old engineering student, in charge of training students for anti-British guerrilla activities in the Suez Canal Zone, an activity he continued until 1954 when Nasir ordered a temporary halt on such operations.[8] Khalaf met ʿArafat, whom he described as full of "energy, enthusiasm and enterprising spirit," through the PSU, "a sort of umbrella organization grouping Palestinian students of various political stripes."[9]

During the period immediately following the defeat of the Arab armies in Palestine, the Communists and the Ikhwan (Muslim Brethren) were the predominant transnational political currents in the Arab world. Arab nationalist organizations were still in their infancy. The Ikhwan in particular had a clear commitment to Palestine, which it had demonstrated through its participation in the 1948 war. It called for the liberation of Palestine[10] and it alone in Egypt allowed for non-Egyptian participation.[11] For these reasons, many of those who joined the PSU in the early years leaned toward the Ikhwan. Communist elements were also present, but never in a majority. In any case, political inclination does not equal direct coordination. The connection between the Ikhwan and the union probably involved an overlap of political program, not more.[12]

Alan Hart states that ʿArafat was an independent who allied himself with the Ikhwan only as a matter of temporary convenience, while Khalaf was a staunch Ikhwan partisan.[13] The former GUPS members interviewed for this study—some former members of the ANM, most now with Fateh or independents—confirmed that the predominant trends in the PSU at the time were the Muslim Brethren and the Communists. All referred to 'Arafat as at least sympathetic to, if not a member of, the Ikhwan, with whom he reportedly had fought in Gaza during the 1948 war.

Khalaf, on the other hand, maintains that, while he admired the Ikhwan for their devotion to the struggle against the Zionists and the British and for their willingness to die for their ideals, his political tendencies lay in a more secularist direction. According to Khalaf, neither he nor 'Arafat belonged to a particular political party, but both shared the belief, even in the early 1950s, that Palestinians could expect nothing from the Arab regimes and that they would ultimately have to rely on themselves to regain Palestine.[14]

The political affiliations of 'Arafat and Khalaf in these early days remain a point of contention. All interviewees' testimonies converged with emotion, however, on the fact that the disappearance of the word "Palestine" from the political map after the war heightened the students' determination to assert their identity as Palestinians, whatever their travel documents or passports said.[15] Not until West Bank and Gazan students went abroad, and at this time that usually meant Egypt, did they have the opportunity to assert openly their Palestinian identity, to group together as Palestinians, and to work for Palestinian political goals.

According to Khalaf, in 1952, on a simple platform of Palestinian identity and self-reliance, he and 'Arafat decided to test the political waters of the PSU and enter the elections for the executive committee. Neither was in a position to marshall material resources from outside political sponsors, but they had established good relations with all the students, irrespective of political affiliation. In the campaign they presented themselves, not as against any particular political party or organization, but rather as *for* the Student Union (the name of their slate of candidates, which included Khalaf, 'Arafat, four other independents, one Communist, one Ba'thi and one member of the Muslim Brethren). And the formula proved successful: the Student Union list won an overwhelming majority. 'Arafat was elected president, a position he retained until his graduation in 1956. He was then succeeded by Khalaf, who had served for four years as his vice-president.[16]

Two months after the elections, the Arab League Council once again cut student subsidies. The students responded by declaring a strike and occupying the league headquarters. By this time, however, they were dealing with a different regime. Since their first major demonstrations, Egypt had witnessed its revolution. The new regime was still in the process of consolidating power and not in the mood to cave in to protesting students. Using considerable force, the police dislodged the students. Nineteen were arrested. Khalaf, who gone into hiding in the ʿArafat family apartment in the Cairo suburb of Heliopolis, finally turned himself in and was again imprisoned in ʿAbdin. His release came thirty-five days later following Shuqayri's personal intervention.[17]

At the time, the All-Palestine Government, weak and devoid of content as it was, was the only Palestinian political body to whom Gazans and other Palestinians in Egypt could turn. As a result, they found themselves effectively in a political void. Indeed, the PSU was the only Palestinian organization that held democratic elections, thereby rendering it the only group that could legitimately claim to represent Palestinians.

The growing importance and power of Egypt in Arab and international circles and Cairo's location—at the crossroads of the Arab, African, and Islamic worlds—heightened the potential influence of the PSU, for it presented wide-ranging possibilities for making political contacts and engaging in informational work. Cooperation and participation with the Egyptian Students Union helped the Palestinians ease into what might otherwise have been closed circles. The PSU grew in size and importance in the 1950s with the influx of more students and the ascendancy of President Nasir.

As a result of their activism, ʿArafat and Khalaf were selected to head the first Palestinian student delegation to attend an international event as part of the Egyptian delegation to the July 1954 youth festival in Warsaw (although, a few hours before their plane was to leave, Khalaf was arrested on the grounds that he was "too dangerous" to leave the country). While such a conference and Palestinian participation in it may now appear a rather minor affair, at the time it was a major breakthrough. With the name Palestine erased from the political map and with no Palestinian body of international standing to represent Palestinians, participation in such an event was a significant achievement. It was the first opportunity for the PSU to participate—if under the auspices of an Egyptian delegation—in an international gathering where Palestinian identity could be asserted and the cause explained and promoted. For Palestinians it was an initial step toward reminding the world of their existence and problem.

Then came the students' opportunity to take on the Egyptian regime directly. In protest against the Egyptian army's inability to defend the population of Gaza (as demonstrated by a February 28, 1955 Israeli raid into the Strip which claimed more than three dozen lives), Palestinian students in Cairo organized strikes concomitant with strikes in Gaza and publicly called for bringing down the regime. They began a sit-in and hunger strike at the PSU's headquarters and presented the Egyptian authorities with three demands: the abolition of the visa system imposed on Palestinians entering and leaving Gaza; the resumption of train service between Cairo and Gaza (interrupted when the strike broke out); and the introduction of obligatory military training for Palestinians to enable them to defend themselves against Israeli attacks.[18] The students further demanded that Nasir discuss their grievances with them in person.

Although Nasir first asked to see a delegation of students, he finally agreed to give audience to all two hundred strikers. According to Khalaf, the atmosphere of the meeting soon became relaxed. After the session ended, the Egyptian president asked four of the students, Khalaf among them, to stay. A lively discussion ensued in which Nasir sought to learn from the students more about their organization as well as their feelings and aspirations. As Khalaf remembers, "We soon fell under the immense charm of the man, who seemed a great patriot."[19]

The students scored their first victory in an international organization in 1955, when a delegation to the International Union of Students (IUS) Congress, composed of ʿArafat, Khalaf, and Zuhayr al-ʿAlami, managed to thwart the efforts of the Israeli delegation and won for Palestinians full membership in the IUS.[20] In 1956, in a natural extension of their ever-broadening realm of activity, the students took up arms. In the wake of the combined French, British, and Israeli aggression against Egypt following Nasir's nationalization of the Suez Canal Company, they assembled a Palestinian commando unit to serve along with Egyptian volunteers. ʿArafat, a reserve officer in the Egyptian army, was sent to Port Saʿid to participate in a mine-sweeping operation. Khalaf, still "too dangerous," was refused authorization to go to the front, and instead had to content himself with keeping watch at Cairo's bridges.[21]

According to ʿArafat, none of these activities was as important as winning official Egyptian approval to publish and distribute a student magazine called *Sawt Filastin* (Voice of Palestine). According to the PLO chairman,

> to Palestinians it was so clear and obvious that our magazine was not for the student union. It was much more serious than that. . . . In the *Voice of Palestine* I was speaking to those of our Palestinian brothers who could be organizers of secret cells in other countries. The magazine was distributed in many places—in Gaza, Jordan, Syria, Iraq, Lebanon and so on. It was, in fact, our first

underground way of making contact with those who could organize.[22]

Just as the nature and range of PSU activities gradually changed, so did its political complexion. Repressed by Arab governments and suspect in many circles because of internal splits and controversy over its stand on the establishment of the State of Israel, the Communist party had never been able to win a mass following. Although the anti-Ikhwan campaign in Egypt that followed the attempt on Nasir's life in 1954 might have otherwise given the Communists an opportunity to expand their influence in the union, it was already too late. And, even had the Ikhwan not been pursued in Egypt, its strength was also waning. For a number of political and economic reasons, Nasir's strength and Arab nationalist line increased the appeal of pan-Arab parties like the newly ascendant Ba'th and the secret, well-organized ANM throughout the Arab East. While these parties were not permitted to operate openly in Egypt, PSU members came increasingly to identify with them.[23]

In addition to the rising Arab nationalist feeling in the region, the Ba'th and later the ANM partisans were aided in their efforts to win control of the PSU by the arrival in Egypt of two groups of Palestinian students expelled from Lebanon and Iraq to Egyptian universities. In 1954, the American University of Beirut expelled more than eighty students, among them a large number of Palestinians, for their participation in political activity on campus, which was against university policy. (In this way the university sought to avoid providing government security forces with a pretext for entering the university campus.) The group, which included a large number of ANM activists, proceeded to recruit aggressively among students in Egypt. In the union elections held in 1957, the Ba'this secured four seats, the Ikhwan four, and the independents one. These elections were the Ikhwan's last stand. It was then the Ba'th's turn for prominence.[24] The second group of students came from Iraq after the failure of the al-Shawwaf revolution in March 1959 in Mosul.[25] Like their AUB predecessors, these highly politicized students actively promoted greater political awareness and involvement among their Palestinian counterparts in Egypt.[26]

THE MOVE TOWARD GENERAL UNION

By early 1957 'Arafat, Khalaf, Qaddumi, and other members of the PSU old guard (those who later formed the core of Fateh) had graduated and left Egypt, many for employment in the Gulf states. Their hard work and activism laid a solid foundation for further expansion of the student movement. It was only a matter of time before the PSU took a leading role in the establishment of a diasporawide Palestinian students' organization.

To examine the origins of the idea of a general union of Palestinian students, the discussion must return for a moment to Iraq. After 'Abd al-Karim Qasim assumed power through a July 1958 coup, he began to establish Iraqi popular organizations along sectoral lines, including students. From this idea, the Palestinian students in Iraq, who had no prior permission from the government, conceived of setting up a secret office to work toward establishing a federation to unify the disparate Palestinian student groups.[27] In late 1958, Zuhayr al-Khatib, president of the PSU, also urged the Palestinian students in Iraq to organize formally. Negotiations followed between the Ba'thi and ANM elements among the Palestinian students in Iraq. After agreeing upon the structure of the secret office, they then contacted the Palestinian student organizations in Egypt, Lebanon, and Syria regarding establishing a student federation. However, in 1959, the deterioration of Egyptian-Iraqi relations, particularly after the abortive Mosul revolt, led Qasim to expel Palestinians with Nasirist tendencies, among them the student leaders. Many went first to Syria and then, after meeting there with Nasir, to Egypt.

In Cairo, the PSU's pro-Nasir Ba'thi majority proposed to the Egyptian president the idea of establishing a general union of Palestinian students. Nasir lent full support to the idea of establishing a Palestinian student federation with headquarters in Cairo.[28] Plans for gathering together Palestinian student leaders from across the diaspora were set in motion. Finally, on November 29, 1959, representatives of Palestinian student groups in Cairo, Asyut, Alexandria, Damascus, and Beirut attended the first conference of the General Union of Palestine Students (GUPS), held at Cairo University.

According to Egyptian law, organizations like the PSU, which registered with the Ministry of Social Affairs, were not permitted to operate transnationally. In the case of the GUPS, Nasir waived the restriction. Jurisdiction over its affairs was transferred to the executive branch of the Egyptian government, that is, Nasir.[29]

POLITICAL HISTORY OF THE GUPS[30]

The list below presents chronologically the prevailing political trends in the PSU (Cairo) and then the GUPS in general.[31] It should be noted that as the individual country branches of the GUPS developed, they tended to take on the political coloring of the host regimes or their dominant parties.

pre-1958: Ikhwan majority with Communist minority
1958–1963: Ascendancy of the Ba'th party
1963–1965: ANM holds power
1966: Brief period of power held by the independents (supported by Fateh) and problems between the GUPS and Nasir
1967–1987: Fateh takes over the leadership, sometimes in coalition with PFLP or DF elements or others, depending upon the country

Most of the work of the November 29, 1959 conference that proclaimed the establishment of the general union dealt with organizational and constitutional matters. One of the most significant issues, and one that has plagued the other Palestinian unions established subsequently, was whether the union was to be a student guild or a political movement. What was the union's purpose? What sort of constitution should it have? The PSU had no set ideas, just as it had no organizational regulations. In fact, guest delegations from North Africa—the General Union of Tunisian Students, the National Union of Moroccan Students, and the Muslim Algerian Students Union—helped the GUPS founders draft a formula to combine the two faces of the union.[32]

The political rivalries that characterized GUPS (and subsequently PLO) politics surfaced immediately in the first conference. For example, ANM members clashed with the Ba'this over proportional representation in the union's executive council. At the time, the ANM controlled the Beirut organization and had a majority in the student organizations in Damascus and Alexandria. Strengthened by the Egyptian-Syrian union, the Ba'th had also attracted large numbers of Palestinians, and it held sway in Cairo, the seat of the union. Thus, it was the Ba'th that ultimately prevailed. Not to be so quickly defeated, the ANM resolved to oust the Ba'this from their position of GUPS dominance through stepped-up organizing both inside and outside the union.[33]

The political posturing of Palestinian students was a serious matter, for, in the absence of a Palestinian political entity, the GUPS was the sole forum in which Palestinians could express themselves politically as Palestinians. For those students committed to their cause, GUPS elections and political debates evoked enthusiasm and passion. Clearly, Arab leaders also knew that the student organization was more than just youngsters playing at politics. From Nasir of Egypt to Faysal of Saudi Arabia, Arab presidents and kings met with and listened to the student leaders. They treated the GUPS as a political organization of consequence: they subsidized it to increase their influence and swiftly repressed it when the subsidies failed to work their political magic.

On the inter-Arab student level, one of the GUPS's first acts following its establishment was to conclude an agreement with Jordanian student groups that designated West Bank students as a GUPS constituency alone. In practice, this meant that if a West Banker wanted to join a student group it had to be the GUPS. The move aimed at strengthening the young Palestinian union.[34] As it matured, the GUPS not only assisted the Arab student groups with their activities, but also helped to found several of them and was the moving force behind the establishment of the General Union of Arab Students.

The second GUPS conference was originally scheduled for the summer of 1960, but the leadership did not fulfill its responsibilities and thus was forced to postpone the conference. The decision to postpone the conference created a crisis between the executive committee and the branches. The executive committee continued to oversee the union as the dissolution of the UAR led to a second postponement of the conference and further deterioration in executive committee–branch relations.

As was the case in later disputes and feuds, the natural political rivalries and disagreements that characterize such an organization became inextricably tied to inter-Arab developments. In this case, the dissolution of the Egyptian-Syrian union led the Ba'this to turn on Nasir (and he on them) and turn to Syria for support. From the "president's party" in the GUPS, the Ba'th was transformed into the "not-so-loyal" opposition.

The heads of the chapters assembled and requested a meeting with the Ba'th-dominated GUPS executive committee in Cairo, but their request was refused and the ANM-dominated Alexandria and Beirut chapters were charged with "sabotage." When the second conference was finally convened in Gaza on October 25, 1962, the effects of the infighting were obvious. The GUPS executive committee succeeded in preventing the Aachen, Germany representatives from attending while it gave an unelected representative from Asyut delegate status.[35] Despite the controversy that marred the conference, the delegates approved several historic resolutions. They called for the establishment of a Palestinian entity, a liberation army, and a liberation organization—the first resolutions of their kind.[36]

The political infighting continued. Following the second conference the non-Ba'thi Cairo-based members of the GUPS administrative council, with the backing of the Egyptian regime, moved to expel a number of the Ba'this from the executive committee. They then assembled a temporary executive committee, composed of independents and ANM members from the administrative council, which took over on August 14, 1963.[37] To help purge the union, the Egyptian government expelled several Ba'thi students and prevented certain members of the administrative council from coming to Cairo. The expelled Ba'this gathered in Damascus where they declared themselves the legitimate representatives of the union—the first *inshiqaq* (split).[38] After forming their own executive committee, they attacked the Egyptian authorities and charged the new executive committee in Cairo with both collaborating with outside powers and plotting against the union. Despite its less than democratic origins, the new, temporary executive committee in Cairo did reflect the political orientation that prevailed among the students at the time. The other branches of the GUPS responded by announcing their support for the anti-Ba'thi "coup."[39]

The ANM members finally gained numerical control of the union during the third GUPS conference, held in February 1964. To do so they had made an alliance with Fateh (whose power base was in the chapters in Germany) and independents (who drew support from the chapters in Port Sa'id and Alexandria). To ensure victory, the ANM had mobilized the previously unorganized Palestinian students to open new chapters and thereby increase its influence. As shown above, the decline of the Ba'th—a direct result of Syria's withdrawal from the union with Egypt—greatly facilitated their efforts.[40] Others have suggested, however, that by using its pro-Nasirist orientation against the Syrian Ba'th, the ANM was also able to enlist the support of Egyptian intelligence in its quest for GUPS control.[41]

During the period between the third and fourth conferences, the PLO was established. The GUPS was certainly not opposed to the establishment of a liberation organization: it will be recalled that it was the first Palestinian organization to call for such an entity. However, the leadership of the PLO was overwhelmingly composed of members of the traditional Palestinian elite, many of whom were viewed by the younger generation as ineffective and in part responsible for the loss of Palestine. Just as important, the GUPS had continually tried to maintain its independence of host states, and the Arab League had in fact recognized it as a distinct entity. Its political achievements, which were substantial, and its growing power and importance have been detailed above. Nevertheless, the charter of the new PLO refered to the GUPS as one of the bases of the liberation organization without even consulting it. The students resented what they considered an obvious attempt by Shuqayri to assert control over the union. Mistrustful of the PLO's leadership, political style, and intentions vis-à-vis the GUPS, the students issued a sharp criticism of the PLO on June 18, 1964.[42] Nasir, although a supporter of the students, was also Shuqayri's main patron; and thus arose the first dispute between Nasir, the students, and, by extension, the ANM.[43]

When the GUPS administrative council met on October 12, 1964, determining the relationship between the union and the PLO topped the agenda. The agreement worked out between the students and a PLO representative who attended the meeting included the following points: the PLO agreed to help fund the GUPS; it would not interfere in internal GUPS affairs; and former PLO officials or "members" would not try to join the GUPS. The administrative council of the GUPS did vote to consider the union one of the popular bases of the PLO, but stated its intention to remain aloof from Arab and Palestinian parties, organizational fronts, and political currents.

In 1960 the union had embarked upon a program of developing ties with student organizations in socialist and African countries and, to a more limited degree, groups in the United States and Europe. The GUPS began sending delegations to conferences of friendly student unions and in turn inviting foreign delegations to its conferences. These ties also involved various forms of expression of solidarity, the issuing of communiqués or drafting of resolutions on matters of importance to the sister unions.

In 1965, the GUPS undertook its first major international activity by organizing a large Palestine Symposium held in Cairo on March 30, 1965. Attended by delegations from fifty-eight countries, the conference was the first of its kind and thus constituted an important public relations, informational, and political breakthrough not just for the

GUPS, but for the Palestinians at large. Nasir provided financial and organizational support for the symposium to which not students, but political leaders and intellectuals from around the world, were invited. To the surprise and satisfaction of Nasir and the students, the conference was a tremendous success. Well attended, it made an invaluable contribution to publicizing the Palestine issue on an international level.[44]

Despite PLO promises, the organization offered the GUPS only minimal support for the symposium. The honeymoon was over, and PLO-GUPS relations began to deteriorate further at about the time of the fourth student conference (held in Cairo beginning December 22, 1965). The PLO abandoned its vow not to interfere in the GUPS, and so the GUPS set to work to change the PLO leadership.[45]

Another development with far-reaching implications for the GUPS and the PLO was that with Syrian support Fateh's military wing, al-ʿAsifah, had begun to carry out guerrilla operations in early 1965. Lack of consensus on the need for independent Palestinian military action (undoubtedly influenced by the sad state of Egyptian-Syrian relations and the fact that Fateh was Syrian supported) led the GUPS administrative council to pass a resolution in which it neither supported nor criticized al-ʿAsifah's activities. The committee's equivocation on the issue of military activity refueled internal GUPS disputes, and the fourth GUPS conference was convened in December 1965 in the midst of these tensions.

At the time of the branch and chapter elections that preceded the fourth GUPS conference, two election lists were submitted: one included pro-PLO members, including the Palestine Liberation Front (PLF), Fateh, and some independents; the other consisted of ANM supporters and some independents. Since the PLO was beginning to stress mass organizing, Ahmad Sidqi al-Dajani (PLF), who headed the efforts, was charged with lobbying the GUPS on the PLO's behalf in Egypt. The results were impressive: in the chapters in Egypt, the PLO-supported list won overwhelmingly. However, latent tensions surfaced as PLO chief Shuqayri attended the GUPS conference and tried to force the election of a leadership composed of his supporters. As a result, Fateh and ANM partisans alike withdrew and the conference was unable to complete its session.[46] A split in the union was narrowly avoided when the competing factions agreed to form a new executive committee (with Muhammad Subayh, an independent, as president; Taysir Qubʿah, an ANM member, as vice-president for external affairs; some members of Fateh, and some independents) and published a charter of national action to guide the union until the fifth conference was convened.[47] In other words, they agreed to disagree until the next conference.

The fifth conference, scheduled for December 1966, was first postponed for administrative reasons until July 1967. However, the disruption caused by the June 1967 war forced a further delay, as many GUPS members left their places of study to join the Palestinian resistance movement. Their departure upset the results of branch elections held before the war, which had continued to give a majority to the ANM. In the aftermath of the war, student interest in the GUPS skyrocketed. Twenty-six new branches participated in the fifth conference, which was finally convened in Amman on July 31, 1969.

Much had changed since the fourth conference. Shuqayri, discredited by association with Arab regimes, had been ousted as PLO chief, and after Yahya Hammudah's brief term in office, former student activist Yasir ʿArafat assumed the PLO's chairmanship. Meanwhile, Palestinian-Jordanian relations neared the precipice as *fidaʾiyyin* activity expanded and challenged the Hashemite regime.

More critical for the future development of the union was that the rise of the resistance and the change in the nature of the PLO to a more mass-based organization with legitimacy among the vast majority of Palestinians deprived the GUPS of its most basic, former role, that of a widely accepted Palestinian representative. The new PLO leadership, most of whom were GUPS "graduates," took over as legitimate spokesmen of the Palestinians—a role over which the GUPS and the PLO had battled. The GUPS never regained its former position. It had created the skilled leadership, whose assumption of the reins of the PLO rendered its most dynamic contribution, to a certain extent, redundant.[48]

It was in the fifth national conference that the GUPS leadership finally passed to Fateh, which had become the preeminent political faction among Palestinians at large. The new political composition of the union was immediately reflected in changes in GUPS policy. The union amended its constitution to give it a more Palestinian nationalist character (as opposed to its former Arab nationalist stance) and to stress the centrality of armed struggle. The union even established a special committee to study ways of increasing GUPS participation in the armed struggle.

The sixth conference was held between July 30 and August 7, 1971 in Algeria, far from the battlefield. Unlike the prevailing climate at the fifth conference (which had been characterized by the growth of the

Palestinian revolution, especially on the Palestinian-Jordanian front), this conference was convened in the aftermath of fierce fighting in Jarash and ʿAjlun through which the Jordanian army had liquidated the PRM's military presence in the country. Given the precarious political situation, delegates exercised great caution in discussions, so as not to prejudice other Arab regimes' relations with the resistance and the PLO. To this end, democratic procedure was compromised. Some delegates were not permitted to speak, topics were placed off limits for discussion, and sessions were closed when they could no longer be controlled.[49] The limitations were no doubt also in part responsible for the absence of bitter election fighting for control of the administrative council and the executive committee. And, for the first time, the factional alliances in the branches neither replicated the alliances of the center (Egypt), nor were they directed from it.[50]

ADDRESSING STUDENT NEEDS

Before examining post-1970 developments in the GUPS, particularly in Egypt, it is useful to examine the union's role in students' daily lives. When the GUPS was formed in 1959, its goals included serving the general needs of Palestinians and defending their rights.[51] Moreover, it brought together Palestinian students from each of the diaspora communities, and to a certain degree recreated a Palestinian society. In so doing it helped to bridge the gaps that might have developed between a Palestinian from Jordan and a Palestinian from Gaza, or Egypt, or anywhere else in the diaspora.[52]

As part of its efforts to serve students, the Cairo chapter provided temporary housing for new students until they found apartments. Later, after the chapter's membership grew, it opened special dorms for Palestinian students and arranged for free or low-cost medical checkups. Upperclassmen assisted freshmen with registration and in general facilitated their adjustment to university life away from home. Every Thursday the chapter sponsored cultural symposia which included films, speeches, and discussion. It also organized short field trips and sponsored sports teams to create a healthy social atmosphere. GUPS parties marked occasions of national significance. In addition, two monthly magazines, *Jabal al-Zaytun* (Mount of Olives) and *al-Ittihad* (The Union), were published in Cairo by the GUPS.

The students took an interest in the entire Palestinian community and tried to include it in their events. Especially in the early period, students served as vehicles of political consciousness raising in the community as they engaged in political organizing on behalf of the organization or party to which they belonged. The GUPS also arranged short trips and outings for members of the community to increase their ties with the union.[53]

On balance, what the GUPS had to offer to improve the material lot of Palestinian students was minimal. As an outsider in every country of its operation, the union had no mechanism to press for student academic demands other than through cooperation with the student union of the host state. Thus, it was generally a student devoted to his or her people and their cause who joined the union. Students gave to the union rather than the reverse, both in terms of time and money. Often a member's only compensation or reward were frequent interrogation sessions with the Egyptian police.[54]

FUNDING SOURCES AND MEMBERSHIP

Funding sources for the PSU were limited to membership dues, contributions, and revenue from parties and films it sponsored. In 1953, it began to receive assistance from the All-Chinese Students League. After the founding of the GUPS, members of the executive council, located in Cairo, made yearly fund-raising trips through the Arab world, but concentrated on the Gulf where many former union members worked. The trips used to bring in JD (Jordanian dinar) 15,000 ($42,000) annually.[55]

Former members insist that the union accepted financial contributions, but without political strings. The political diversity of the donors no doubt assisted the union in its drive for independence of operation, but attempts to balance the demands and whims of monarch and soldier, reactionary and revolutionary, often incurred the wrath of the host regimes. Prior to the establishment of the PLO, and even until 1967–68, the GUPS constituted the sole political voice of the Palestinians with a mass support base. As such, in the course of their efforts to solicit contributions, open new chapters, and publicize the Palestinian cause, the young leaders of the GUPS were initiated into the world of international and inter-Arab diplomacy. The extensive and diverse sources of financial support that the union enjoyed are witness to the seriousness with which the Arab heads of state viewed the union. In effect, they accepted the GUPS as a legitimate Palestinian voice. The lessons in diplomacy and statecraft were probably unparalleled for men and women so young. Schooled in the art of compromise and pragmatism from an early age, they established contacts that continue to serve them to the present.[56]

Although the problem of finance weighed heavily in the early period, student recruitment developed as a much greater problem.[57] Many students feared expulsion, a common fate of those who became too involved in politics, particularly if their activity did not conform to the prevailing orientation of the regime.[58] Others could not afford the time that active union membership demanded. Some paid dues but appeared at union headquarters only at election time.

Most of the former GUPS officials interviewed spent several years beyond the four normally required to complete a bachelor's degree. For them and for many others, the union became the center of their lives to the near exclusion of their studies. Although the preoccupation clearly had its drawbacks, it demonstrates the extent of the union's role among students. As one former GUPS member stated, "The union office was the Palestinians' mosque and church." As a hub of political and social activity, the union engendered a camaraderie among adherents of diverse political persuasions which, according to former members, continues to this day.[59]

THE SURGE IN EGYPTIAN ACTIVISM

As with many of the trends that crystallized after Nasir's death, Egyptian student activism really began to reemerge in the 1967–68 period, in the wake of the humiliating June 1967 defeat. Egyptian students had been quite vocal in the 1940s, but under Nasir they had remained quiescent, in part as a result of their support for the president and in part as a result of pervasive regime control and repression after 1954. However, in February and November 1968 they exploded in the most serious expressions of public discontent following the 1967 defeat. The February uprising actually began among workers in the industrial area of Hilwan, south of Cairo, after the announcement of what were considered to be excessively lenient verdicts against the leaders of the Egyptian air force (who were generally held responsible for the 1967 defeat).

Thousands of students from both Cairo and Alexandria universities (including GUPS members)[60] participated in the unrest, which lasted until February 27, with students from the engineering faculties playing a particularly notable role. In Cairo alone two workers were killed, 77 civilians and 146 policemen were injured, and 635 people were arrested. Although moved to act by the court verdicts, the students focused their demands on the question of democracy in the country as a whole and in the university in particular.[61]

It was at least in part as a response to the student unrest that Nasir issued his program of March 30 for a relative liberalization of the political system. Nevertheless, a second wave of student unrest erupted in November 1968 in the Delta city of al-Mansurah following the promulgation of a new education act limiting the number of times secondary school students could take the college entrance exams (al-thanawiyyah al-'ammah). Disturbances spread to al-Azhar and Alexandria. Again, some students were killed and many others were arrested.[62]

Although relative calm reigned during the 1969–1971 war of attrition, activism continued. Students organized numerous societies, published a multitude of "wall magazines," and held conferences.[63] The societies differed in nature, but some were clearly political, most prominent among them the Society of the Supporters of the Palestinian Revolution (SSPR), established in Cairo University's faculty of engineering by a group of activists, some of whom had visited refugee camps in Jordan or had experience with the Palestinian resistance. A major impetus for their founding was the November 1971 assassination of Jordanian prime minister Wasfi al-Tal in Cairo at the hands of the Black September group. Composed overwhelmingly of Egyptian students (although there were some Palestinian members), the SSPR's primary aim was to secure the release of the four guerrillas responsible for the killing.[64]

These student committees, particularly the SSPR, gradually became involved in a more generalized protest against Sadat's policies and in fact came to constitute the nucleus of the 1972 campus riots. Sadat had spoken of 1971 as the year of decision for action against Israel. But 1971 came and passed with no new initiatives. The Egyptian president faced crises on both the economic and military fronts, yet lacked the popularity or legitimacy that had enabled his predecessor to survive similar challenges. The most overt manifestation of these crises was the student movement. While student demands covered a wide range of domestic issues (students of both the right and the left joined the battle), Palestine and Egypt's role (or lack of role) in the conflict was a major concern of many.[65]

Indeed, one analyst attributed the spark that rekindled student activism to Palestine Week, held at the end of December 1971 and sponsored by students in the engineering faculty of Cairo University. Sadat's January 1972 speech about the postponement of the "decisive year" had included a condemnation of the "group of sympathizers with the Palestinian revolution" who had organized the event. The unrest, which began two days after Sadat's speech and lasted into February, involved students from both Cairo University and al-Azhar, and resulted in the arrest of thousands of students.[66] The government accused the Palestinian resistance—which Sadat claimed had 20,000 students in Cairo[67]—of being behind the 1972 riots and arrested a number of Palestinian students.[68] Despite Sadat's claim, the student unrest should be understood as an Egyptian reaction to Egyptian policies, not as Palestinian inspired, organized, or triggered. The issue of Palestine and the Palestinians was a factor not in and of itself, but because of Egypt's integral involvement in the Arab-Israeli conflict.[69]

Again in March 1972, when Palestinian students demonstrated outside the Jordanian embassy in Cairo against Husayn's newly proposed United Arab Kingdom (a federation of East and West banks under his leadership), Egyptian security forces stepped in to protect the embassy. The Palestinian students sent a strong note of protest to the Egyptian government.[70] Sadat's expulsion of the Soviet advisors, announced on July 23, 1972, only served as an additional focus for mounting discontent among various sectors, particularly students. When the GUPS openly criticized the move, the regime responded by dissolving the joint Egyptian-Palestinian student committees and arresting some of their members.[71]

Egypt's participation and performance in the 1973 war apparently placated many in the Egyptian student movement and gained for the regime the legitimacy it so sorely needed. Although in November 1976, following January workers' strikes in Cairo, March textile workers' strikes in al-Mahallah al-Kubra, and September strikes by bus drivers, five hundred leftist students demonstrated for the right to form new political parties,[72] the uprisings of 1972 were not repeated. Egyptian student activism was largely relegated to the waning left[73] (until 1977 witnessed a resurgence in the power of Islamic groups which continues in Egyptian universities to the present).

Palestinian student activity was closely tied in this period to activity among Egyptian students, as the surge among the Egyptian students opened the way for a similar flourishing of Palestinian activism. On a purely Palestinian level, the major concern of the post-1973 war period was the proposal, which had come from certain Palestinian quarters, for the establishment of an independent Palestinian state in part (as opposed to all) of Palestine. This suggestion created a great deal of controversy in the union (as it did throughout Palestinian society) since it marked the abandonment of the goal of total liberation and indicated the acceptability of a diplomatic rather than a military solution. Many felt that this contradicted the PLO charter.

Palestinian cooperation and coordination with Egyptian students, notably the leftists, grew. But repression also increased. At the same time, internal GUPS conflicts and debates were further exacerbated by the civil war in Lebanon, and specifically the Syrian intervention. Many students abandoned their former political affiliations. Some joined new parties. Divergence of opinion among Fateh supporters was so great that two election lists were entered under its name in 1976 GUPS elections.[74]

As dissatisfaction with Sadat's policies mounted (especially following the conclusion of the second Sinai disengagement agreement in September 1975), the regime felt compelled to clamp down more forcefully on student activism, particularly among Palestinians. Members of the administrative council of the GUPS were expelled in 1976 as were other Palestinian activists who supported the students against the regime.[75] No new Palestinian students were accepted into Egyptian universities in Cairo, and the tuition exemption, even for those Palestinians who came from the community in Egypt, was canceled. From then on all Palestinians were required to pay for their education, and in hard currency.[76]

The breaking point came in November 1977, when Sadat journeyed to Jerusalem. Anger among Palestinian students exploded in anti-Sadat demonstrations. The regime had finally had enough. Its change in political course on the international level—from confrontation to accommodation—had already become clear; the demonstrations simply led to the natural domestic conclusion. Among the measures of repression, large numbers of Palestinian students were expelled and the union was closed. (The GUPS activity was not officially halted—by the PLO—until 1979, when the PLO froze its relations with the Egyptian government upon the signing of the Camp David accords.) Despite the crackdown, at the end of 1979 there were still nearly 12,000 Palestinian students studying at Egyptian universities.[77]

Beirut remained until 1982 as a GUPS center and refuge, but the GUPS never regained the power and stature of its Cairo days. While the advent of the Mubarak regime marked the beginning of a new era of gradual, if cautious, improvement in the sorely strained Egyptian-

Palestinian relations, the GUPS alone among the Palestinian unions has not been reopened. Fearing that the timing is not yet right and the request may be denied, the PLO has not asked for permission to remove the lock from the door of the pre-1977 GUPS headquarters which is, ironically, the former office of the All-Palestine Government.

[5]
The Search for Community:
The GUPW, GUPWom, GUPT, and PRCS

Few in number and scattered throughout the country, Palestinians in Egypt were virtually engulfed by overwhelming numbers of Egyptians. In order to blend in with their surroundings, many Palestinians in Egypt adapted their dialect and customs to those of Egypt; and marriage to Egyptians, often the only sure route to a more secure residency, was not uncommon. Many people lost track of where their former compatriots were and often, at least in terms of outward indicators, became virtually indistinguishable from their Egyptian hosts.

As a result, organizing among such a group on the basis of Palestinian identity, and reestablishing community, posed severe problems. This chapter examines efforts by Palestinians to organize laborers, women, and teachers, and to construct an affiliate branch of a health organization. As the case studies below demonstrate, the impetus for reorganizing did not come initially from members of the indigenous Palestinian community, but rather from Palestinians from outside whose presence was often temporary. Moreover, when mobilizing efforts succeeded, they owed their success in no small measure to support from the Egyptian regime, which in some cases subsidized activities at home and in others sponsored union efforts to expand abroad.

THE WORKERS

Labor or trade union organizing among Palestinians first began in 1925 under the auspices of the Palestinian Arab Workers Society, headquartered in Haifa (for a discussion of the labor movement in Jordan, see chapter 10). The society actively defended workers' rights and played an important role in the Arab Palestinian national struggle against increasing Jewish immigration to Palestine. The establishment of the State of Israel and the destruction and human displacement that followed ended the activity of the branches of the society in the areas over which Israeli sovereignty was established—most notably the two strongest branches, those in Haifa and Jaffa. The Palestinian dispersal and the lack of a sovereign national base from which to organize complicated the development and goals of the trade union movement. After the Palestine war, many trade union activists regrouped in Nablus, the major industrial city of the West Bank, and attempted to continue their work. However, a military coup attempt in Jordan in 1957 brought the imposition of wide-ranging political restrictions, and some Palestinian labor leaders were forced to seek political asylum in Syria and then, after the breakup of the Egyptian-Syrian union in 1961, in Egypt.

Despite the small size of the Palestinian working class in Egypt, Cairo provided the most conducive conditions for the major reorganizing thrust. In the first place, given Egypt's rising influence in the 1950s, Cairo was the political and cultural center of the Arab world. The International Federation of Arab Trade Unions (IFATU) was headquartered in Cairo. Furthermore, after the breakup of the Egyptian-Syrian union, Nasir undoubtedly felt he could boost his standing in the Arab world by supporting Palestinian reorganization. As with the students, such mobilization in Egypt posed little or no security threat. The Palestinian community was too small to be, by itself, a political force of any consequence and Egyptian intelligence could easily keep an eye on the union leadership. And, as was the case with Palestinian students in Egypt, the workers who pushed for the reestablishment of a Palestinian trade union in Egypt, best known among them Husni Salih al-Khuffash of Nablus, came from Palestinian communities outside Egypt.

Khuffash, who had come to Egypt from Syria in 1961 as a political refugee (for which he drew a salary from the UAR), began his efforts to regroup Palestinian workers from within the IFATU. In May 1962 he sent a letter to, and later met with, the head of the IFATU, Muhammad As'ad Rajih. In the letter he stressed the importance of having an experienced Palestinian capable of explaining the Palestine issue present as a delegate in the union and he asked that the IFATU include such a representative in its conferences. Khuffash and Rajih also discussed the need for organizing Palestinian workers. Khuffash found the IFATU president sympathetic, for in both cases he offered to put all the facilities of the general secretariat of the union at the disposal of the Palestine issue.[1]

At first all Khuffash asked for was a small office. Then on May 25, 1962 he issued a statement in the name of the General Committee for Palestine Workers calling upon Palestinians to unite. Another former Palestinian trade unionist, Naji al-Kawni, then joined the ranks. Kawni, also from Nablus, had been a port worker in Haifa, but in 1948 had returned to Nablus, where he helped organize the electrical and municipal workers. The committee, composed only of Khuffash and Kawni, began to produce a weekly publication, *al-Nashrah*, which was circulated primarily in Gaza, but throughout the Arab world as well. The committee subsequently enlisted the aid of two other former labor activists, Husayn al-Husayni and Ruhi al-Zamr. On October 27, 1962, Khuffash became supervisor of the IFATU newspaper and publications, through which he began to introduce with greater frequency articles dealing with the Palestine question.[2]

After launching the publication, the men began their efforts to organize the workers. Kawni, originally a mechanic, was responsible for the Hilwan area, where the auto factories and the iron and steel works had originally caught the committee's attention. Kawni visited Hilwan virtually every day, going from factory to factory to talk with workers. As an outsider, unknown by the workers, his task was a difficult one. According to him, the greatest hurdle was convincing the men that the government was not opposed to the idea of their organizing.[3] After Kawni convinced them that such an organization would serve their interests, the Chapter of Palestine Workers in Hilwan was established, composed of Kawni and six others.

In 1963, Khuffash made a series of trips abroad related to his organizing efforts. As head of an IFATU mission to the People's Republic of China, he succeeded in having the Palestine issue put on the agenda, and the conference published several decisions in support of the Palestinians and their cause. At the time, such an achievement in an international arena was virtually unprecedented. Khuffash also continued his efforts on the Arab front. In February 1963 he visited Kuwait with an eye toward organizing the large Palestinian working class and then in August 1963 went to Gaza to investigate working conditions there.[4]

As the only part of Palestine that had not been annexed by Jordan or become a part of Israel, Gaza, in the minds of Khuffash and others, constituted the most natural place for the reemergence of a strong Palestinian labor movement. Khuffash's memoirs describe the terrible working conditions in the Strip and place substantial blame on the Palestinian upper classes which, in conjunction with the Egyptian military administration, worked to block efforts at trade union organizing.[5] Kawni confirmed that the Gazan upper classes opposed their labor organizing efforts, but he claimed that they were able to work out an arrangement to avoid inter-Palestinian conflict.[6] In 1963 six unions were opened in Gaza for the metal industries, carpentry and construction, agricultural workers, public services workers and commercial employees, drivers, and tailors and weavers.[7]

In the meantime, Khuffash and Kawni had been continuing to recruit among Palestinian workers in Egypt. Their initial successes in Hilwan were followed by others in Cairo, Kafr al-Shaykh, Suhag, Qina, Alexandria, al-Buhayrah, Tanta, and Qalyubiyyah (where Palestinians worked in the largest chemical factory in Egypt). On August 3, 1963, their efforts finally culminated in the proclamation by the chapters of Palestinian workers in Egypt of the establishment of the General Union of Palestine Workers (also known as the PTUF, the Palestinian Trade Union Federation). The secretaries of each of the local chapters were tapped to form the executive committee of the new federation. The primary target of the organizers remained Gaza, but resistance to their efforts had been negligible in Egypt itself, and Khuffash and his cohorts believed that the proclamation of the union would assist in organizing attempts elsewhere, particularly in the Strip.[8]

As part of the Gaza campaign, on March 28, 1964, the IFATU sponsored the Palestine Conference in Gaza. Since many of the Palestinians who participated had not seen each other since 1948, the conference served to reinforce national ties, boost morale, and spur them on to greater action. Attended by labor representatives from throughout the Arab world and beyond, the conference encouraged Palestinian workers in Gaza and elsewhere to mobilize and demand more freedom to organize. In its wake, the GUPW increased the frequency of publication of *al-Nashrah* and its circulation widened. Meanwhile, Khuffash continued to visit concentrations of Palestinian workers, and in 1964 branches of Palestinian workers in Kuwait and Baghdad joined the GUPW (see chapter 7).

Its successes not withstanding, the growing GUPW suffered from a lack of formal consensus upon principles and goals. Therefore, the GUPW general secretariat received permission from As'ad Rajih for Palestinian labor representatives from Egypt, Gaza, and elsewhere to attend an IFATU educational symposium in order to elect an executive committee and unify the union's political stance. Several meetings were held during the symposium in late July 1964 in which the representatives adopted a temporary constitution, selected an executive committee from their ranks, and elected Khuffash general secretary. The GUPW declared itself a base of the PLO and on August 30, 1964, sent the PLO a letter to that effect.[9]

Despite its growth, by virtue of its origins and, more important, its source of monetary support, the GUPW remained a part of the IFATU. In a meeting in late 1964, however, Khuffash effectively declared the union's independence by refusing to take further monetary assistance from the IFATU. The separation was not the result of political differences or anger over treatment. Khuffash simply felt the time had come—and that it was possible—for the GUPW to stand on its own. Until that time all its needs had been taken care of by the IFATU, to the extent, according to Kawni, that the workers wondered why it was they were paying membership dues.[10] Therefore, the GUPW general secretary insisted that the union would rely solely on membership dues for support and proceeded to rent an independent office on Ramsis Street in downtown Cairo.[11]

Despite the boost that came with the GUPW's founding, union organizing efforts in Gaza continued to encounter problems with the military administration. Kawni downplayed the difficulties encountered in Gaza as perhaps stemming from security considerations.[12] He insisted that the government never imposed any restrictions. Khuffash, on the other hand, notes in his memoirs, for example, that the military governor of Gaza, at that time General Yusif al-Aghrudi, pushed for the transfer of GUPW headquarters to Gaza where Gazans (presumably cooperative Gazans) would have occupied leadership positions and where, presumably, the military would have had direct control. He also contends that the military administration tried to pressure the Gazan unions by making licensing contingent upon their remaining separate from the GUPW. Clauses tacked onto labor and work legislation placed additional pressures on the unions.[13]

While Gaza was still the primary focus of their organizing efforts, even had there not been some opposition to free organizing, moving the GUPW headquarters to the Strip was not deemed desirable by the leadership. Cairo had embassies, Arab and international labor organizations, and cultural centers and activities. To have transfered the headquarters to Gaza would have meant severely curtailing the union's informational work and restricting its access to its major sources of moral and financial support.[14]

Ironically, then, yet certainly appropriately, the GUPW's first conference was held in Gaza in April 1965. At the time, the GUPW was controlled by independents close to Nasir who enthusiastically supported the new PLO and its chairman Ahmad al-Shuqayri[15]—hence the GUPW support for the PLO while other organizations, like the GUPS, expressed reservations. The union proclaimed itself one of the bases of the PLO, supported the decision of the Gazan legislative council that imposed conscription and a liberation tax on Gazans, and called upon Palestinian workers to make themselves available to the military council of the PLO and to take advantage of all opportunities for military training.[16]

It was decided at the conference that the GUPW executive committee should include three Gazans and one representative each from the branches in Egypt, Lebanon, Syria, and Iraq (in addition to General-Secretary Khuffash). In the elections, Naji al-Kawni secured a seat on the eight-member executive council. The three Gazans elected were Mahmud Abu Satit, ʿAbd al-Rahman Darabiyyah, and Muhammad Abu Layl. In addition, the eighteen-member higher council of the union, from which the executive council was chosen, counted three members from the Egypt branch and five from Gaza.[17] The heavy representation of these two communities in the union hierarchy may have been due, at least in part, to Egypt's invisible hand of control. The first conference witnessed a political struggle between the independents, led by Khuffash, and the ANM members, headed by Ahmad al-Yamani from the GUPW branch in Lebanon, although a Palestinian historian described the struggle as more of a clash of personal followings than of political differences.[18] Khuffash electorally strongarmed Yamani to be elected general secretary.

The nature of the resolutions published by the conference accurately reflected the union's goals, as the political content dominated. Despite the fact that the GUPW was ostensibly a trade union, none of the conference's resolutions dealt with traditional workers' concerns. Although one of the studies presented to the conference on strengthening the organizational aspect of the union stressed that each branch needed a meeting place where ties among workers could be solidified, and where workers could gather for discussions and consciousness-raising sessions, even here, the goal was clearly political mobilization.[19]

When the GUPW higher council met in mid-March 1966, it issued a plan of action, again with high political and low trade union content, although it did call for educational symposia for workers. More important, the council mentioned the need to try to coordinate efforts with fellow Palestinian workers in Jordan: "We all know the conditions of our people in Jordan and the sensitivity stemming from fear of working on a Palestinian basis. . . . At the same time we all realize that it is very difficult or impossible to liberate Palestine without the participation of our Palestinian people in Jordan."[20]

The GUPW's second conference was held in Cairo in April 1967, on the eve of the June war. In addition to the usual political resolutions, it named Jordan the primary base for launching the national struggle and called upon the people to bring down the Jordanian regime.[21] In the union elections, Khuffash held on to his post as general secretary. The higher council was enlarged from eighteen to twenty-two members, with three from Egypt and five from Gaza. Palestinians from Egypt and Gaza continued to dominate the hierarchy as the executive committee counted two from Egypt and three from Gaza, while the five-member general secretariat included Khuffash, Kawni, and Darabiyyah.[22]

Cairo was also the host for the third GUPW conference (1969), but by the time of its convening much had changed: PLO leadership had passed to the *fida'iyyin*. Resolutions remained highly political; however, the union did call for the establishment of productive cooperatives and agricultural projects aimed at employing Palestinian workers and preparing them for entering productive fields.[23] It called for a concomitant development of the fighting potential of the workers.

In the early days the union's political inclination had been independent/Nasirist. With the rise of the commando organizations in the PLO, only Fateh was allowed to operate in Egypt. The third conference, however, marked the end of Egyptian dominance of the GUPW, as the union subsequently transferred its headquarters to Damascus. From then on, former ANM members, based primarily in Syria and Lebanon, who came to constitute the core of the PFLP, dominated the general union.

The Egypt Branch

The first conference of the Egyptian branch of the GUPW was held on July 24, 1965. From its activity report, it appears to have been involved in numerous labor-related issues. It had requested that Egyptian companies accept certificates of vocational proficiency from the secondary vocational training center in Gaza and had in fact had success with several companies. The branch also contacted employers to seek the reinstatement of workers who had been dismissed. It sought the assistance of the Office of the Military Governor of Gaza so that workers might more easily receive job appointments after completing their military service (which had become mandatory), and contacts were underway with the Ministry of Industry and Production to strengthen cooperation in order to intercede to solve workers' problems.

Among other services, the branch made available monetary assistance and loans to workers or workers' families. It issued identification papers to union members to be presented to Arab consulates, and provided good conduct documents (required for employment in some countries) and birth certificates. With infrequent success it worked to facilitate the movement of Gazans to Egypt and to secure residency for workers. And it acquired land in four governorates that could be used as cemeteries for Palestinians, who naturally had no family burial grounds in Egypt.[24]

Fellowships for workers was another sphere of activity. Many of the Palestinian workers in Egypt were the products of vocational schools in Gaza, young men who had not done well enough in school to continue at a more advanced level. The union from time to time received offers from Eastern European countries—East Germany, the Soviet Union, Yugoslavia—to send workers abroad to improve their trade union and technical skills. The union would choose recipients of the fellowships (which sometimes were for a year or two) and then see to it that the worker's job was secure and that his family would continue to receive his salary in his absence. Clearly, both the worker and his factory (after his return) benefited from the skills acquired while abroad. Indeed, in a few cases, "graduates" of such programs were later sent to university by the union and became engineers.[25]

Local chapters in Egypt participated in celebrations of national and local holidays. They held weekly lectures and discussions on Palestine, issued a monthly publication, and sponsored sports teams in some of the governorates. In Suhag and Qina, the chapters formed military units—part of the National Guard—which participated in several military parades.[26] Funding sources expanded initially from membership dues alone to occasional assistance from other branches—usually for specific projects—as well as money from the DPO. The branch also sponsored benefit parties and solicited contributions. During the 1960s, the Egypt branch of the GUPW enjoyed good relations with the Federation of Egyptian Trade Union Workers (FETUW), from which it often received donations of medical supplies, blood, clothing, and blankets.[27]

Although it is difficult to reconstruct the exact nature of the branch in Egypt given the paucity of sources available, it appears that the most significant contribution of the branch in Egypt was the spark it gave to organizing among Palestinians in other diaspora communities. Branch activities as reported in records of its fifth conference indicate an involvement similar to that of the earlier period: providing modest assistance to workers' families in need (usually no more than a modest LE10 or LE20 per month); receiving delegations from abroad; making field visits to the chapters throughout Egypt; celebrating national days with the other popular organizations; and the like.[28]

In the post-1970 period two developments stand out. The first is that of the movement of the headquarters of the GUPW from Cairo to Damascus. As a result, it seems, the number of Egypt and Gaza branch members on the executive committee decreased. For example, at the fifth conference of the GUPW, held in Damascus on August 21–25, 1974, the executive committee included three Palestinians from Syria (including the general secretary), and one each from Gaza, Kuwait, Lebanon, and the Federal Republic of Germany.[29] Egyptian influence was clearly on the wane.[30]

More important for the community at large was the deterioration in Palestinian-Egyptian relations after 1975, and particularly after Sadat's 1977 trip to Jerusalem. The workers' union was the only popular organization that the PLO allowed to remain open during the 1979–1983 period. With chapters in virtually all the governorates it was the one agency that remained to enable the PLO to keep track of what was happening to Palestinians in Egypt. Although the documents of the period (for example the record of the seventh branch conference held in 1981) do not indicate in detail any curtailment of activity, those who lived the period readily admit that Palestinian activity during the 1979–1983 period was highly restricted.[31] Perhaps the branch's most important role during this period, in addition to being the one PLO-affiliated office that remained officially open, was that of arranging more lucrative work contracts for Palestinians (many of them teachers) in Libya, North Yemen, and Tunis, and in sending workers to Lebanon and Syria for military training. Hundreds of Palestinians from the community in Egypt volunteered and went to fight with ʿArafat in Tripoli in late 1983.[32]

Sadat's passing and the 1982 Israeli invasion of Lebanon led both Egyptian popular opinion and official policy to move in a more sympathetic direction. Since 1982 the branch has again begun to operate more freely, participating in national day celebrations and coordinating with the GUPWom branch and the Palestine Red Crescent Society more openly. It has also carried out a census of Palestinians for the PLO office. While Palestinians are relieved at the passing of the overt repression and anti-Palestinian propaganda that characterized the 1977–1981 period, the damage to the Palestinian community remains. The privileges of free education (except for the children of Palestinians working for the Egyptian government), free health care, and employment appointments on an equal basis with Egyptians are gone and seem unlikely to be restored. The Egypt branch of the workers' union, therefore, has its work cut out for it. Its members include some of Egypt's poorest Palestinians, in need of far more than it can offer— given cur-

rent capabilities—in the way of subsidies, scholarships, and interces-
sionary powers. Barring a major upheaval, there is little likelihood of
significant improvement.

THE WOMEN

Although Palestinian women in Jordan and Lebanon reestablished numerous societies directly after the 1948 war, the League of Palestinian
Women in Egypt (Rabitat al-Mar'ah al-Filastiniyyah fi Misr) was not
founded until 1963. Several women engaged in graduate study in the
early 1960s—Samirah Abu Ghazalah, Zaynat 'Abd al-Majid, Jihan
Salamah, and others—led the way. The impetus for founding the league in Egypt came from an experience at a doctors' conference in Cairo
to which Mrs. Abu Ghazalah had been invited. During the conference
she found, by coincidence, that she was seated next to another Palestinian woman. The fact that in Egypt there were Palestinians so close
to each other sharing the same problems and struggle yet not knowing
about each other was a problem that needed to be remedied.[33]

It is significant that the women graduate students who founded the
league in Cairo were all *wafidat* students, Palestinians from outside
Egypt, not from families residing there and therefore unlikely to stay
after the completion of their studies. This common theme—the transitory nature of the Palestinian presence—may be found in all the Palestinian institutions in Egypt. Indeed, it is a feature to be noted among
diaspora Palestinians in general.

At its founding in 1963 the league set straightforward and overwhelmingly political goals for itself: 1) to bring together and strengthen
the bonds of solidarity and cooperation among Palestinian women; 2)
to mobilize Palestinian women's talents and skills to serve the Palestinian cause; and 3) to raise the social and cultural consciousness of
Palestinian women. The constitution forbade interference in Egyptian
domestic political affairs. Membership was open to all Palestinian
women as well as non-Palestinians who supported the Palestinian
cause.[34]

The already well established GUPS lent an organizational hand to
the women by making its offices available for the women's meetings
and by assisting with various programs. More important for diasporawide organizing, however, the women in Cairo became involved in ongoing efforts among Palestinian women throughout the Arab world,
though primarily in Lebanon and the West Bank, to unify the scattered

Palestinian women's societies. A meeting of representatives of Palestinian women was finally convened in Jerusalem in 1965 and proclaimed the establishment of the General Union of Palestinian Women (for a more detailed discussion of the emergence of the GUPWom, see chapter 11). With the founding of the GUPWom, the League of Palestinian Women became the Egypt branch of the GUPWom.

The union was originally headquartered in Jerusalem and when the Jordanian regime closed PLO offices in 1966, it closed the GUPWom office as well. Following the occupation of Jerusalem in June 1967, it was decided to move the headquarters of the GUPWom temporarily to Cairo. With new responsibilities, the Egypt branch began to expand its contacts with Egyptian women's organizations and develop ties with women's groups abroad. Cairo's centrality as an Arab and African diplomatic and cultural center greatly facilitated the women's efforts. When part of the union leadership decided in 1969 to move the headquarters from Cairo to Amman, the Egypt branch refused to relinquish its position. Not until 1974 did it acquiesce in the move.

On the domestic front, the Egypt branch began to organize by holding small parties to enable women to get acquainted. Regular meetings followed. As noted above, the branch enjoyed the cooperation of the GUPS as well as the moral and financial support of Egyptian women's groups like Nadi al-Sayyidat, Ittihad al-Jam'iyyat, and Jam'iyyat Huda Sha'rawi.[35]

Two sources of financial support included membership dues and contributions. Some additional funds came from the PLO's DPO, but they were cut in 1969 when the branch refused to acknowledge Amman as the new seat of the general secretariat. The branch's major fundraising vehicle was its yearly bazaar in which pieces of clothing and embroidery produced in the branch's small workshop were sold. The sewing and embroidery workshop constitutes an integral part of numerous Palestinian institutions and societies. Palestinian women, primarily villagers, have long produced embroidery for their own needs. Thus it was not a skill that women had to be taught, nor was it work that required they leave home. If a women could not or preferred not to work outside the home, she could still engage in embroidering. The needlework enabled women to secure additional income and thereby, at least in part, ease the difficult financial conditions in which they lived. Furthermore, embroidery production served to protect and assert Palestinian cultural identity. Whether on shawls, pillowcases, skirts, vests, or the traditional Palestinian dress, the *thawb*, in all cases traditional patterns were preserved. Through its sale of embroidery, the branch annually raised LE3,000 to LE4,000 ($7,000 to $9,000) which served most of its budgetary needs.[36] Although its first products were clothing for sale, with the rise of the resistance movement, the workshop also produced clothing for the *fida'iyyin*. Egyptian currency restrictions in the 1960s forbade sending support abroad in the form of money.[37]

In 1965, using proceeds from the first bazaar, the chapter built a dormitory for 50 female students in the al-Duqqi area, near Cairo University. Dinners and cultural events held at the hostel enabled the women to raise funds that then went to a scholarship fund for needy students. After the 1967 war, the branch used the donations to found a Palestinian Students' Fund designed to help cover the educational expenses of the students in the hostel who had lost contact with their families in the then recently occupied territories. Between December 1, 1967 and June 30, 1968, the fund provided assistance to 35 young women.[38] The hostel has been criticized by some former residents, however, for catering primarily to wealthy students and for ousting women if they became involved in political activity. Critics of the dormitory compare it with the more than thirty dorms operated and subsidized by Fateh during the 1972–1977 period, which housed some 650 young Palestinian women.[39]

In 1968, the branch opened a self-help center for mothers and children in a poor section of the 'Abbasiyyah area. It was called Markaz al-Wijdan after Wijdan al-Shawwa, a woman who had been very active with the union. Using contributions from local businessmen to supplement its own funds, the center served seventy-two poor Palestinian families, offering free medicine and treatment. Also part of the center's program were literacy classes conducted by young women from the hostel. More than one hundred Palestinian women took embroidery, nursing, and secretarial classes. The nursing graduates immediately found work with the center's public health personnel who staffed the clinic and canvassed areas of high Palestinian concentration to demonstrate the essentials of hygiene, preventive medicine, and nutrition.[40] For children the center sponsored feeding programs, group outings, and a scout troop.[41]

The involvement particularly of the young women students in the center's activities served to reawaken a Palestinian identity among the people of the area who, living in an overwhelmingly Egyptian environment, had not preserved their Palestinianness. They formed a folk group, recorded and taught folk songs, and brought older women to the center to talk about villages in Palestine. The folk dance troupe participated with the Egyptian national dance troupe and traveled and performed throughout the Middle East. Later, a group that performed Palestinian songs was established and often participated with the dance troupe in national celebrations. Both served to raise revenue and to publicize the Palestinian cause abroad.

The young women activists also contacted Palestinian engineering students, who agreed to explore putting new roofs on some of the houses in the ʿAbbassiyyah area. (The roofs were described as worse than those in many refugee camps.) But these various activities—particularly those with high Palestinian national content—began to appear to be too political to some elements in the union leadership. As a result, and in order not to precipitate more serious problems, the center was closed in 1974–75, although it was reopened briefly by the GUPS in 1976.[42]

Among its other activities, the branch occasionally sponsored Palestinian dinners. It also organized several conferences of four- to five-day duration, as well as regular day-long symposia on topics as diverse as "the Palestinian family" and "America and the Palestine question." Throughout the early period the Arab Socialist Union (or ASU, Egypt's "government party" from 1962–1978) lent its headquarters for these gatherings. Special efforts were made to involve young Palestinian women in the national movement by encouraging their participation with the GUPWom, particularly in such conferences.[43]

Aside from the studies produced for the symposia and conferences, and a monthly bulletin issued for a short period, the branch appears to have produced only one publication, entitled *Kifah al-Marʾah al-Filastiniyyah fi-Zill Thawratiha* (The Palestinian Woman's Struggle Under the Auspices of Her Revolution). The book discusses the general background of the Palestine question, gives a brief history of women's participation in the national struggle from the time of the mandate, and includes short biographies of individual *fidaʾiyyat* (women commandos). Significantly, the official organ of the ASU, then headed by Anwar al-Sadat, subsidized the book's publication.[44]

The Alexandria Chapter

Shortly after the founding of the league in Cairo, Mrs. Abu Ghazalah made several trips to Alexandria in hopes of establishing a sister organization. At the time she was unable to assemble sufficient numbers; however, a league of Palestinian women was finally formed after the 1967 war. The wife of the governor of Alexandria even assisted the women in their search for a meeting place.

Several women who had been attending meetings and symposia at the PLO office in Alexandria initiated the organizing efforts. Their primary goal was to raise political consciousness on the Palestine question among Egyptians. Nevertheless, one of their first activities was to provide shelter and food to the Palestinians who had come to Alexandria as refugees from the 1967 war. A workshop that the women opened then began to produce clothes for needy families. Other products of the workshop as well as most of the receipts from league activities went to Fateh. Later, the women sponsored events similar to those of the GUPW branch in Cairo: charity bazaars, displays of Palestinian embroidery, and the like. However, the activities of the women in Alexandria remained quite limited as the active membership did not exceed eleven.[45]

Beyond 1970

During the period 1965–1970, all the women interviewed stressed the high level of activity that characterized the Egypt branch, despite the size of the community. They attributed it in large part to the absence of intra-PLO feuding in Egypt[46] and to the supportive nature of the regime and the Egyptian people through the early 1970s. The women described the years 1965–1970 as "the golden years of the revolution."[47] The beginning of fida'iyyin activity generated great sympathy among all strata of Palestinians especially after the battle of Karamah in March 1968. Women everywhere began to participate gladly in whatever ways they could. At the same time several women gained notoriety for their involvement in skyjackings.

Branch membership lists were not available for examination. Members stated that the number of those who attended meetings and served in leadership positions probably did not exceed twenty.[48] Some two to three hundred participated on an irregular basis.[49] A lack of full-time workers, which limits the field for expansion of activities and services, has always plagued the branch. Another problem that surfaced more seriously after 1970 lay in the branch's failure to develop strong ties with poorer Palestinian women. Finally, the transitory nature of the community in Egypt has continually depleted membership ranks. Many of the young women who participated with the branch while they were students eventually settled elsewhere. Consequently, the leadership has not been infused with new people and ideas with any regularity.

The gradual deterioration in PLO-Egyptian relations, particularly after Sadat's Jerusalem visit in November 1977, forced the GUPWom members to terminate their activities as a branch of the union. Any work they carried out thereafter had to be in the name of the League of Palestinian Women, under which they had first organized in 1963. Between 1978 and 1982 activity was restricted to the holding of the yearly fund-raising bazaar.

Not until the 1982 Israeli invasion of Lebanon did the atmosphere change. At that time, the women began to put out a regular bulletin on developments in Lebanon for distribution to Palestinians and other interested individuals. Egyptian security, however, claimed that this was a secret publication. The women were instructed to cease publication, and several were threatened with expulsion from the country.[50]

In general, however, conditions continued to improve for organized Palestinian activity in Egypt following the invasion. In the flurry of work that the invasion sparked, the women, again operating cautiously as a branch of the GUPWom, set about to develop a broader organizational base. Attempts were made to mobilize younger women and students in particular. For example, the branch became involved in improving educational conditions among the 5,700 residents of the Canada refugee camp (located in the Egyptian sector of Rafah). By March 1984, after four months' work, the union had succeeded in: adding two classrooms to the new Palestinian high school; providing scholarships for 80 Palestinian students to pursue their studies; building a kindergarten for 700 camp children; opening a library; and providing the camp schools with instructional materials and books.[51]

The cultural committee began developing a library and organizing regular cultural discussions and film showings. It also began to sponsor seminars on such topics as "rejection of the peaceful solution." And, in the new and gradually improving political climate, celebrations of national days such as March 30, the Day of the Land, and limited demonstrations (such as one that took place outside a PLO office in November 1983 protesting the inter-Palestinian fighting then going on in Tripoli, Lebanon) were once again permitted.

The problem of reaching beyond the women who are already members (and who tend to be wealthier women) in order to reach those Palestinians who are in need of a wide range of social services remains. The community is in serious need of the revival of the Wijdan center or a similar facility. However, the experiences of the Sadat era continue to affect the behavior and attitudes of women. They are hesitant to undertake as bold a project as reopening such a center. The reason given for failure to act on the idea is that of lack of funds; a more basic concern is that the branch's conservative leadership is hesitant to submit for approval a project that the Egyptian government may reject.[52]

THE TEACHERS

Statistics of the General Union of Palestinian Teachers (GUPT) placed the number of Palestinian teachers in Egypt at 3,000 in 1970.[53] Most were from Gaza and had been appointed according to the 1962 law that provided for the employment of Palestinians on the same basis as Egyptians. (Some of these Gazans had been working in Saudi Arabia and were expelled along with the Egyptians King Faisal expelled in 1957. Nasir responded by appointing them to positions in Egypt.) A few had been in Egypt since 1948. Others had come in 1967 and were appointed to teach throughout Egypt in government schools; they received their salaries from the Office of the Military Governor of Gaza. Only a handful of Palestinian teachers received appointments between 1967 and 1977.

Members of the GUPT in Egypt serve at all levels (although they are employed in greater numbers in preparatory and secondary schools), in the various higher and technical institutes, as well as in the financial and administrative sections of educational institutions. They may be moved from administration to teaching and vice versa, from school to school, or from level to level. Most teach in government schools; a few teach in private schools, and their employment is more precarious.

When the call came from the PLO's Department of Popular Organizations in 1969 to organize Palestinian teachers (for details of the founding of the GUPT see chapter 11), those in Cairo, like their colleagues in other parts of the diaspora, formed a preparatory committee for a branch and in 1970 held their first country (qutri) conference. Prior to the founding of the GUPT, teachers in Egypt had belonged to the GUPW. (And during the 1975–1983 period, representation of the teachers reverted to the GUPW.) With the founding of the GUPT teachers were given a choice: most chose the new GUPT, but a few preferred to remain members of the GUPW.

Early activities of the union did not differ from those of the other mass organizations. First among their activities were seminars (nadawat). The branch, at that time still lacking facilities, would contact sister unions in Egypt, which helped coordinate events and lend their headquarters for holding events. The Egyptian unions also contributed financially and supported the union's informational work.

As relations between the PLO and the Egyptian government deteriorated, Palestinians faced greater restrictions in their organized political work. For example, it became more difficult for members of the GUPT's secretariat to attend events in Egypt: they needed PLO permission to do so, and this was not always forthcoming given the strained relations; they also needed permission to enter Egypt, which the Egyptian government was more likely to refuse in the post-1975 period. Moreover, Egyptians tended increasingly to stay away from Palestinians: they needed permission from internal security to meet with them, and that, too, became more and more difficult to obtain.

It was not the deterioration in PLO-Egyptian relations alone that gradually paralyzed the branch in Egypt, however. Internal developments, primarily problems with finances, led the secretariat to freeze the activity of the branch in 1975. Since these internal problems coincided with the deterioration in PLO-Egyptian relations, there was little room for maneuver for the branch, either domestically or vis-à-vis the PLO which, by 1979, had officially frozen its relations with Egypt.

Nevertheless, some movement did occur. Some of the teachers in Egypt complained to the PLO that the secretariat's punishment of the branch was severe in comparison with the mistakes that had been made. Had political conditions in Egypt been better, it is likely that the problem would have been solved more quickly. At the time, however, both the union and the PLO were concerned with other, more pressing issues. Eventually, with the support of the PLO, the teachers were able to convince the GUPT secretariat that they had been dealt with unfairly. Having solved the problem with the secretariat, the branch, like branches of the other popular organizations in Egypt, had to await an improvement in general PLO-Egyptian relations in order to begin anew. The Israeli invasion of Lebanon in 1982 opened the door to improved relations. By early 1983, the teachers had begun to prepare for the GUPT's fourth conference. And in July 1983, two members from the Egypt branch, at the invitation of the secretariat, attended the conference in Aden. Since that conference the branch has been officially reactivated. By the end of 1983 it was again holding regular meetings, using offices in the GUPW headquarters.

As of 1986 there were about 600 active members of the union, in addition to 250 to 300 teachers who had belonged to the Egypt branch, went elsewhere to teach, but have returned, and are not currently engaged in teaching. The teachers are located in all the governorates. The largest numbers live in Cairo and Giza; but there are also chapters in Alexandria, Tanta, and the Fayyum, in addition to a preparatory com-

mittee in Shibin al-Kum. The branch itself has only two full-time employees: the general secretary and his assistant. They make regular visits to areas where Palestinian teachers are concentrated. The fact that
some members of the branch's executive committee live outside Cairo—
in Alexandria, Tanta, and Damanhur—helps the branch keep abreast
of local problems. Occasionally, the branch may dispatch a member to
investigate a problem if a member of the executive committee is not
nearby.

In the mid-1980s the branch in Egypt faced two pressing problems.
The first concerns residency for teachers returning from abroad. These
are Palestinian teachers who had been residents of Egypt, who left for
more lucrative teaching opportunities elsewhere in the Arab world, and
who now seek to return to Egypt. The renewal of their residence is
uncertain. The government often requires that they change a certain
amount of hard currency on their arrival in Egypt. Some return without
a place to live. The second problem is a related one: children of these
returning teachers are forbidden to work, and the teachers themselves
may not be reappointed after returning from abroad. (Since 1977 it has
been forbidden to appoint Palestinians to government jobs.)

Before its activities were frozen, there was the possibility that if a
problem arose, the branch could help a teacher, either through the GUPT
secretariat or through the PLO. The PLO had substantial funds at the
time to provide assistance; and the union itself was central in arranging the placement of Palestinian teachers elsewhere in the Arab world,
where salaries were often higher. Those who received appointments
abroad further assisted by establishing additional contacts. After 1983,
however, some Arab countries began recruiting teachers directly, not
through the GUPT.

The union has been urging the PLO to push the Egyptian government to review the condition of Palestinian teachers in Egypt, especially those from Gaza. They argue that Egypt, as the former admin-
istrator of Gaza, bears a responsibility toward its inhabitants and,
therefore, that it is unfair for new laws to be passed that apply to all
Palestinians. Gazans were a separate case before, they argue, and their
privileges should be preserved. Whereas in the past assistance in such
matters was at times sought from Egyptian unions, despite the fact
that contacts are again permitted, neither side has approached the other.
Even though the PLO has also tried to intercede with the Egyptian
government on behalf of the teachers, as of the writing of this study
no response has been forthcoming.

THE PALESTINE RED CRESCENT SOCIETY (HILAL)

Among the privileges accorded the Palestinians in Egypt prior to 1977 was free medical care on a par with the Egyptian host population. Hence, no special need arose among the community in Egypt to develop its own health care services.[54] Moreover, Egypt, although it sheltered some *fidaʾiyyin* in Gaza and Sinai, was never the launching ground for Palestinian military operations that Jordan was.

For these reasons, the founding of a chapter of the Palestine Red Crescent Society in Egypt proceeded not so much from local needs as from the declaration of the founding of the society in Jordan in December 1968, which called for the establishment of chapters of the society in all places of Palestinian concentration (for details on the founding of the PRCS see chapter 10). Like other Palestinian institutions in Egypt, the PRCS is treated as operating under the auspices of the PLO. It is subject to the Egyptian Ministry of Health only to the extent that any new facility that wishes to open must be certified by the ministry.[55]

The original PRCS in Jordan was in desperate need of financial and a wide range of material support because of the large numbers of refugee camp residents and *fidaʾiyyin* it served. Although the community in Egypt was small, it counted many wealthy and well-educated Palestinians able to contribute to the struggle. Even the less well-to-do, it was argued, could become involved in the production of clothes for the commandos. Moreover, Cairo's centrality and status as a diplomatic center and leader of the Arab world meant that Egypt's PRCS members also had an important, early role in the informational aspect of the society's work through participation in international gatherings.[56]

From a variety of professional backgrounds, but largely from traditionally prominent Palestinian families, the following people came together to found the PRCS in Egypt: Jamal ʿArafat, Khadijah ʿArafat, Hind Abu Saʿud, Mufidah Dabbagh, Arab ʿAbd al-Hadi, Hayfa al-Husayni, Nahidah al-Husayni, ʿIsam al-Agha, Zaki Susi, and Ribhi Badr. The PRCS operated on the principle of self-sufficiency. Therefore, in the beginning the chapter counted only three salaried workers, and volunteers—many of them students—played an important role.[57]

To raise money, memberships in the society were solicited from community members. As it expanded, the chapter opened an embroidery and sewing workshop in the same building that housed its hospital (see below) and began collecting contributions to support the hospital and clinics in Jordan. The campaign to collect clothing and supplies for the Jordanian facilities brought donations from many Palestinian wholesale merchants and from the textile centers in the Delta town of al-Mahallah al-Kubra.[58]

Because of limited facilities, at first the PRCS in Egypt operated out of a wing in the Egyptian Red Crescent Society hospital, where it treated those wounded in *fida'i* attacks and Israeli raids in 1969. Shortly thereafter, the society opened its first hospital—eight beds and an operating room—in the Heliopolis home of In'am 'Arafat, sister of the PLO chairman. During the 1970 civil war in Jordan, all the wounded from the Amman area were brought to Cairo. The small PRCS hospital received some, while the Egyptian Hilal hospital took others.[59] The Palestinian facility was also used to care for casualties from the war of attrition. The presence of these health facilities captured the interest of Palestinian doctors in Egypt just as it had in Jordan. Some fifty Palestinian doctors enlisted to serve in the various centers, so many that the society could not use all of them on a full-time basis. Instead, each worked either six hours weekly, or one day per week.[60]

In addition to the clinic/hospital in Heliopolis, between 1974 and 1976 the PRCS opened clinics in downtown Cairo (Jawad Husni Street), in the Manyal area, 'Ayn Shams, and Alexandria, as well as a four-story convalescent center in Duqqi (Giza).[61] The society also operated a mobile dispensary which served Tanta. These clinics are still in operation and each serves an average of fifty to sixty patients per day.[62]

At the end of 1972, a villa in Heliopolis was rented for use as a 35-bed hospital. It received victims from both the 1973 war and the Lebanese civil war. In 1978, the society purchased the villa as well as the land around it. The villa was then torn down and work was begun on a new seven-story, 350-bed hospital. All those employed in building the hospital—carpenters, plumbers, electricians, and contractors—were Palestinians from the community in Egypt.[63] In the interim, a villa next to the land was rented and the hospital facilities transferred there.[64]

However, the concentration of attention on Lebanon and the deterioration of Egyptian-Palestinian relations brought work on the new Palestine Hospital to a halt and inhibited the development of any other PRCS facilities in the country. In the wake of the 1982 invasion of Lebanon, with the PRCS's headquarters and facilities there either destroyed or under daily assault, and many of its personnel either missing, detained, or known dead, the society was forced to choose new ground on which to regroup. Egypt, in the less restrictive atmosphere of the Mubarak government, emerged as the most logical choice.

Work on the hospital was begun again and in September 1983 the first stage of Palestine Hospital was completed. At about the same time the Jerusalem Nursery School was opened in Heliopolis to accommodate 125 children. In October 1983 a nursing school opened and accepted a first class of one hundred students, most of them from the occupied territories. Students do not pay tuition and receive a monthly stipend of LE30. In return, after graduation they are expected to work for the PRCS for the same number of years as they spent in the training course.[65]

Although as of 1987 the full seven floors of the hospital had not yet been completed, three floors as well as several labs and operating rooms were in full use and the nursing school had moved from a single-floor facility in Heliopolis to a five-story villa in Madinat Nasr. The hospital now provides a place where young Palestinian doctors can do their internships, since they may not work in Egyptian hospitals.[66]

Moreover, in early 1984, the PRCS founded two new clinics: in Mudiriyyat al-Tahrir and in the Palestinian camp in Rafah. An attempt was made but permission was not forthcoming from the government to open a clinic in the Delta town of Zaqaziq, but a center for handicapped children was opened in the ʿAyn Shams area. The public relations division has grown and a new planning committee has been formed to focus on health service development strategies. The PRCS in Egypt staff counts more than 250 employees and 50 volunteers.[67]

The PRCS is responsible for the health care of the ʿAyn Jalut Brigade of the PLA (based in Egypt), members of Fateh based in Cairo, families of martyrs, PLO employees, employees of the Office of the Military Governor of Gaza, and some Palestinians who come from the occupied territories.[68] Nevertheless, the society's services are open to all, and many Egyptians avail themselves of the PRCS's facilities, which have a reputation for quality. For those who have PRCS health insurance, medical care is free (unless they want a private or semiprivate room). PRCS workers automatically are covered by this insurance; employees of the PLO pay a fee of LE3 per month. Those without insurance pay regular fees; however, no one who needs help is turned away. If patients are unable to pay, the cost is absorbed.[69]

In addition to health care, the Hilal has stressed the social aspect of the Palestinian movement and opened the Social Affairs (Shuʾun) Section to develop strong ties with the community. Women have overwhelmingly staffed the Shu'un section of the society. Some were rel-atives of *fida'iyyin* and sought some way to contribute. Others were simply concerned women who wanted to participate in whatever ways were available. They sewed clothing for the fighters and later devel-oped the PRCS's extensive embroidery program.[70] Other Shu'un pro-grams have included weekly meetings at the homes of members, which feature talks on various aspects of the Palestine problem. During the summers, the workshop becomes a hub of activity as schoolgirls come in large numbers to the office to volunteer.

The Shu'un sends teams on field visits to meet with needy Palestin-ian families and determine what type of assistance they require. How-ever, "no taking without giving" is a PRCS slogan. In practice this has meant that whoever seeks assistance from the Hilal receives it free of charge; however, the society then asks the recipient to contribute whatever he or she can in the way of time, sewing, or some other ser-vice. The intention is to prevent the development of a welfare men-tality which debilitates and deprives people of dignity.[71]

In this way, the PRCS represents the social side of the movement and serves all who are in need—not just Palestinians—wherever it op-erates. Its functions differ substantially from those of the popular or-ganizations examined in this study. As a humanitarian organization, it stresses the right of all human beings to be recognized and treated as such. For that reason, many Palestinians who have preferred not to join a particular Palestinian political faction have enthusiastically sup-ported the PRCS.[72]

[6]
Opportunity in Exile

Although relief agencies began to provide assistance to the Palestinian refugees as early as 1948, the magnitude of the problem meant that demand, even for basic needs, far outstripped supply. The Arab states also contributed to the relief efforts, but with the exception of Syria, none of the states bordering Palestine was capable of absorbing such large numbers of newcomers. Even Jordan, which did grant citizenship to the Palestinians shortly after their arrival, was incapable of providing employment or assistance commensurate with the tremendous need. Stateless, jobless, and often penniless, many Palestinians found that their survival and the survival of their families dictated that they seek economic opportunities beyond the countries of first refuge.

In the late 1940s, Kuwait was still a British protectorate, a small and relatively poor trading center at the westernmost end of the Gulf. The desert to its back, its face to the sea, and constantly tested by a punishing climate, at the time of the *nakbah* Kuwait was only beginning to reap the benefits of its oil wealth. Indeed, Kuwait's drive to develop its nascent state structure and economy coincided with the expulsion from Palestine of both an educated class that in effect constituted a "ready-made" bureaucracy and a largely peasant class that, through loss of its lands, was transformed into a large pool of unskilled or semi-skilled labor.

Although the Kuwaitis welcomed the arrival of the expatriates, the harsh climate and the isolation experienced by single males—who made up the majority of the community in the 1950s and early 1960s—made life very difficult for many of the Palestinians who came during this period. Palestinian writer Ghassan Kanafani, who lived in Kuwait in the late 1950s, described the situation in the following way: "Circumstances themselves led us there. We accepted a kind of hero's choice: exile in exchange for providing our families with subsistence. We did our best to make life bearable in one way or another."[1]

For those who went to Kuwait with work contracts, the remuneration was substantial—housing was generally provided in addition to a generous salary—and residence secure. For those who did not have work contracts and entered the country illegally, the trip was dangerous, and the possibility of arrest and expulsion ever-present. Yet, the hazards deterred few: the prospect even of manual labor and tenuous residency in Kuwait meant escape from the hunger and degradation of refugee camp life as well as the chance to provide the family—often a large, extended family left behind—the means to rebuild.

Kuwait did not offer citizenship to its Palestinian guest workers, nor were Palestinians granted any special privileges as refugees, as they were in Egypt and Syria. Furthermore, unlike the situation in the Arab East, the division between Kuwaiti and expatriate gradually became more pronounced, eventually finding expression in most aspects of life. Nevertheless, economic opportunity combined with Kuwait's relatively liberal political atmosphere continued to attract expatriate workers, Palestinians and other Arabs alike.

It should be noted, however, that while Egyptians, Lebanese, and Syrians also came to Kuwait in the early 1950s, usually to fill positions in the bureaucracy or the educational system similar to those filled by the educated Palestinians, it was the Palestinians more than any other single expatriate group who helped shape the country's social, economic, and political development. The length of their residence, the size of the community, their dedication to work in both the public and private sectors, and their consequent entrenchment in the bureaucracy, economy, professions, and the media enabled the Palestinians in Kuwait to develop into one of the most cohesive and active communities in the diaspora.

THE POLITY

Kuwait's six thousand square miles of largely barren, riverless desert far from the Arab-Israeli battlefield have been ruled by an amir of the al-Sabah family for over two hundred years. In the early 1950s, Amir ʿAbdallah al-Salim (1950–1965), the father of modern Kuwait, began to institute a far-reaching program of reforms and development in the young oil state. He laid the groundwork for an elaborate social welfare system and in 1952 established the Development Planning and Welfare Board to implement it. In the same year, he initiated a program of overseas investment through the Kuwait Investment Board in London. In this way the amir sought to ensure sufficient revenue for Kuwait's needs if and when the oil ran out. Furthermore, well aware of the small country's external political vulnerability (given its powerful Saudi, Iraqi, and Iranian neighbors), the amir and his finance minister Jabir al-Ahmad established the Kuwait Fund for Arab Economic Development (KFAED) in 1962. The fund was to serve both to enable Kuwait's oil wealth to aid other Arab states and to secure political support or noninterference from Kuwait's neighbors through awards of economic assistance.[2]

After its independence from Britain (June 1961), Kuwait alone among the Gulf states promulgated a constitution (1962) which called for a cabinet-parliamentary form of government. Ultimate power continued to rest in the hands of the amir; yet, although the National Assembly rarely initiated policy, it developed an independence not envisioned by its drafters. Political parties were prohibited by law; however, opposition blocs emerged regularly—in 1963, 1967, 1971, 1975, and in the mid-1980s—generally around issues concerning Kuwait's role in the Arab world, the dominance of the oil companies, the state's relationship with the United States and Britain, or domestic issues like the 1982 Kuwaiti stock market (suq al-manakh) crisis and its repercussions.

THE ECONOMY

The characteristics of the Kuwaiti economy—an oversized service sector, a high level of consumerism, and underdeveloped indigenous productive forces—have their roots in the pre-oil era. In this period, British imperial policy effectively dislocated regional carrying trade and transferred capital out of the country rather than investing it in ways that would have promoted local development.[3] Therefore, when exploitation of the country's oil wealth demanded industrial expertise and a swift expansion of the bureaucracy, the state of the indigenous economic productive base forced Kuwait to import already-trained technicians and bureaucrats from abroad. Subsequent trends have been similar, as the Kuwaiti economy has developed almost independently of the labor of the indigenous population. This situation has been exacerbated by the fact that the economy has evolved into a monoproduct one based on oil, a commodity that requires expensive, sophisticated technology in all aspects of its production and marketing. All of these factors have rendered Kuwait even more dependent upon imported technology and skills.

THE BEGINNINGS OF PALESTINIAN IMMIGRATION

In the early 1950s, the hungry Kuwaiti labor market began to attract large numbers of immigrants—many of them Palestinians—from Jordan and Lebanon, where unemployment was rampant and skilled personnel were numerous. Prior to 1957, Palestinian and other immigration to Kuwait took two forms. The first was illegal, individual immigration through the "underground railroad," the kind described by Ghassan Kanafani in his novel *Rijal f-il-Shams:*

> [He] began the trip with two childhood friends; from Gaza, across Israel, across Jordan, across Iraq. Then the guide left them in the desert before they crossed into Kuwait. . . . And he buried his two friends in that unknown land. He took their identity cards with him so that when he reached Kuwait he could send the cards to their families. . . . After several months had passed he returned to Iraq where they arrested him and he is now spending his second year in some horrible prison.[4]

Whether by land across the desert or by sea from Faw, the journey was fraught with danger and many died along the way.[5] Those who survived the journey generally found work as unskilled or manual laborers—a type of employment not coveted by Kuwaitis. The second type of immigration was by contract with the government, the Kuwait Oil Company, or a private sector firm. As oil production rose, massive capital resources available to the Kuwaiti government enabled it to initiate development projects that led to an expansion of other forms of economic activity.[6] As a result, work opportunities multiplied, and educated Palestinians were particularly valuable in commerce because they were generally proficient in English as well as Arabic.

Because visas, work permits, and residency have become such important parts of the expatriate's life in Kuwait, it is useful to digress for a moment and describe the legalities that have conditioned migration to Kuwait since the late 1940s.[7] According to an 1899 treaty, the British were responsible for Kuwait's foreign relations; however, there was no British military presence in Kuwait as there was in Palestine and Bahrain, only a British commissioner. In all offices that dealt with internal affairs, a shaykh, a member of the al-Sabah family, had complete authority.

In the 1940s, few Kuwaitis had enough money to go abroad, so passports were not much of an issue. If one did need to travel, he was issued a document recognized by the British, since Kuwait's inhabitants were considered residents of a British protectorate. As a result, those Kuwaitis who did travel abroad were treated by other Arab countries, not as Arabs, but as foreigners. A complaint about this situation was finally taken to the amir who, in consultation with the British, decided in 1948 to set up a bureau of passports and residency. He brought a Palestinian refugee from Jaffa, Hani al-Qaddumi, to set up and oversee the new office.[8]

During the pre-1950 period, most of those who came to Kuwait came for specific jobs. Those who came illegally were few, and in any case there were no frontier posts at the time. Even after border posts were established, the country was in such need of manpower that Kuwaiti employers generally did not check to be sure a non-national had a work permit or residency. The problem arose for the "illegals" when they wanted to leave Kuwait in order to bring wives and families back with them. In such cases, a man would usually appeal to his employer, who would then go to the British commissioner to request approval for the issuance of a visa.

In the 1950s a series of reciprocal agreements were concluded between Kuwait and other Arab states that canceled the need for visas. The first was with Lebanon in 1951–52; an agreement was signed with Egypt a few years later. Most important for Palestinians, the visa requirement for Jordanians was canceled in 1958–59. This opened the door of legal immigration for all those who were Jordanian citizens— East and West bankers alike. According to the arrangement, any Jordanian could go to Kuwait as long as he or she had a valid passport. The only Palestinians who continued to encounter problems were those who carried travel documents, because there was no government to which they were legally subject which could conclude such an agreement on their behalf.

The Palestinians who came to Kuwait immediately after the *nakbah* played a critical role in arranging for the immigration of others. For example, if a Palestinian employee had earned the respect and trust of his Kuwaiti superior, the Kuwaiti would generally approve the Palestinian's hiring recommendations. Similarly, having earned the Kuwaiti's trust, the Palestinian was not likely to bring to Kuwait someone who he himself was not sure would perform well. Those who were best known were, naturally, family members or friends from the same refugee camp or village. The Ministry of Electricity (in which 'Abd al-Muhsin al-Qattan of Jaffa worked as general inspector until 1963 and which was nicknamed a *musta'mar yafawi* or a Jaffa colony) and the Ministry of Public Works became well known for the large number of Palestinians among their employees.[9] Thus, the early Palestinian pioneers paved the way for a continuous movement of family and acquaintances to Kuwait as the bureaucracy and economy expanded.[10]

KUWAITI AND NON-KUWAITI

Perhaps the most striking aspect of social and political life in Kuwait is the distinction or division that has developed between Kuwaitis and non-Kuwaitis. Most of those who went to Kuwait prior to 1948 were non-Arabs involved in the oil industry and therefore lived in al-Ahmadi, south of Kuwait City.[11] After 1948, as other companies and the government began to attract more expatriates, the number of non-Kuwaitis living within the reddish brown walls of Kuwait City began to rise. Until 1957 Kuwaitis and expatriates lived together within the city's walls.[12] In 1957 the walls were torn down and there began to be built carefully planned residential districts—each with its own school, police station, clinic, market, and the like—that spatially laid the groundwork for later legal and political distinctions between Kuwaiti and expatriate.

While Kuwait welcomed large numbers of expatriates in the 1950s and 1960s, by the late 1960s and certainly by the mid-1970s, the state was concerned that Kuwaitis had become a minority in their own country. The country's feelings of vulnerability because of its population composition—the expatriate mosaic and the Sunni-Shi'i ratio—surged during the civil war in Lebanon in 1975–76, and again with the rise of fundamentalism in the area and the outbreak of war between Iran and Iraq. Kuwait faces a dilemma in dealing with its guest worker communities: it acknowledges and appreciates the many years of service of so many expatriates, yet it has not yet come to terms with the idea of granting permanent residency to them because of its citizens' concern regarding their own smaller numbers. Moreover, Kuwait's recent experiences with terrorism—the series of explosions that rocked the country in December 1983, the attempt on the life of the amir in May 1986, and additional explosions the following June—have led the Kuwaitis to be particularly suspicious of Iranians, Iraqis, Lebanese, and Syrians. However, expulsions of members of these nationalities have only increased the feelings of insecurity among the others, including the Palestinians.

Let us turn to an examination of the status of expatriates under Kuwaiti law. The first Kuwaiti nationality law was issued in 1948 (Law Number 2 of 1948); however, probably owing to the general lack of development in the Kuwaiti bureaucracy, the law had little effect. Not until 1959 did Amiri Decree Number 15 formally establish nationality requirements. Residency regulations for foreigners were also clearly delineated in 1959 by Amiri Decree Number 17.[13]

According to Article 1 of the citizenship law of 1959 (which was later amended in 1960, 1965, and 1966), Kuwaiti citizenship belongs to those (and their descendants) who resided in Kuwait before 1920 and maintained residence there through 1959. All others are non-Kuwaitis, including many of the bedouin who carry Kuwaiti passports, but not citizenship.[14] As the figures below demonstrate, continuing tight naturalization restrictions combined with large-scale immigration have rendered the Kuwaitis a minority in their own country.[15]

In the field of employment, until 1967 the system of reciprocal visa agreements rendered Kuwait fairly easily accessible to expatriate Arab workers. However, the influx into Kuwait of thousands of Palestinians in the wake of the 1967 war forced Kuwait to reassess its policy. Rather than single out a particular country for cancellation of the visa agreement, new measures—the requirement that one obtain a visitor's card, a work card, or a no-objection certificate—were instituted in 1968–69. These official papers are issued only at the request of a Kuwaiti through the Ministry of the Interior or the Ministry of Social Affairs and Labor. The Kuwaiti then becomes responsible for the non-Kuwaiti whose immigration he requested in all legal and financial dealings.[16] This, then, was the beginning of the *kafil* or guarantor system, a system that has become a basic feature of employment in Kuwait.[17]

Residency in Kuwait for a nonnational is guaranteed through one's employer, father, or spouse. Officially, non-Kuwaitis must leave the

Table 6.1: Population of Kuwait, 1957–1975

	1957	1961	1965	1970	1975
Kuwaitis	113,622	161,909	220,059	347,396	472,088
Non-Kuwaitis	92,851	159,712	247,280	391,266	522,749
Total	206,473	321,621	467,339	738,662	994,837
Kuwaiti % of Total	55%	50.3%	47.1%	47%	47.4%

country upon termination of their employment. A company may be willing to continue to sponsor the residency of a longtime employee; however, each company is allotted only a certain number of residencies. Therefore, continuing to sponsor someone who is retired reduces the number of active workers a company can sponsor. Alternatively, there is the option of al-mulhaq b-il-ʿaʾil, changing one's residency sponsor to a son working in the country. But many longtime residents find this option humiliating.[18] If neither of these options can be or is chosen, no matter how long the person has lived in Kuwait, he or she must leave.

A few final points should be made to complete the picture of the status of nonnationals in Kuwait. In the realm of social welfare, non-Kuwaitis enjoy free or nearly free medical care and public education is available according to a quota system (see "Economic Development and Education," below). However, with the exception of diplomatic missions, they may not own immovable property (Law Number 5 of 1965).[19] They also may not vote or be elected to any legislative body—local, regional, or national—nor may they join political parties or organize political meetings (Law Number 13 of 1963, Article 10).[20] In the labor market, expatriates may not organize. They may join Kuwaiti unions, but only after a period of five consecutive years of work in the country.[21] In the case of Kuwaiti professional societies, the non-Kuwaiti may be required to join in order to practice; however, he does not have the right to vote or be elected.

In the realm of business, in 1965, the government passed a series of measures regulating the activities in the private sector. The Industrial Law of 1965 gave the government extensive control over all sectors of the economy. All industrial firms were nationalized: 51 percent or more of the company had to be controlled by Kuwaiti shareholders. An Industrial Development Committee was established to grant or withhold import licenses, building permits, and the like with the goal of promoting the development of Kuwaiti-owned enterprises. Moreover, regulations were enacted that banned non-Kuwaiti firms from setting up banking and financial institutions.[22]

Aware of the potential threat posed by the unenfranchised, expatriate Arab communities, especially during periods of increased regional tensions between rival regimes, Kuwaiti national planners have emphasized forecasting labor force requirements and instituting educational policies to meet these demands by employing nationals.[23] While the policies have served to ease the Kuwaitis' understandable concern about the need to assert greater control over their country's political, educational, and economic systems, they have concomitantly raised fears for job security and continued residency among expatriates.

In the application of the laws detailed above, Palestinians are treated no better or worse than other nonnationals, and there are no restrictions specific to Palestinians as Palestinians. However, when retirement age is reached and a Palestinian is forced to leave Kuwait—even though he may have lived most of his life there—his situation diverges from that of other workers. For when a Pakistani reaches retirement age he returns to Pakistan, the Iraqi returns to Iraq, and the Egyptian to Egypt. But the Palestinian, unless he is fortunate enough to hold a passport (usually Jordanian), faces the dilemma of where to go.

Even for those who do hold Jordanian passports, the limited economic base of that country and its high unemployment levels, especially among professionals, constitute serious problems. Moreover, Palestinians who have been involved—not even necessarily active—politically while abroad often face imprisonment or confiscation of their passport upon returning to Jordan. Some have even been denied renewal of passports while still abroad because of their political involvements. As a result it appears likely that a major challenge for the Palestinian communities in the Gulf in general, and in Kuwait in particular, where they have reconstituted a sense of national identity and cohesion unparalleled in other host states,[24] will be the consequences of the economic slowdown of the late 1980s and, more important, of the policy of gradual replacement of expatriates by nationals.

THE SOCIOECONOMIC STRUCTURE OF THE PALESTINIAN COMMUNITY IN KUWAIT

The earliest population figures available for Kuwait are those of 1957, which list the number of Jordanians and Palestinians as 15,173, 16 percent of the total immigrant population and 7.3 percent of the total population. According to 1961 statistics, the number of Palestinians in Kuwait had reached 37,327 or 11.6 percent of the population and 23.4 percent of all non-Kuwaitis.[25] The statistics do not indicate from which country the Palestinians came, nor do they include separate categories for Palestinians and Jordanians; that is, they do not distinguish between Jordanian citizens of East Bank origin and Palestinians. However, it is generally accepted that 95 percent of the Jordanians in Kuwait are Palestinians.[26]

By 1965, the number of Palestinians/Jordanians had risen to 77,712,

31.4 percent of the expatriates and 16.6 percent of the total population. By 1970, the statistics counted 147,696 Palestinians, 37.7 percent of all non-Kuwaitis and 20 percent of the total.[27] By 1975, the number of Palestinians had risen to 204,178.[28]

Using Jordanian emigration figures, Bilal al-Hasan concludes that five times as many Palestinians in Kuwait have come from Jordan as from all other Arab countries. Several factors account for the large emigration from Jordan. Far more Palestinians reside in Jordan than in any other Arab country and the country's traditionally weak economic base has led to chronic unemployment. Furthermore, the development priority enjoyed by the East Bank stifled West Bank economic growth and led to emigration. The generally higher level of education of West Bankers in comparison with East Bankers may also have served as an incentive to Palestinians to migrate to areas that offered opportunities for more remunerative employment.[29] Finally, the 1967 war and the Israeli occupation of the West Bank triggered the movement to Kuwait of entire families, whereas prior to the war generally only a single male provider went abroad.

As mentioned above, in the 1950s and early 1960s, migration to Kuwait—Palestinian or otherwise—was usually on an individual basis. One person, usually a male, emigrated, leaving the family behind. As a result, the expatriate communities consisted of an unusually high proportion of males. As females increasingly came singly to the Gulf, primarily as teachers, the ratio of males to females gradually moved closer to one. The most significant change in the gender ratio occurred between 1965 and 1970, as immigration developed into a family affair. The 1967 war and the occupation of the West Bank and Gaza by the Israelis forced many Palestinians out of the newly occupied territories. Some headed for Kuwait, but, in addition, many of the male family supporters in the Gulf decided to bring their families from the occupied territories to join them.[31]

With the exception of a small number of very wealthy Palestinians

Table 6.2: Gender Ratio in the Palestinian/Jordanian Community, in Kuwait, 1957–1970[30]

	1957	1961	1965	1970
Males	11,616	25,586	49,744	79,934
Females	3,557	11,741	27,968	67,762

working primarily in the private sector, the majority of the community may be divided into three main groups. The first comprises large numbers of farmers and unskilled or semiskilled workers with low incomes. Because of the type of jobs they hold, their position is most tenuous: if a problem arises, a Palestinian mechanic is easily replaced by a Korean or an Indian. The second group, whose residence is somewhat more secure, includes a small sector of skilled workers of modest income and others like them from the middle and lower classes: government workers, private sector employees, small businessmen, grocers, bakers, and the like. The third sector, the middle and upper classes, which enjoy a slightly higher income, includes many professionals (journalists, engineers, doctors, lawyers, and teachers), among them large numbers of the politically aware and nationally conscious.[32]

Thus, despite the perception abroad that the community in Kuwait is wealthy, in reality many Palestinians, especially in the light of the cost of living (particularly rent), which increased markedly in the late 1970s, struggle just to make ends meet. A visit to residential areas with a high Palestinian concentration makes this clear. Two areas in particular, Hawalli-Nuqrah, close to the downtown area, and Farwaniyyah, near the airport, have been nicknamed the "West Bank" and the "Gaza Strip," respectively. No luxury villas or expensive cars are to be seen here. Living conditions are crowded and many of the buildings are in obvious need of repair. Because the frequently large Palestinian families require additional income, many of the family providers hold two jobs and in some cases both husband and wife work.[33]

Especially in the areas where the percentage of Palestinian residents is high, family bonds and, in some instances, village structure, have been reconstituted. Visits to the West Bank or Gaza Strip, or in cases where that is impossible, to other centers where family members have gathered, such as Amman, reinforce the sense of identification with the larger family, and by extension, Palestine. The strength of the attachment to both family and homeland among all sectors combined with the economic power of the members of the professional class has been basic to the development of an organized and cohesive Palestinian community in Kuwait.[34]

ECONOMIC DEVELOPMENT AND EDUCATION

Following the June 1967 war a new strain was placed on the Kuwaiti budget in the form of an annual £ 50 million ($120 million) subsidy which Kuwait provided to the confrontation states according to a decision of the Arab League Council summit meeting at Khartum (1967). This and other steps led to a decrease in monetary liquidity in the country. Commercial activity declined, wage levels dropped and, for the first time, unemployment appeared.[35]

The economic slowdown also affected the educational system. Originally, sufficient room had existed in Kuwaiti government schools for all who sought to enroll, including the non-Kuwaitis. However, the change in the migration pattern of Palestinians—from that of single males to families (and usually large ones)—combined with the tighter fiscal policy meant that the government schools were no longer able to accept all school-age Palestinian children. The problem had first appeared in the mid-1960s but was exacerbated by the effects of the 1967 war.

In 1965, the number of non-Kuwaitis accepted into government schools was limited to 25 percent of total enrollment and was then lowered again in hopes of reducing the figure to 10 percent. The quota system had a greater impact on the Palestinians than on other expatriate groups because of the size of the community and because of the family nature of the Palestinian presence. In response to the increasing demand, both out of concern for the children of the community and because it was generally a profitable venture, members of the community established several private schools: Dar al-Hanan (1963), al-Jayl al-Jadid (1963), al-Munhil, al-Fahahil al-Wataniyyah, al-Mujahid, al-Bara'im al-Namuthijiyyah, al-Nahdah, al-Farwaniyyah, and al-Ahliyyah (all after 1967).[36] Children who could not be accommodated by the government schools had to enroll in private schools. While the opening of these schools solved the problem of alternative educational institutions, the new problem of paying the tuition for these private schools arose.

Members of the Palestinian community appealed to the PLO for assistance when the problem first surfaced. As early as March 1967 the PLO requested the Kuwaiti Foreign Ministry to increase the number of Palestinians admitted into government schools. The situation improved somewhat; however, the population influx that followed the June 1967 war sent the PLO and the Palestinians back to the drawing board.[37]

In August 1967 the PLO again appealed to the government to raise the quota for Palestinians, but the Kuwaitis argued that government resources were insufficient. After further study and discussion, an agreement was concluded between the government and the PLO whereby the PLO was permitted to operate its own schools. The Ministry of Education agreed that some of its teachers could be used to teach afternoon or evening sessions in PLO schools and the ministry provided the building and furnishings for the schools without remuneration. The PLO took responsibility for the general program of the schools and for paying for the services of the teachers it needed, but the curriculum was to conform to that of the ministry.

In November 1967 students began to register; classes began on December 2, 1967. In 1967–68 eight schools were used for 4,721 students. By 1975–76, the last year of the program, twenty-two schools served 16,616 children.[38] The schools catered primarily to children of Palestinians who had come to Kuwait after the 1967 war; however, there were families who had sent their children to government schools who then transferred them to the PLO schools.

Palestinian teachers played a leading role in supervising the schools and their programs. Many either volunteered or took token salaries. Members of the Palestinian Teachers Chapter helped devise pay scales for the instructors and established a scale of charges based on the number of children and family income. Kuwaiti government schools continued to accept at the elementary and junior high levels those Palestinian children who lived far from the PLO facilities; and they accepted all Palestinian secondary school children. The government also promised to ensure that the 10 percent quota of non-Kuwaitis accepted into government schools would include a reasonable number of Palestinians.[39]

In his study of Palestinians in Kuwait Bilal al-Hasan argues that the Kuwaiti decision not to raise the Palestinian quota derived from the government's desire, for political or demographic reasons, to discourage the 1967 immigrants from remaining in the country. However, some officials may have believed that the government's financial capabilities would not allow for it to educate all the new immigrant children and that if the situation was left unaddressed the newcomers might return home.[40] The PLO insisted that, in accordance with a decision of the Arab ministers of education which stated that Palestinian students were to be treated the same as children of the host state, it was incumbent upon Kuwait to accept the children into government schools. The PLO continued to operate its schools but at the same time persisted in pressing for the inclusion of Palestinian children into government schools.[41]

Money to finance the schools came from the Kuwaiti government; payments from families, although some who were supposed to pay were unable to do so and others, children of Palestinians killed in battle, were exempted from tuition; contributions from wealthy Palestinians and other Arabs; and other smaller contributions. Expenses for the first year were KD (Kuwaiti dinar) 77,587 ($263,000), but by 1975–76, the final year of the schools' operation, they had reached KD600,000 ($2 million).[42] Student payments never exceeded KD220,000, while the Kuwaiti government's contribution ranged between KD155,000 and KD200,000 annually.[43]

Because of the many problems they faced, PLO schools were unable to maintain the same academic standards or working conditions as the government schools. Financial constraints took their toll: transportation, material, and teachers' costs were substantial. One result of the budgetary problems was an insufficient number of buses to serve the large numbers of children living far from the schools, thus hampering access. This particular problem took on added significance because of the generally harsh weather conditions in the country and because the children returned home from school at night (classes were held in the afternoon and evening after the regular school hours).[44]

Despite the problems, the PLO school experience contributed immeasurably to the development of national consciousness among Palestinian students. Children saluted the Palestinian flag each day, participated regularly in Palestinian cultural and social activities, and joined scouting troops as well as the Zahrat and Ashbal (associations that provided children with paramilitary and political training). For educational, financial, and political reasons the PLO schools were closed after the 1975–76 academic year and the children were reintegrated into Kuwaiti government schools.[45]

Unfortunately, overcrowding in government schools again became an issue for the Palestinians in the early 1980s. To solve the problem, the Kuwaiti government decided that only children of expatriates who had been in Kuwait as of January 1, 1963 would be permitted to register in government schools. Children already matriculating in government schools were not affected. Other children would have to enroll in private schools, tuition for which the government subsequently moved to subsidize by 50 percent for children affected by the new ruling.

Palestinian children were particularly hard hit by the government's decision. The majority of those who were coming of school age in the early 1980s were children whose parents had come from the West Bank and Gaza in the wake of the 1967 war and who are generally among Kuwait's poorest Palestinians. Least able to afford to put their children in private schools, and often having large families, these parents, already burdened financially by rising rents and depressed economic conditions, have been forced to economize further where possible and often to choose which (if any) of their children to send to private school.

The threat of the spread of illiteracy among Palestinian children— among a national group that has come (or been forced) to value education as its key to survival and its most important weapon in its struggle for self-determination—has greatly alarmed many in the community in Kuwait.[46] The branch of the General Union of Palestinian Women in Kuwait became involved in the problem to a limited degree when it first arose. But its program of tuition subsidies for needy children (which assisted about 300 children in 1983–84) expanded so quickly that by academic year 1986–87, some 3,000 children were able to go to school at the union's expense (see chapter 7). Just as important as the union's financial assistance is the degree to which its efforts have been responsible for alerting the rest of the community to the extent, seriousness, and urgency of the problem.

Palestinian youth also face difficulties when they reach the university level. Kuwait University sets aside only 10 percent of available seats for foreign students. While in 1986 Palestinians, who have a reputation for excellence in school, were accepted for 200 of the available 276 seats,[47] this does not approach the number of Palestinian high school seniors seeking to continue their education. For those who are accepted, tuition is free and other expenses are minor; the others must face the challenge of being accepted in universities elsewhere in the Arab world (where economic retrenchment has hit Palestinians hard), Islamic countries, or in the socialist bloc countries. More and more often, despite the tremendous cost, families opt to send their children to Europe or the United States.[48]

The difficulties do not end with overcoming the admission problem and coping with the financial burden. The Palestinian male who goes abroad to study faces the likelihood that he will never be able to return to Kuwait to live: it is extremely difficult for a non-Kuwaiti male from Kuwait who studies abroad to renew his residency after age twenty-one. In some cases, merely obtaining a visa to return "home" to visit requires special influence. And some countries will not issue visas to Palestinians from Kuwait unless they have at least one year's residency left, thus leaving the student in a Catch-22 situation: he is unable to renew residence in Kuwait because of living abroad and unable to stay abroad because of the inability to renew residence.[49] No solution is in sight. As a result, expatriate frustration and insecurity increase, and the further splintering of many already severely fractured Palestinian families appears to be a likely consequence.

PALESTINIAN-KUWAITI RELATIONS

Throughout the years the Palestinian community has enjoyed relatively good relations with the Kuwaiti government. Palestinians have been in the country longer than most of the other expatriate communities, so they are better known and are generally trusted. They have even volunteered to fight for Kuwait on several occasions: when it was threatened by Iraq in 1962 and more recently, when the Iran-Iraq war threatened to spill over into the tiny amirate.

The large Palestinian presence in the bureaucracy has given the community some influence in policymaking as well as in appointments, although as more and more Kuwaitis enter government service, Palestinian influence declines. Their role in the media and at the university has also opened opportunities for discussing the Palestine problem and for influencing public opinion because of the freedom of the press and expression that Kuwait has enjoyed.[50] The relatively liberal nature of the Kuwaiti political system has traditionally tolerated more political activity and expression than have many other Arab states. It was in Kuwait that the first central committee of Fateh was formed by Yasir ʿArafat, Khalid al-Hasan, Khalil al-Wazir, and Salim Zaʿnun, all of whom were living in the country at the time. Kuwait remained Fateh's central meeting place until its headquarters were moved to Damascus in 1966.[51]

The good relations between the Kuwaiti government and the PLO are attested to by the fact that since the late 1960s the government has collected 5 percent of its Palestinian employees' salaries as a "liberation tax," which is then given to the Palestine National Fund. Nor has Kuwait sought to influence PLO politics by sponsoring its own commando group in the way that Syria sponsors al-Saʿiqah or Iraq sponsors the Arab Liberation Front. Fateh predominates—its office in Kuwait serves as a headquarters for Fateh for the entire Gulf area—and is really the foundation of all Palestinian activity in the country. Other *fasaʾil* have offices, but operate only semiofficially,[52] largely owing to their leftist-oriented programs, which have elicited much more government opposition and much less popular support than Fateh.[53]

Surprisingly, the community's allegiance to ʿArafat hung in the balance for some time after the summer 1983 revolt in Fateh. There was, at least until early 1984, a chance that the Palestinians in Kuwait would side with Abu Musa's rebels. However, it appears that Syria's heavy-handed interference ultimately alienated many who otherwise might have opposed 'Arafat.[54] Despite the waivering on the Abu Musa issue the PLO in Kuwait has been, by virtue of its leadership and desire to preserve its position, basically conservative in nature. That stance, combined with the privileged position it has achieved, has led some to conclude that the Kuwaiti government actually relies on the PLO to control and monitor the Palestinian community.[55]

Palestinian political activity in Kuwait proceeds through four channels: the PLO office (opened in October 1964 and first headed by Khayr al-Din Abu al-Jubayn, who was seconded from his job in the Ministry of Electricity);[56] the branches of the popular organizations; the *tanzimat*; and the participation of individual activists in political work through Palestinian and Kuwaiti official and popular channels. The *tanzimat* constitute the backbone of union leadership and of all political or mass organization work.

Palestinian political activity in Kuwait consists of various types of work. The popular unions sponsor ongoing social or cultural programs and are in regular contact with Kuwaiti unions and other political forces to coordinate activities. Government permission is required only for special festivals and demonstrations, although in emergency circumstances, displays or demonstrations that spring from the pressure of political events outside Kuwait have been allowed without prior permission. Kuwait does not, however, permit a Palestinian military presence,[57] just as it has made clear that it will not tolerate its territory's being used as a battlefield for inter-Palestinian disputes.[58]

Unlike any other Palestinian community, the community in Kuwait formed a council to coordinate popular organization and *tanzimat* activity. The "enlarged council" includes representatives of each of the *tanzimat* as well as resident PNC members and the leaders of the popular organizations. The council coordinates Palestinian union, political, and community activity in Kuwait and discusses issues of concern to the community. Representatives of the popular organizations also meet regularly to deal with similar issues. For example, the first annual Conference of Palestinian Popular Organizations, convened on December 18, 1977, discussed the general state of the Palestinian revolution and its relations with Arab and other states; the implications of Sadat's trip to Jerusalem and how to react to it; Palestinian popular work in Kuwait; and PLO institutions in general. Among its decisions were to set up the Sunduq al-Sumud (a fund to support the occupied territories); to hold a yearly Palestinian culture celebration; to strengthen Palestinian-Kuwaiti relations and work to solve local Palestinian problems through Kuwaiti authorities; and to assemble a committee to visit the Syrian and Iraqi embassies to try to solve the problems between the two countries. It also recommended that the PLO and resistance organizations give the popular organizations a greater role in the PNC and that more precise ways of choosing representatives for the PNC be established.[59]

Relations between the Kuwaiti government and the Palestinian community are largely influenced by external events related to the Palestine question. Since its independence in 1961 Kuwait has played a leading role, both in Arab and international forums, in support of the Palestinians and the PLO. It has traditionally provided monetary support to the PLO and has sent emergency aid during periods of crisis in Lebanon in the 1970s and 1980s. Throughout the years Kuwaiti officials have been prominent participants in Palestinian cultural festivals, celebrations of national holidays, and even political protests.

The 1950s and 1960s were a honeymoon period for the Kuwaitis and the Palestinians, as both communities were swept up in the Arab nationalist fervor of the time. Since then relations have fluctuated. The first episode that cooled relations between the two was the civil war in Jordan. Kuwaiti concern stemmed from a fear that similar events might occur in other countries with large concentrations of Palestinians. In 1974–75, as the crisis in Lebanon unfolded and discussions of possible parallels between the demographic structure of Kuwait and the Lebanese ethnic and confessional mosaic began to appear in the media, renewed concerns were voiced. In 1976, in the wake of the first round of the Lebanese civil war, the PLO schools were closed and Palestinian children were reintegrated into Kuwaiti government schools.

Because of their large numbers and their strategic location in the government, the professions, and business, Palestinians gradually became suspect as Kuwaitis strove to come to terms with and address their continuing position as a minority in their own country. When explosions at the U.S., French, and British embassies and the Kuwait International Airport rocked the country in December 1983, Palestinians waited nervously, hoping none of their countrymen would be found to have been involved. Already suffering from increased visa and residency restrictions, problems with educating their children, and with the economic recession in the Gulf, evidence of Palestinian involvement in the explosions, many believed, would trigger the imposition of even greater restrictions, and perhaps—the greatest fear of the community in Kuwait—mass expulsions. The fact that there was no Palestinian involvement in these bombings (or in any of the subsequent terrorist incidents that Kuwait has witnessed), combined with the community's expressions of support for Kuwait when it felt threatened by the Iran-Iraq war has largely dispelled the sentiment, formerly held by some Kuwaitis, that the Palestinians might at some point try to subvert the government. The Palestinians' feelings of insecurity, on the other hand, have yet to recede.

Despite Palestinians' numbers, cohesion, and influence, their political activity remains hostage to the events, both external and internal, that guide or force the hand of Kuwaiti policymakers. Concern for continued residence, which has been particularly acute since the events in Lebanon in 1975–76, has led to a decline in the community's political activism. Kuwaitization policies are also constant reminders of the tenuous nature of their presence. Even those who have what seem to be secure jobs nonetheless worry about the educational and employment future of their children, as well as their own lives once retirement comes. As a result, some have withdrawn completely from active political involvement; others have diverted their political energies into activities that are more social or cultural; finally, some of the more financially secure have opted to fill the PLO's coffers as a substitute for publicly proclaiming its slogans or shouldering its kalashnikovs.[60] Given the prevailing climate of pessimism about the likelihood of movement toward a solution to the Palestine problem, combined with the heightened sense of insecurity felt by all in Kuwait because of developments in the Gulf war, many Palestinians are unwilling to engage in activity that may jeopardize their jobs and, by extension, their residence, when the potential returns at this stage must be viewed as dubious at best.

[7]
Workers and Women

During the early years of Palestinian migration to Kuwait, the community was characterized by a preponderance of men. Some were single and supporting parents and siblings back home; others were married but had left their families behind. However, after the 1967 war many of these men sent for their families from the newly occupied West Bank and Gaza Strip. The number of women and children thus increased dramatically, transforming the nature of the community in Kuwait to one dominated by families.

These changes in the composition of the Palestinian community have affected the type and degree of popular organizing in which Palestinians have engaged. Although some important strides were made in labor organizing in the wake of Kuwaiti independence, the Palestinians' nonnational status and increasing concern for residence once the men were joined by their families combined with a weak indigenous labor movement to limit severely the range of activities in which a Palestinian trade union could become involved. In contrast, because of its overwhelmingly social as opposed to political program, organized activity among Palestinian women, which was almost nonexistent in the early period owing to their small numbers, came to play a greater and greater role in the community.

THE WORKERS

As the lifeline of the developing states of the Gulf, oil was both politically and economically the most sensitive sector. In the mid-1950s, Palestinian workers supported by indigenous nationalist elements who opposed the continuation of Western economic domination led a series of strikes throughout the Gulf to protest conditions in the oil sector. Deportations of Palestinians from Saudi Arabia, Iraq, Libya, and Kuwait followed. The governments and oil companies involved then moved to ensure that a larger percentage of oil sector workers would be host country nationals. For example, a 1957 agreement between the

Saudi government and American oil companies gave priority in job recruitment to *citizens* of Arab League countries, thereby excluding all Palestinians who remained stateless. In Kuwait a similar agreement was concluded between the government and the oil companies; however, in the case of Kuwait, the amir was empowered to choose whomever he wanted for employment, without regard to whether the Arabs were citizens of Arab League states. Therefore, in Kuwait the potential impact of the new agreements was lessened.[1]

The suppression of the strikes of the mid-1950s and the subsequent deportations no doubt hindered the reemergence of labor organizing both through depletion of ranks and intimidation of prospective recruits. Although Kuwait has had relatively liberal policies in some fields, labor organizing traditionally has not been one of them: a combination of the mono-product nature of the economy and the policy of large-scale labor importation has kept the Kuwaiti trade union movement small and weak.[2]

The beginnings of labor organizing in Kuwait may be traced to the efforts of members of the Arab Nationalist Movement (ANM). The ANM was in the vanguard of clandestine political organizing in the 1950s. In addition, however, it sought a more mass-based mobilization in the form of federations or unions of blue-collar workers. The large number of workers among the Palestinians in Kuwait made the country and the community an important ANM organizing target as early as the 1950s.[3]

In late 1959, interest in trade union organizing began to manifest itself in other quarters. A committee of three independents—Musa al-Basyuni, Fathi Raghib, and ʿAwni Battash—began making informal visits to the major places of Palestinian worker concentration: Ford, Mercedes, Fiat, Pepsi-Cola, the Municipality, and the Ministry of Public Works. Unlike the ANM, this committee sought to organize bureaucrats and technocrats as well as blue-collar workers. The men met with the workers, informally discussed their problems with them, and tried to determine who constituted the natural leadership in each workplace. The three-man committee then approached these "leaders" and suggested the idea of forming a Palestinian labor union.[4]

In the early 1960s, Fateh—toward which these independent labor organizers inclined—was still in its infancy. Its lack of an elaborate political apparatus (unlike the ANM, which had an elaborate hierarchical structure) and its policy of noninterference in the internal affairs of Arab states rendered it less of a threat; indeed, it was therefore allowed to grow and gradually develop a wide base of largely nonideological popular support. The ANM, on the other hand, with its secret cell structure and more revolutionary line, continually encountered problems: its members were considered suspect and were periodically expelled from Arab states for their political activism. In 1962, Fateh began attracting members from the Palestinian community at large. Its partisans in Kuwait worked among the members of the nascent Palestinian workers' movement to convince them to become supporting, if not full-fledged, members of the Fateh political organization.

Eventually, those who had been recruited by both the ANM and the independents formed the first Palestinian trade union council, which comprised thirty-two members representing each of the major places of employment.[5] The council held its first conference in October 1963. Each company sent representatives according to the number of Palestinians employed: a company with 100 or more workers was allowed two delegates while those with less than 100 but more than 50 were permitted one. A neutral committee supervised the elections. The workers' council was able to agree on an organizational program; however, the divergent political views of its members precluded consensus on all but the most minimal political principles: noninterference in the affairs of Arab states; national and not class-oriented work; collective and not individual leadership.[6] As its first activity, the Kuwait branch organized a Palestinian workers' protest at the Mercedes company, an action that led to the dismissal of union activist Fathi Raghib from his job.[7]

Also in 1963, Palestinian trade unionist Husni al-Khuffash began to push for the establishment of a General Union of Palestine Workers (for details of the founding of the GUPW, see chapter 5). Working out of Cairo with Egyptian president Nasir's backing, Khuffash sought the restoration of a Palestinian workers' movement within a Nasirist framework. Having heard of the labor organizing activity in Kuwait, he came for a four-day visit. Some members of the workers' council in Kuwait were prepared to join with Khuffash immediately, while others preferred to wait until political conditions improved: that is, until chances seemed better for joining *and* maintaining independence. They stipulated that to win their support such a union must not be dominated by any political party nor should it interfere in the affairs of the host state. They did express a desire to coordinate action with other unions and join the International Federation of Arab Trade Unions (IFATU), but Khuffash left Kuwait without convincing them to become members of a general union led from Cairo.[8] The Palestinian Workers' Council in Kuwait did not join the GUPW until 1964.

Husni al-Khuffash's version of the evolution of the branch in Kuwait differs somewhat from the account above. His memoirs note that as part of a labor-organizing tour, he departed Baghdad on June 7, 1964 for Kuwait. Khuffash claims that prior to the Kuwait visit he had met in Cairo with Fayiz Faddah, a former Palestinian trade union activist from Haifa residing in Kuwait, and Faddah agreed to take responsibility for establishing a branch of the GUPW in the oil state. However, when Khuffash arrived in Kuwait in 1964, not a single worker had embraced the idea of the union. Therefore, he took it upon himself to visit workers' groups and explain the purpose of the GUPW. On June 16, 1964, he called for a meeting of interested workers and designated them as a founding committee. An administrative committee was also assembled which included Fayiz Faddah, Yasir al-Karmi, and Fayiz al-Khuffash. The ranks of the branch quickly expanded with the addition of Palestinian workers on Faylaka Island (just off the coast of Kuwait).[9]

The contradictions in the story of the early days of organizing the branch in Kuwait deserve discussion.[10] Although the detailed recollections of ʿAwni Battash and ʿAli Qubʿah do not match, Khuffash's contention that nothing had been done toward establishing a branch by 1964 when he came to Kuwait seems unlikely. Khuffash himself in his address to the first GUPW conference only a year later called the branch in Kuwait one of the strongest.

One possible explanation may lie in Khuffash's statement to the first GUPW conference on the Kuwaiti branch in which he remarked that in addition to its other accomplishments, the branch had achieved gratifying results in its efforts "to gather together the workers' energies and to unify their word."[11] His remark implies the existence of divisions in the past which the branch had managed to overcome.

According to Battash and Palestinian historian ʿAbd al-Qadir Yasin, Khuffash had an independent/Nasirist orientation that in the early 1960s would have put him in or near the ANM camp.[12] Battash, on the other hand, noted the growing popularity of Fateh in Kuwait during this period. The labor organizers differed, not over the idea of organizing, but over the framework; that is, the principles on which the organization would be founded. Battash insisted that Khuffash's association with Nasir put off many workers who feared domination of the organization by Cairo. If Khuffash, supported by Cairo, found upon his arrival in Kuwait that Palestinian workers were not convinced of a Palestinian labor organization along the lines he was proposing, or if divisiveness among the workers over this issue had paralyzed further efforts, he might have expressed his dismay by claiming that "nothing had been done."[13]

Despite the lack of consensus on specifics, general trends emerge from the evidence. Members of the ANM and, later, independents (many of whom subsequently became Fateh supporters) were involved in efforts to mobilize the large concentration of Palestinian workers in Kuwait. By 1963, the workers had begun to elect representatives, and by 1964 the workers' council had become the Kuwait branch of the GUPW, which then declared itself a base of the PLO, supportive of and subject to its political line.

The branch in Kuwait sent a delegation of fourteen men headed by branch secretary Fayiz Faddah to the first conference of the GUPW in 1965. In Khuffash's address to the conference he praised the work of the Kuwait branch and called it one of the strongest of the union because of the size of the Palestinian working class in Kuwait and because of its potential for participating in funding the GUPW. He singled out the chapter on Faylaka Island and commended it for its activity.[14] From the delegation from Kuwait, four members were voted seats on the GUPW higher council while two—'Adil Ibrahim Hasan and Subhi Husayn 'Ali—were selected for the eight-member executive committee of the general union.[15]

Faddah, still secretary of the branch, headed its delegation to the second GUPW conference in April 1967. The delegation included three members—Faddah, Fathi Raghib, and Muhammad Naffa'—as well as six auxiliary members, among them 'Awni Battash.[16] In the branch elections of 1969, Raghib took over from Faddah as secretary. Shortly thereafter, he was elected to the post of general secretary after Khuffash retired. In 1971 'Awni Battash became secretary of the branch, a post he held until 1974.[17] He was succeeded by Hamid al-Faris, and then in 1978 by 'Abd al-Ra'uf al-'Alami, who continued to hold the post in 1987.

Branch Activities

Although Kuwaiti law forbids the establishment of non-Kuwaiti unions, an exception was made in the case of the Palestinians. The government has not licensed the GUPW: rather, it treats it as part of the PLO, in whose headquarters it has its office. Agreement exists among the members of the IFATU that the labor union of the host state is responsible for Palestinian workers' affairs: the GUPW can play a direct role only if the conflict or disagreement is between two Palestinians. Like all non-Kuwaitis, Palestinians may, and in some cases must, join Kuwaiti unions, but they cannot vote or be elected, nor do they derive any privileges from membership, thus limiting the appeal of joining.

From about 500 members in 1960, the workers' organization grew to 3,000 by 1963 and to some 10,000 by 1965 after it had become a branch of the GUPW. At the time of the GUPW's third conference, held in 1969, the Kuwait branch boasted 11,000 members and by the fourth conference, convened in 1971, 14,000. However, the numbers alone do not indicate the level of branch activity. Many "members" are recruited around election time and their participation ends with voting.[18] As of 1986 the union counted more than 31,000 members, among whom 5,000 are considered active.[19]

Membership dues render the branch self-sufficient. In fulfillment of the role that Khuffash envisioned for it and according to the GUPW constitution, the Kuwait branch is responsible for sending 30 percent of its yearly receipts to fund the general union. In the past, contributions from members and concerned individuals supplemented members' dues, but the deterioration in economic conditions and in the general Palestinian political situation has triggered a drop in contributions.

In Kuwait itself the branch's resources are used for several major projects. One is its program of "car guaranteeing." In order to prevent people from taking cars (generally inexpensive in Kuwait) out of the country in order to sell them, Kuwaiti law requires a KD5,000 ($17,000) deposit as a guarantee that a car driven out of the country will return. This provision affects many expatriate workers who drive home to Syria, Jordan, and Lebanon to visit family or to attend to business. KD5,000 is a substantial sum, and one that few Palestinian workers in Kuwait would have in cash: therefore, the union pays the deposit for its members. The deposit is refunded upon the car's return to Kuwait.[20]

The branch's remaining financial reserves are deposited in an assistance fund used by its social affairs committee to help between fifty and sixty poor families and to provide scholarships to outstanding children of union members. (This committee, composed of older union members, also handles ten to fifteen cases a month in its additional role as mediator in domestic, neighborhood, and financial quarrels.) Unfortunately, many of the neediest Palestinians are those who came from the West Bank in the wake of the 1967 war, who still have strong ties there, and are, consequently, hesitant to seek GUPW assistance for fear of repercussions from the Jordanian authorities on their return to Jordan for involvement with a PLO-affiliated organization.[21]

The GUPW has viewed military training and participation in the armed struggle as a central duty of workers. Therefore, although far from the field of battle, the branch has an official in charge of military mobilization. Palestinian worker volunteers from Kuwait fought in the 1973 October war, in Lebanon in 1975–76, and again in Lebanon in 1982. Fateh (although not the other *fasaʾil*) has an agreement whereby the union pays the salaries of Fateh workers who enlist to fight.[22] Just as important, unlike some other Arab governments the Kuwaiti government has permitted the return to the country of those men who volunteer for military service with the PLO abroad.

Despite military involvement outside Kuwait, the union has not become embroiled in Kuwaiti domestic affairs and thus enjoys good relations with the Kuwaiti government. As long as the PLO premises are used, the Ministry of the Interior does not require the branch to obtain special permission to publish its journal, hold symposia, or sponsor events. Only one conflict with the government was reported: in 1969, several branch officials were expelled for their involvement in what were described as "leftist activities."[23]

The 1983 revolt in Fateh and the subsequent split in the PLO did not affect the branch internally. Interestingly, it strained relations with the Kuwait Trade Union Federation (KTUF), which, like the GUPW, was originally strongly influenced by the ANM. Unlike the GUPW (which is now overwhelmingly Fateh oriented), the KTUF has its strongest ties in the Palestinian community with supporters of the DF and PFLP.[24] When the 1983 rebellion broke out in Fateh the KTUF cooled relations with the GUPW, but did not take an official position on the internal PLO strife. A visit from the GUPW-Kuwait leadership and a KTUF delegation trip to Syria dispelled initial KTUF sympathy for the rebels and relations between the two unions returned to normal in 1985.[25]

No discussion of the GUPW would be complete without some mention of its effectiveness. Several factors have served to limit its activity. For example, some Palestinian workers in Kuwait prefer not to take an active part in or even to join the union for fear that *any* political involvement may jeopardize their jobs. Heads of households (usually men) are particularly vulnerable because they shoulder the financial responsibility for their families and because the expulsion of a nonnational results in the expulsion of his or her dependents as well. Lack of time is another factor inhibiting active worker participation. All chapter members have one job. Many work at two jobs and consequently have little spare time. Aside from Fathi Raghib, the activist dismissed after the first strike, the union has had no salaried, full-time employees. Work and time are contributed on a completely voluntary basis.

The fact that the union has been able to maintain any level of activity is due in large part to the fact that it is dominated by Fateh, a political organization with broad mass Palestinian nationalist appeal and which, in order to survive, has steered clear of internal Kuwaiti issues and involvements. Many argue that attempts to increase activism in a real trade union sense, efforts that would inevitably collide with domestic Kuwaiti concerns, would have precipitated the union's closure long ago. The resulting paucity of benefits in the social, economic, and labor realms has certainly sapped the union of some potential vitality. While the union's activities may not seem dynamic, its program (like that of Fateh, the predominant party) may be characterized as conservatively survivalist, perhaps the most appropriate posture for the political environment in which it operates.

THE WOMEN

The women's union is generally regarded as the most active of the Palestinian popular organizations in Kuwait, yet its beginnings were, at best, inauspicious. Five years passed between the proclamation of the GUPWom (1965) in Jerusalem and the formation of a preparatory committee to establish a branch in Kuwait (1970). In 1966 a women's committee was launched that had an office at the PLO headquarters, but Palestinian women in Kuwait were few, and those who took part in the committee were even fewer. Lack of transportation and spouse resistance were major barriers to joining. Moreover, the policy of leadership appointment (rather than popular election) during the Shuqayri era undermined the group's pretention to mass representation. At the same time, however, Fateh recruited growing numbers of women who worked on general political as well as women's issues, but it opened no separate office for women within the organization.[26]

With the post-1968 ascendancy of the *fasaʾil*, the new PLO leadership resolved to invigorate the popular organizations, among them the General Union of Palestinian Women. In 1969, according to a directive of the PNC executive council, a delegation from the GUPWom secretariat traveled to Kuwait to assemble a preparatory committee. The committee's formation marked the beginning of a new era for Palestinian women's political, social, and cultural work in Kuwait.

A problem that arose when the branch was first formed concerned goals. Some women felt that the union should serve the purely political purpose of implementing PLO policy. Others questioned the limited nature of this approach and wondered if the branch was not also bound to serve the community. Gradually, the women realized that they could integrate political and social work into an effective program.[27]

The branch first turned its attention to the needs of the *fidaʾiyyin*. The women collected contributions in cash and in kind with which they initiated a program of sending packages to fighters. Community members assembled such items as pajamas, shirts, socks, and soap. In each package of supplies they placed a note of support. The packages were then shipped for distribution among the *fidaʾiyyin*, first in Jordan and later in Lebanon.

An important boost to women's organizing came from an unexpected source in the wake of the 1967 war. It will be recalled that the large influx of Palestinians into Kuwait that followed the war led the PLO, in cooperation with the Kuwaiti government, to open its own schools in order to accommodate all the children who had come with their families from the occupied West Bank and Gaza. As an unplanned side benefit of the educational program, the schools began to serve as a convenient place for Palestinian women to gather for discussions, consciousness-raising sessions, and films.[28]

The women continued to maintain their first office in the PLO complex; however, Salwa Abu Khadra, one of the branch's most dynamic members, had opened a nursery school on the first floor of a rented villa. Gradually, the second floor of the building came to be used as a meeting place for the women. No special permission was sought by the GUPWom to expand in this way. Permission was simply "acquired" through use of the building.[29] The branch continues to be headquartered in two floors of a villa not far from, but not part of, the PLO complex.

Branch Activities

The GUPWom in Kuwait sponsors a wide range of cultural activities and social services. One focus has been the preservation of Palestinian cultural heritage, particularly through a program of embroidery production. The women have collected traditional patterns and colors and assembled elaborate files of regional designs and styles. They have also assembled a collection of more than 100 Palestinian dresses *(athwab)* which are on display in a small museum at the union headquarters.

As elsewhere, embroidery production enables women to secure additional income. However, the significance of the economic aspect is secondary to the role of embroidery production in creating ties between Palestinian women and the union.[30] Just as important, the opportunity afforded the young to see traditional embroidery at home serves to reinforce the younger generation's attachment to its cultural heritage.

In addition to the embroidery program, the union sponsors sewing and typing classes for women and girls who normally would have had virtually no chance of employment. More recently, the branch has offered literacy classes and, depending upon the availability of teachers and the number of interested students, knitting classes and English lessons. The union has also sponsored a tutoring program run by volunteer university students. For these activities, the location of the union's headquarters outside the PLO office has removed a potentially damaging obstacle, for some would have found it awkward to attend classes held in an overwhelmingly male office building. The fact that the GUPWom courses are open only to women also gives the union's classes an edge over private institutes that offer similar courses that are open to both men and women. Families more readily accept women's activity outside the home if it is under union auspices, especially since the branch has provided buses to transport the women to and from the classes.

In the early 1980s, the branch initiated a program of providing monthly financial subsidies to poor Palestinian families. Need is determined after careful study of a family's situation by the union's social committee. Since the assistance the branch is able to offer is quite modest (KD25 or $85 per month), the GUPWom tries to help family members find work, sometimes by training women in its sewing or typing classes. When the number of families seeking financial assistance exceeds the branch's capabilities it refers cases to the Kuwaiti Lajnat al-Zakah (an Islamic welfare fund) for assistance.

The program that has taken on greatest importance—both in terms of its contribution to the community and the time the branch devotes to it—is the tuition subsidy program. As was discussed in chapter 6, with only a few exceptions children of expatriates who were not in Kuwait as of January 1, 1963 may not enroll in Kuwaiti government schools.[31] As a result only about 50 percent of all Palestinian children are accepted into government schools.[32]

Consequently, the prospect of the spread of illiteracy among children is considered one of the most serious problems facing the community. The PLO and, indeed, 'Arafat himself, have taken a special interest and the GUPWom has taken the lead in addressing the problem. In 1983–84 the branch paid the tuition for 200 to 300 children.[33] In 1985–86 the number had risen to 1,500; in 1986–87 some 3,000 children were able to attend private schools thanks to the union's assistance.[34]

The expansion of the GUPWom's services has been facilitated by the fact that Palestinians tend to live in the same areas. People learn of available services through friends, and women from the union hear of needy families in the course of their visits to families already identified as needy. Some additional cases are referred to the women by the PLO.[35] The tuition subsidy program has become so well known that during the period just prior to the commencement of the academic year, the headquarters is filled to overflowing with parents seeking assistance.[36]

In addition to the training and educational programs, the union, which in 1984 counted some 1,800[37] (not all active) members, also sponsors social events. Large dinners serve both to bring together Palestinian families and to increase their ties to the union. Dinners usually focus on a particular political issue and are used to raise funds for scholarships for outstanding female students engaged in graduate study. The union also sponsors an annual Palestinian cultural festival, which lasts several days and features embroidery, traditional handicrafts from the occupied territories, music, food, dance, and films.

Despite the general perception of affluence of the Palestinian community in Kuwait, the branch does not enjoy a surplus. It depends upon several funding sources. It operates a market in which it sells at a fraction of their market value goods donated by local merchants, but this is more a service to the community than a revenue source. It takes in some money in the form of fees for its sewing and typing classes and from sales of embroidery and other products at the yearly cultural festival. Finally, it receives a certain amount from membership dues, contributions from the community, and fund-raising events for specific projects.

Participation in the branch has depended upon a number of factors. The first is access: the headquarters is in Jabariyyah, near the PLO office and close to the areas of Hawalli-Nuqrah and Salmiyyah where large numbers of lower- and middle-income Palestinians reside. The availability of transportation to and from the office has enabled many women, who otherwise might have been excluded, to participate. The relatively liberal political atmosphere in Kuwait over the years, combined with a higher social rather than overtly political content of its program, has also undoubtedly facilitated the branch's operation and expansion.

But there are also factors that discourage participation. As with the workers, primary among them is the availability of time. Palestinians traditionally have large families; therefore, the women are often bound to their homes because of the children or to jobs to help support the family. Such women have little or no time to devote to the union. Most of the women who hold leadership posts come from upper middle-class or upper-class families, and their children are grown or are at least in school; even if they do have young children, they also have live-in nannies to look after them. Therefore, these women have the time, the freedom, and the financial security to engage in nonremunerative work outside the home.

Political considerations also affect a woman's decision to participate. Some believe mere association with the union may lead to political problems in Kuwait. More often, they fear possible repercussions from the Israeli or Jordanian authorities when they return to the East Bank, West Bank, or Gaza Strip to visit. Another, but secondary, factor is the degree of politicization. Politicized women, who are generally fewer in number, tend to work with the union on a long-term basis; on the other hand, the unpoliticized tend to give or participate only in times of national crisis or special need.

Despite the constraints or obstacles, the GUPWom in Kuwait, particularly in the 1980s, has been very active and successful with its program. Certainly, the relatively large number of financially secure Palestinian women in Kuwait who have the time to participate has been important. Just as significant has been the quality and effectiveness of leadership that the branch has enjoyed. The government's tolerance of social work as opposed to pure political work has also given the women freer rein to expand. Moreover, the difficult economic situation in which many poorer Palestinians have increasingly found themselves has created additional needs which the state has not been prepared to address and which, therefore, Palestinians themselves have been forced to confront.

Finally, some women feel that if the national movement encounters setbacks in the inter-Arab or international arena—as has certainly been the case since 1982—and work there appears futile, Palestinians throughout the Arab world have genuine, pressing social needs which the women can address. In the same way, the union's efforts in the realm of revival and preservation of culture are considered basic to the Palestinian long-term struggle, whatever the political crisis of the day may be.

[8]
Changing Organizational Horizons:
The GUPS, GUPT, and PRCS

The relatively liberal political atmosphere in Kuwait and the general sympathy for the Palestinian cause in both Kuwaiti and expatriate circles were critical to the development of separate Palestinian institutions. Nevertheless, other factors intervened to narrow the sphere for expansion of some of the organizations. In the case of the students, Kuwaitization has meant the imposition of a quota on the number of foreign students accepted into the university. Kuwaitization has also had implications for educators; teachers constitute one of the largest Palestinian professional groups, but the increasing number of Kuwaiti graduates of teachers' training programs has narrowed the employment field for nonnationals. Finally, in the case of the Palestine Red Crescent Society, the state's provision of free or low-cost health care to all residents, national or expatriate, has made redundant many of the functions the PRCS carries out in other host states. Hence, its role has been limited largely to that of fund raiser for other branches.

THE STUDENTS

Efforts to establish a branch of the GUPS in Kuwait began in 1968, the year following the opening of Kuwait University, and came to fruition in 1969. At the time, the university had a student body of only 1,763 and of that number only 192 came from non-Gulf, Arab states (including the Palestinians from the community in Kuwait).[1] The GUPS branch, therefore, began with only tens of members.

The first crisis encountered by the branch arose shortly after its establishment and took the form of a major conflict over type of membership and representation in the branch's hierarchy.[2] GUPS members in Kuwait fall into two categories: those who attend Kuwait University and those who are registered in correspondence programs and travel abroad to their universities only to take exams. The conflict, which nearly split the branch, arose over the membership in the branch of the far more numerous correspondence students *(muntasibun)*. Most of the *muntasibun* worked in Kuwait; therefore, the students from Kuwait University contended that they were not students as much as they were workers and should therefore join the GUPW. Furthermore, although more numerous, the *muntasibun* took a far less active role in the branch. Yet, according to the agreement worked out when the branch was founded, the administrative council of the branch included seven *muntasibun* and only two students from Kuwait University. Thus, students who otherwise played an insignificant role in the union were given a two-thirds majority on the administrative council, a situation KU students found unfair and intolerable.

But this was not the real point of contention: the real question was that of who would control the union and how they would maintain that control. Two issues were involved. First, the general democratic nature of the union, that is, the concept of independence of the branch from outside political organizations, was called into question. The second issue was related to the first and involved the larger struggle between the *tanzimat*. A majority of the correspondence students were Fateh supporters: Fateh even had its own office to assist them. Among the KU students there were partisans of most of the other Palestinian *tanzimat*, but a majority there supported Fateh as well; nevertheless, a *muntasibun* majority on the administrative council ensured Fateh's predominance in the branch, a predominance it had no intention of surrendering.

In 1970–71, a process of adjustment began. The Palestinian students at Kuwait University demanded the establishment of a separate GUPS branch for them even though, according to the GUPS constitution, branches—not to be confused with chapters—are not established at individual universities. To reinforce their demands, the KU students seceded from the branch and set up their own administrative council. When news of the split in the branch reached GUPS headquarters in Cairo, the union's executive committee sent representatives to investigate the situation. The KU students discussed with them their demand that the correspondence students join the GUPS branches in the countries of their respective university affiliations, not of their residency (i.e., Kuwait).

After long discussions, a compromise was reached whereby the KU students' representation on the administrative council was increased to five seats, and the *muntasibun*'s reduced to four, with the understanding that the seventh GUPS conference (which was held in July

1974) would further discuss the problem. That conference in fact voted to reduce the *muntasibun*'s representation to only two, leaving the KU students seven seats on the administrative council.

In the period that followed Fateh suffered another blow in the arena of student politics. Across the diaspora, the post-1973 war period witnessed a clash between the idea of a political or negotiated solution to the Palestinian question and the traditional call for armed struggle. Differences between the *fasa'il* began to crystallize in Kuwait in the GUPS bloc programs in 1973–74. In the 1973 elections, the Progressive Bloc (associated with the PFLP and opposed to a political solution) won two seats. However, in 1974–75 it won five seats and thereby took control of the branch. Its position had been further enhanced by the development of divergent opinions within Fateh, a reflection of conditions in the main political arena, Lebanon.[3]

The 1975–77 period saw the rise of an organized and active group of women in the union. The most important catalyst was Shirin ʿAbd al-Raziq, who had been expelled from the American University in Beirut after large-scale students strikes in 1973–74. After her return to Kuwait to continue her university studies, she set out to organize the students at the women's college in Kifan. Through hard work, a core of activist women came to constitute such a powerful force that Fateh's student leadership had no choice but to consult with them. And it was the women who were largely responsible for Fateh's return to power in 1975–76 with the election of a new GUPS Kuwait branch president, Muhammad Jabir. The women remained a powerful force until the graduation of the activist core in 1977–78.[4]

This period of debate and controversy was followed by several years of forced retrenchment. In 1978, trouble between Kuwaiti students, which culminated in campus clashes, led the government to freeze all student activities. The freeze was lifted in 1979, but only the Kuwaiti Student Federation (KSF) was permitted to reopen. The GUPS did begin to operate again, but not on campus. It could organize activities from campus, but any activities had to take place at the PLO headquarters. In some cases the GUPS was able to work through the student societies attached to each faculty (*jamʿiyyat al-kulliyyat*). The range of activity was limited, but the societies were at least able to reserve lecture halls and invite speakers. Since 1985, however, even that has been forbidden, as are student posters—the famous "wall newspapers" that had been such an important part of student politics—or any other student publications inside the university.[5]

A more serious challenge to the branch arose in 1980, this time from the Islamic right. At the GUPS general conference held in Suq al-Gharb, Lebanon in 1978 it was decided for the first time that the union should be bound by the Palestine National Covenant. Prior to 1978, the GUPS constitution had stated that the union was "a base of the Palestinian revolution," but not a "base of the PLO." Palestinian students of the Islamic fundamentalist persuasion objected to the covenant on several grounds: the type of revolution it called for, the secular nature of the state it envisioned, and the exclusivity of PLO representation.

In Kuwait, the Islamic tendency was strong enough (especially since it was also in ascendance in the KSF, from which the Palestinian fundamentalists received both moral and financial support) to secede from the union. In 1980, a separate Palestinian Islamic Students' League, comprising eighty former GUPS members (out of a total branch membership of about 790) was founded.[6] It drafted its own constitution, opened an office, and began to hold annual conferences. Its membership was active, but never exceeded a few hundred students, even at its peak.[7] Although the splinter group received a great deal of attention at first, its importance has waned. While its informational activities continue, it has never been able to provide real services to students. Its strength lies in the funding it receives from sympathetic Kuwaitis and Palestinians. By 1986 it appeared that the Islamic tendency among KSF members had peaked: although it still won a majority in student elections, its margin of victory had narrowed.[8] Since the future of the Palestinian Islamic Students' League is very closely tied to the power of the fundamentalist current among Kuwaiti students,[9] a continuation of the decline that began in 1986 would not augur well for the future of the Islamic league.

In addition to the internal political challenges detailed above, the GUPS in Kuwait has faced other problems. Pressures exerted by the state or even the PLO during periods when it feels the need to improve its relations with the government have hampered student activities. More critical for the long term is the quota system at the university. The limited number of seats in the university open to Palestinians, combined with the policy of preferential acceptance of Kuwaitis, has virtually put the high prestige faculties (medicine, engineering, and the like) out of the non-Kuwaiti's reach.[10] While the potential for the League of Palestinian Secondary Students (see below) to recruit and mobilize among high school students remains high, general political conditions—especially in view of the July 1986 closure of the Kuwaiti parliament and the resultant curtailment of press and certain other freedoms—do not bode well for GUPS expansion.

Branch Activities

As noted at the opening of the chapter, foreign student enrollment at Kuwait University is limited to 10 percent of the student body. Palestinians from the community in Kuwait have traditionally made up the majority of these students. For example, in 1986, of 276 slots for foreigners, 200 were filled by Palestinians. The quota system would not have nearly the same impact were the traditional centers of Palestinian education, Egypt in particular, still open to them. Further exacerbating the situation, other Arab universities have also reduced the number of places open to nonnational students. As a result, the problem for Palestinians in Kuwait has grown so acute that the GUPS opened a special office of scholarships and grants to assist in placing students from the community in universities in Arab, Islamic, or socialist countries. It has also made available limited funds to support outstanding students who study abroad.[11]

For those Palestinians who are accepted into Kuwait University, the GUPS Kuwait branch sponsors activities similar to those of other GUPS branches: orientation for new students, regular symposia on cultural and political topics, sports teams, a magazine, group trips, a scout organization, and parties that have Palestinian cultural heritage as their theme. To address students' everyday needs, it helps new students to adjust to university life, it lobbies to improve the educational environment, and it has a council for student affairs responsible for examining requests by needy students for financial assistance for books and other expenses. The university does not charge tuition.

Since GUPS membership dues are only token, contributions play a major role in funding the union. The most important revenue source is the students' annual four-day party, which in the past has been attended by as many as eight thousand people. However, the major goal of fund raising has never been domestic consumption but, rather, supporting the fida'iyyin. Most of the money raised or material collected has gone to the PRCS, although the branch occasionally designates individual schools or projects for funding.[12]

Overshadowing this social and cultural side of the branch's activities is, in the words of former members, "the far more important political side" of GUPS work. The branch in Kuwait is distinguished by the presence of political blocs, groups that enter elections with their own slate of candidates and programs, but not under the name of the tanzim with which they are affiliated. For example, Fateh has had a bloc within the union called Shabab al-Thawrah (Youth of the Revolution), while partisans of the PFLP formed al-Kutlah al-Taqaddumiyyah (the Progressive Bloc). The Democratic Front did not have its own bloc until 1979. It is no secret that each of these blocs is affiliated with a particular *tanzim*, but for security reasons it is not officially acknowledged: lack of such official political ties means potentially less trouble for students with the Kuwaiti authorities. In fact, the blocs serve as a bridge between the *tanzimat* and the branch. Each has had its own leadership and program in addition to the branch leadership.

The union's political program includes regular symposia and discussions. The administrative council of the branch issues political statements as do the political blocs within the union. But the involvement of the GUPS members has not been limited to political posturing: they have also participated in GUPS-supervised military training in Syria and Lebanon, and fought in the civil war in Lebanon, where some branch members were killed.[13] Kuwait may be distant from the battlefield, but the students do not consider themselves far removed. Consequently, the nature and extent of the political work of the branch, as well as the rivalries played out in it, have traditionally reflected developments on the main battlefront, Jordan or Lebanon.[14]

The fact that the GUPS has never been officially licensed has enabled the government to "persuade" the students to remain quiet when problems have arisen within the Palestinian community or at the university: notably, in 1975, when the Palestinians opposed the Sinai II disengagement agreement between Egypt and Israel, and in 1976 when the Syrian intervention in Lebanon led to direct confrontation with the Palestinian resistance. At each of these junctures the government feared not only the effect of such developments on the Palestinian community, but also the possibility that their discontent might incite Kuwaiti students to action as well. Internal security concerns have dictated regular interrogation sessions for some student activists as well as periodic expulsions.

Although throughout most of its history the GUPS branch in Kuwait has encountered few obstacles to its activities, its good relations with the Kuwaiti Student Federation have been critical, since it is the only officially licensed student organization. To a certain extent, the Palestinians have depended upon the Kuwaiti students, who have a budget to cosponsor events as well as easy access to university facilities. In fact, the use of university facilities by the Palestinians can be officially secured only by first obtaining a letter of approval from the Kuwaiti Student Federation. The GUPS's only office is a small room in the PLO complex. Without access to outside facilities, its small size would have severely restricted branch activity. Until the rise of the Islamic current among Kuwaiti students and their subsequent support for the splinter Palestinian Islamic Students League relations between the GUPS and the KSF were quite good. The Palestinian students enjoyed the solidarity of Kuwaiti students and the two cooperated in a variety of political and social activities, most notably the KSF's successful campaign in the mid-1970s to end the policy of segregated classes at the university.

Before concluding this section it must be noted that Palestinian student activity and activism in Kuwait is not limited to the university level. The activity and influence of the GUPS is multiplied many times by its involvement in scouting organizations for both boys and girls and, more importantly, by its work with its high school auxiliary organization, the League of Palestinian Secondary Students. Founded concomitantly with the GUPS, in 1986 it counted between three and four thousand members in both private and government schools compared with the GUPS's 1,000 members.[15] The league sponsors the same kind of activities as the GUPS, but with a high school audience in mind.

Because it reaches such large numbers of Palestinian youth it has been instrumental in developing strong ties between the GUPS and the community. One indication of its importance is that occasionally government pressure on student activity has focused on the league and not on the GUPS, presumably because of its greater numbers. With the GUPS's possibilities for expansion and influence on the university level limited by the quota system, the league has increasingly become the primary vehicle of politicization and political mobilization among Palestinian youth in Kuwait.[16]

THE TEACHERS

Education was one of the first issues Kuwait sought to address after the drilling of the Kuwait Oil Company's first well promised future increases in state revenue. In 1936, the Council of Education (Majlis al-Maʿarif) was established which then sent a request for teachers to the mufti of Jerusalem, al-Hajj Amin al-Husayni. That same year the first delegation of Palestinian teachers went to Kuwait: it was composed of Ahmad Shihab al-Din, Muhammad Jabir Hadid, Khamis Nijm, and Muhammad al-Mughrabi. The council sought teachers from Palestine because of Jerusalem's Kulliyyat al-Mu'allimin (Teachers College) and because of a heightened interest in Palestine among Kuwaitis triggered by the 1936 great revolt.[17]

At the time, Kuwait had only two schools—al-Mubarakiyyah, inside the city walls, and another in al-Ahmadi, to the south—with a combined enrollment of 600 students. The arrival of the teachers from Palestine was of such importance that the members of the council accompanied by the students went to the Kuwaiti-Iraqi border to meet the four teachers. The men were even housed in the shaykh's residence for the first few days of their stay. The following year, two Palestinian women came to teach at a girls' school, and each subsequent year brought several more teachers—usually Palestinians—to the expanding Kuwaiti educational system.[18]

However, it was the coincidence of the 1948 uprooting of the Palestinians with increasing oil wealth and the Kuwaitis' interest in education that brought large numbers of Palestinians to Kuwait. Indeed, in Kuwait, appointing Palestinians came to be viewed as a national obligation (wajib qawmi).[19] And for those Palestinians who grew up in the wake of the nakbah, teaching as a profession was most attractive: it was a marketable, transferable skill that was in demand throughout the Arab world, particularly in the young oil states of the Gulf. As a result, teachers have come to constitute the largest professional group among Palestinians throughout the diaspora.[20]

Despite their numbers, it was not until 1964, when Kuwait counted some 2,100 Palestinian teachers—50 percent of all educators in Kuwait[21]—that the founders of the PLO focused attention on the need to mobilize Palestinians according to profession and the teachers were accordingly organized into a chapter. Chapter founders contacted teachers through the schools in which they worked and invited them to come to the PLO office, where they selected twenty-five representatives through direct elections. At the time, however, no unifying political ideology guided the chapter,[22] and it lacked the members and the dynamism needed for active involvement in community affairs.

As the nature and composition of the PLO shifted to that of a more mass organization dominated by the commando groups, only a handful of the original chapter members continued to participate. Some had risen to positions they were unwilling to jeopardize through association with the new face of the post-1968 PLO. Others came from a class background that rendered them less sympathetic to the fida'iyyin organizations.[23]

In 1969, the PLO's Department of Popular Organizations, headed by

Faruq al-Qaddumi, set about invigorating the existing popular organizations. The DPO assembled a preparatory committee for a General Union of Palestinian Teachers which then visited Arab countries that hosted large numbers of Palestinian teachers in order to assist in the establishment of union branches. When the GUPT opened a branch in Kuwait in 1969, the response among the majority of Palestinian teachers was overwhelmingly positive.

Since its inception, the branch has sponsored regular symposia on a variety of political, cultural, and informational topics as part of its efforts to raise political consciousness among teachers. The branch has also organized parties that aim in part at entertainment and fund raising, but also seek to spark greater political consciousness. Money raised by the GUPT at these and other functions is not intended primarily for internal GUPT use. The funds are used to support SAMED (the Palestine Martyrs' Works Society); to develop various institutions in the refugee camps; and to purchase basic provisions like blankets and clothes for the camps and the fighters.

As is the case with the GUPW, Palestinian teachers cannot lobby for demands separately from other teachers. Consequently, the guild content of the branch's program has remained low. Branch founders hoped that the organization would eventually implement a program of social insurance; however, despite several attempts, only a small number of teachers have joined the program. To collect payments the GUPT needs salaried workers, of which it has none. A further hindrance has been the Kuwaiti Ministry of Education's policy of taking monthly deductions from all teachers for *its* employee fund from which, unfortunately, non-Kuwaiti teachers do not benefit.[24]

The most important developments affecting the future of the branch stem from Kuwaitization policies. In the early 1970s, Kuwaiti teacher training institutes and Kuwait University began to graduate approximately 200 Kuwaitis per year. Naturally, employment preference goes to these Kuwaitis. Although the absolute number of Palestinian teachers employed in Kuwait has increased over the years, the rate of increase has been declining as has the percentage of Palestinian versus Kuwaiti teachers: in 1966–67 there were 2,733 Palestinian teachers representing 48.7 percent of the total; in 1970–71 the numbers had increased to 3,032, but that figure represented only 33.6 percent of the total; and in 1977–78 4,946 Palestinian teachers constituted only 25 percent of educators in Kuwait.[25] Many of the teachers who went to Kuwait in the early period will soon reach retirement and, therefore, the absolute figure is certain to begin to drop as well. Relations between the Kuwaiti Teachers' Federation and the GUPT have been good, but the gradual replacement of expatriates with nationals means that the branch, which counted more than 5,000 members in 1982,[26] faces a future of slowly declining membership.

THE PRCS

Because of the low-cost or free high-quality medical care that the Kuwaiti government makes available to all residents, citizen and noncitizen alike, Palestinians in Kuwait have not been forced to open their own hospitals and clinics as they have in other parts of the Arab world. Moreover, Kuwait's distance from the battlefield has precluded its becoming a military base of the resistance movement, thus eliminating the demand for primary, emergency health care so desperately needed by the Palestinians in Lebanon, where they are exposed to frequent military attack. The branch of the PRCS in Kuwait was established by decree of the PLO on January 1, 1969.[27] In the beginning, Palestinians in Kuwait viewed paying PRCS membership dues as a kind of donation or contribution, but not as a commitment to work. Thus, the branch quickly gained 5,000 "members." In 1984 the branch counted 550 working—as opposed to mere paying—members, who come from diverse professional and socioeconomic backgrounds.

The PRCS (or Hilal) in Kuwait, unlike branches elsewhere in the diaspora, has served primarily to gather contributions—whether monetary or in the form of food, clothing, medicine, or equipment—to assist the "consumer" branches—those in Lebanon, Jordan, and Syria. Its work also includes support for the occupied territories. For example, it markets traditional products from the West Bank as part of a program intended to enable Palestinians under occupation to secure additional income outside the Israeli labor market so as not to free Israelis from production for fighting. The PRCS sells these products along with others that it produces in annual displays that serve to publicize Palestinian cultural heritage. The PRCS also sends shipments of clothing to the refugee camps in the occupied territories; its headquarters regularly become a center for storing and packing used clothing bound for the West Bank.

Among the Hilal's other programs have been health awareness and first aid training sessions intended to raise general health care consciousness in the community in Kuwait. It has occasionally sponsored Palestinians from across the diaspora—including the wounded from the battlefield—to come to Kuwait for medical treatment. In such cases the PRCS cooperates with the Kuwaiti Ministry of Health and the Kuwaiti Red Crescent Society (with which it has enjoyed close relations) in securing insurance to pay for treatment. The branch also sends a medical team each year with ambulances, doctors, and nurses to Saudi Arabia for the *hajj*, and has assembled and sent teams of medical personnel throughout the Arab world to assist after natural disasters.

In order to send as much money as possible to PRCS health care facilities abroad, the Hilal in Kuwait has striven to keep its own staff small. It does, however, have a social committee, which investigates cases of poor families and offers assistance when need is established, especially in emergency cases, such as the death or illness of a family supporter. Through 1977, the social committee operated an embroidery workshop, which played a role in cultural revival, vocational training for girls and women, and financially assisting needy families. The embroidery project functioned much as it does in the GUPWom, but never reached the same level of development and the two embroidery programs were eventually consolidated.

The Hilal's most important work has been and continues to be raising funds to equip PRCS hospitals, clinics, and offices in the diaspora. But the situation in the mid-1980s called for a reexamination of the Kuwaiti Palestinian community's social needs. The effects of the economic stagnation resulting from the stock market crash in 1982, the drop in oil prices, and the continuing Gulf war have most severely hit the substantial number of large, lower-income Palestinian families. As a result the need for financial assistance among this sector has increased dramatically. A shift in orientation toward the community in Kuwait, or at least an expansion of internal assistance, appears to be the most pressing demand and thus the greatest challenge facing the society in its continuing quest to respond to changing diaspora needs.

[9]
Identity Suppressed, Identity Denied

'Abdallah ibn al-Husayn was only one in a line of Hashemites with aspirations to rule the Arab East. His father, the sharif of Mecca, had treated with the British over the possibility of Arab independence in exchange for cooperation with the British World War I effort against the Ottoman Turks. 'Abdallah's brother Faysal had led the Arab forces that fought with Allenby's armies in Palestine and Syria. He was subsequently proclaimed king of Syria and ruled in Damascus from 1918–1920. In 1921, the British granted 'Abdallah, the next in line, Transjordan, the portion of the Palestine mandate between the Jordan River and Iraq, as his domain. As part of a drive to enlarge his realm, after the 1948 war 'Abdallah succeeded in annexing the West Bank, the part of Palestine that had been occupied by the Arab Legion and the Iraqi army.

The economic crisis created by the 1948 war was staggering. Nearly half of 'Abdallah's 900,000 new subjects were refugees; 160,000 others were separated from their productive land by the armistice lines and although denied their means of livelihood did not qualify for UNRWA assistance. The war also left unemployed those Palestinians who had worked in the coastal regions of Palestine. Further exacerbating the situation, the establishment of the State of Israel disrupted transport and commercial lines between Jordan and its outside markets. With Haifa no longer available as a port, shipping had to move through Aqaba, Transjordan's only sea outlet, or by land to Damascus and Beirut. As a result, shipping costs rose and merchants were forced to seek new markets. The kingdom also found itself with a 650-kilometer border with Israel that required a diversion of resources for defense.[1]

Jordan's Western patrons, first Britain and later the United States, kept the kingdom financially solvent in exchange for pursuance of a policy that also addressed Hashemite concerns: the suppression of Arab nationalist and later, Palestinian separatist movements. The Western powers believed the growth of such movements would lead to instability in the region and eventually threaten their interests. The Hashemites feared that the spread of Arab nationalism might lead to their overthrow and that Palestinian separatism would tear the state asunder.

This chapter will first examine briefly the basic features of the Hashemite Kingdom: the large refugee population, the division between the East and West banks, the role of the army, and the nature of the economy. It will then turn to a detailed discussion of the role Jordan's Palestinian majority has played in the country's post-1948 political development.

THE REFUGEES AND UNRWA

Transjordan's population prior to the partition of Palestine has been estimated at 340,000,[2] divided between nomads and seminomads of the desert on the one hand (160,000) and primarily rural town inhabitants on the other (180,000). The annexation of the territory that came to be called the West Bank increased the population by about 900,000: Jordan acquired the native population of the West Bank (400,000 to 450,000), some 450,000 refugees who had fled or been driven from the area that had become the state of Israel (about one-fourth of whom went directly to the East Bank), and tens of thousands of Palestinians not classified as refugees and therefore not eligible for UNRWA assistance who had managed to find their way into the area controlled by the Arab Legion.[3]

During 1948 and 1949, Arab governments bore the primary refugee relief burden. In August 1949 the United Nations Economic Survey Mission (otherwise known as the Clapp Mission) was charged with examining the repercussions of the 1948–49 war. The mission calculated the total number of refugees to be 726,000, of whom 652,000 were considered in need, although there were some 971,243 on relief in Arab countries as of September 30, 1949.[4] After its investigations, the Clapp Mission recommended the establishment of a new organization to handle the refugee problem. With Resolution 302 of December 8, 1949, the United Nations General Assembly created the United Nations Relief and Works Agency for Palestine Refugees in the Near East (UNRWA) which began operating on May 1, 1950.

When UNRWA began operations, less than 30 percent of the refugees lived in camps.[5] (See tables 9.1 and 9.2) Gradually, however, many exhausted the savings they had brought with them and were forced to move to UNRWA camps. For the first few years tents served as shelter, but as a swift solution to the problem grew less and less likely, during

1955–56 the tents were replaced by small block structures covered with corrugated metal roofs.

Social welfare projects originally undertaken by voluntary agencies and coordinated by UNRPR (United Nations Relief for Palestine Refugees, the forerunner of UNRWA) gradually became the agency's responsibility. UNRWA expanded health care services as well as vocational training programs. Education, vocational training, and a program of small-scale loans for development projects aimed at providing the refugee the skills or resources necessary to support himself or to begin anew in whatever host society he might reside. The goal was development for integration.

While the refugees had no aversion to education or to the idea of providing a decent standard of living for their families, they nonetheless viewed UNRWA with suspicion. It was the UN that had partitioned Palestine and the refugees held it in part responsible for their uprooting. The Palestinian clung to his UNRWA ration card as if it

Table 9.1: List of Refugee Camps—East Bank

Post-1948	Established	Location	Original Population
Al-Husayn	1952	Northern Amman	8,000
Irbid	1951	Northern Irbid	4,000
Zarqaʾ	1949	Southeast Zarqaʾ	8,000
Al-Wahdat	1955	Southeast Amman	5,000
Al-Karamah[a]		Jordan Valley	21,990
Post-1967			
Marka	1968	10 km. northeast of Amman	15,000
Al-Biqaʿah	1968	20 km. north of Amman	26,000
Talbiyyah	1968	35 km. south of Amman	5,000
Al-Suf	1967	50 km. north of Amman	8,000
Al-Husn	1968	80 km. north of Amman	12,500
Jarash	1968	50 km north of Amman	11,500

SOURCE: Compiled from "Briefing Notes," UNRWA Field Office, Amman for each of the camps, January 1984, and UN Document A/2978 (GAOR Session X, Supplement 15, Annex 1.3).

[a]In February 1968, the emergency camps in the Jordan Valley as well as the al-Karamah camp were moved to higher ground as a result of continuous military attacks. No other figures for al-Karamah were available. The other camps moved at the same time were al-Biqaʿah, al-Suf, al-Husn, and Jarash. The al-Karamah population figure is for 1955.

were title to his lost homeland, not a piece of paper to be surrendered when economic self-sufficiency was achieved. The agency's emphasis on developing skills appropriate for the job market of the host society was viewed by Palestinians as but another step in a process intended to deprive them of any chance to return: UNRWA was simply assisting in attempts to solve the Palestine problem through a gradual integration of the refugees outside their homeland.

Immediately after the war, resettlement was commonly suggested as

Table 9.2: List of Refugee Camps—West Bank

Area		1955 Population	
Nablus			
	'Askar	2,247	
	Balatah	4,734	
	Al-Far'ah	4,976	
	Camp Number 1	1,856	
	Nur Shams	2,743	
	Tulkarm	5,343	
Jericho			
	'Aqabat Jabr	30,533	
	'Ayn al-Sultan	15,191	
	Al-Nuway'mah	6,794	(abandoned 1967)
Jerusalem			
	Shu'fat (Mu'askar)	4,428	
	Al-Am'ari	1,878	
	Dayr 'Ammar	2,392	
	Al-Jalazun	3,877	
	Qalandiya	2,081	
Hebron			
	Al-Dahayshah	4,800	
	'A'idah	815	
	Bayt Jibrin	918	
	Al-Fawwar	4,763	
	Al-'Arrub	5,693	

SOURCE: UN Document A/2978 (GAOR Session X, Supplement 15, Annex 1.3).

a solution to the refugee problem. In 1949 the Jordanian government commissioned an English company to study a plan for land reclamation through irrigation in the Jordan Valley. UNRWA subsequently became involved and promised to help fund the proposed project if some of the Palestinians could be settled on the reclaimed land, thereby enabling UNRWA to lower the number of refugees on its rosters. At the time, 93,057 refugees lived in the valley, 64 percent of all the valley's residents and 20 percent of the refugees in Jordan. When Israel voiced opposition to the plan, the United States proposed joint Arab-Israeli exploitation of the Jordan River water. Jordan rejected the plan and no further proposals to settle refugees on reclaimed land in Jordan were forwarded.[6]

Despite the UNRWA and other international aid efforts over the years, the commissioner-general of UNRWA described refugee living conditions in 1964 in the following terms:

A large part of the refugee community is still living today in dire poverty, often under pathetic and in some cases appalling conditions. Despite the sustained efforts of UNRWA and of the host Governments and other collaborating agencies, there are families . . . who still live in dwellings which are unfit for human habitation: some in dark cellars, others in crumbling tenements, others in grossly overcrowded barracks and shacks. . . . Nearly all the UNRWA camps are extremely overcrowded with five or more persons living in one small room. They lack adequate roads and pathways and many camps are deep in mud in winter and in dust in summer. There are rarely any sewers or stormwater drainage. The water supplies are communal and often inadequate, particularly during the hot summer months.[7]

As for other aspects of the UNRWA relief, the commissioner-general stated that "the relief accorded by UNRWA, though indispensable . . . has been no more than a bare minimum. . . . The rations are meagre and unvarying and would hardly sustain a person who depended solely on them for any long period."[8]

The situation in the East Bank camps established for the 1948 refugees has gradually improved. The city of Amman has witnessed tremendous growth, especially since 1967, and has come to encompass the Husayn and Wahdat camps. As a result, services and general living conditions have improved and their isolation has lessened. Even in the 1967 camps, the block house structures have taken on a certain degree of permanence, although the streets remain largely unpaved and sewers are often still open. What has not changed is that, at least in the fields of health care and education, most of the refugees remain dependent on UNRWA services, which although meagre, are nonetheless increasingly threatened by budget cuts.

EAST BANK, WEST BANK

The economic and cultural gap that separated the two banks of the Jordan rendered their integration problematic, despite the legal unity that was formalized in 1950. The East Bank was thinly populated, primarily by bedouin and small peasant farmers. Of the major East Bank cities—Amman, Karak, Irbid, and Salt—none had a pre-1948 population of more than 30,000. Palestine, on the other hand, had had a significant urban sector with concentrations in port cities and towns such as Haifa, Jaffa, and Gaza, as well as in the principal inland towns of Jerusalem, Hebron, Nablus, and Nazareth.[9]

Palestine had also had a flourishing middle class involved in commercial activities and in the elaborate civil service that had developed under the mandate. A substantial labor force had exerted sizable influence in the economic life of Palestine in the form of the Palestinian Arab Workers Society, founded in 1925. Transjordan, on the other hand, had no such trade union tradition. Moreover because of their contact with the West and their struggle against increasing Jewish immigration and British discriminatory policies, Palestinians also tended to be more highly politicized than their East Bank counterparts.[10] West Bankers sent a greater proportion of their children to school, and had more doctors and a lower mortality rate. Combined with the characteristics mentioned above, these features created a sense of Palestinian superiority over native East Bankers.[11]

The Jordanian constitutional structure, which provides for regional representation along East Bank and West Bank lines, has further reinforced the sense of regional communalism. Jordanians tend to think of themselves as either West Bankers (Palestinians) or East Bankers (Transjordanians). Despite preponderant numbers, Palestinians are entitled to only 50 percent of the seats in both houses of the legislature. Minorities in Jordan such as the Christians, Circassians, and Shishens are also accorded a certain number of seats—a number out of proportion to their percentage in the population. Conversely, until the 1986

Election Law, there was no provision for representation of the Palestinian refugees, who constitute approximately one-third of the kingdom's population.

THE JORDANIAN ARMY

The Jordanian army has been the traditional basis of support for the Hashemite regime.[12] Created in 1922, the Arab Legion, as it was then called, integrated the police with the armed forces. Commanded by British general John Bagot Glubb, from 1939 to 1956 the legion developed from "a minor police force into the best-trained and, for its size, best-equipped army in the Arab World."[13] In the beginning, the majority of the legion's soldiers were recruited from the southern Transjordanian bedouin, particularly the Huwaytat, but as the legion expanded in the postwar period, many were also drawn from northern Transjordan and from the West Bank.[14] The legion was sponsored and fully subsidized by the British until the 1957 termination of the Anglo-Jordanian Treaty; at that point the United States assumed the role of primary subsidizer.[15]

Glubb made an attempt to integrate Palestinians into the armed forces through the creation of the National Guard, composed of part-time and not professional soldiers. On the other hand, Palestinians from pro-Hashemite West Bank families were recruited directly into the army and air force as officers in an attempt to prevent the development of a unified armed opposition to the king or to the power of these leading families.[16] As time passed, however, Palestinians joined the army in increasing numbers. In 1976, military service became mandatory for all Jordanian men, thus opening the way for additional Palestinian participation and a resultant change in the army's composition. Palestinians are more likely to have the technical and managerial skills needed by a modern army and have, therefore, gained a significant share of the lower-echelon posts. The upper ranks, however, remain the preserve of the bedouin traditionally loyal to the Hashemites.[17]

The centrality of the support of the armed forces to regime stability has led to the allocation of a disproportionately large share of the national budget to the armed forces and public security. As table 9.3 shows, during the pre-1970 period, the total ranged from a high of 63 percent in 1956–57 to a low of 40 percent in 1967, with an average for the period of 52 percent. These high percentages also support the contention that Jordan's foreign subsidies, particularly those from Britain and the United States have been intended to enable the country to serve as a regional policeman protecting Western interests.

THE JORDANIAN ECONOMY

During the twenty-year period from 1924–25 through 1943–44, more than 50 percent of total government revenues came into Transjordan's

Table 9.3: Central Government Actual Expenditures (In JD Million)

Year	Defense	Public Security	Develop- ment	Civilian Services	Total	Defense and Public Security % of Total
1955–56	9.35	1.28	2.76	4.24	17.63	60
1956–57	12.13	1.36	3.06	4.77	21.32	63
1957–58	11.33	1.64	4.30	6.59	23.86	54
1958–59	14.66	2.07	5.82	6.79	29.34	57
1959–60	15.81	2.24	4.80	7.85	30.70	59
1960–61	16.15	2.27	5.98	8.44	32.84	56
1961–62	16.42	2.29	4.94	9.34	32.98	57
1962–63	16.80	2.31	7.60	10.82	37.53	51
1963–64	18.57	2.45	6.15	12.18	39.35	53
1964–65	18.57	2.46	9.17	13.43	43.62	48
1965–66	18.76	2.84	11.27	14.12	46.99	46
1966[a]	19.41	3.30	15.87	16.29	54.87	41
1967	24.16	3.26	23.50	17.24	68.16	40
1968	35.16	3.25	23.34	18.77	80.62	48
1969	41.47	3.73	23.27	20.03	88.40	51
1970[b]	33.06	4.35	21.17	21.48	80.06	47

SOURCE: Budget Department, *State Budget Law* for various years, as presented in Odeh, *Economic Development of Jordan 1954–1971*, Appendix 8.

NOTE: The value of the Jordanian dinar remained constant at JD1.00 = $2.80 throughout the entire period.

[a]Represents the twelve-month period January 1 through December 31. As of January 1, 1967, the fiscal year was changed to coincide with the calendar year in place of the previous system of April 1 through March 31, which was applicable until the fiscal year 1965–66. To facilitate this change the 1966 budget covered the nine-month period April 1 through December 31.

[b]Preliminary actual.

treasury as grants-in-aid from abroad, the overwhelming majority representing British Treasury contributions.[18] Thus, although 'Abdallah's annexation of the West Bank is usually attributed to his political ambitions to reign over a larger Arab kingdom, he also likely expected that the area and its inhabitants would contribute significantly to his efforts to render his political entity a more economically viable state.

The arrival of the refugees and the bureaucratic requirements of governing a larger and significantly more populous area caused a shift in the Jordanian economy from one dominated by agriculture to one dominated by services (see table 9.4). With the British mandate ended, Jordan embarked upon a program of infrastructure expansion. At the same time, in the private sector the arrival of the Palestinians bearing capital and entrepreneurial skills stimulated the housing and service sectors, causing especially the latter to grow rapidly.[19]

Although political crises triggered fluctuations, the Jordanian economy did make moderate progress in the 1950s and 1960s. Some of the progress owed to the fact that large numbers of Jordanians, most of them Palestinians, left the country for work opportunities in the oil states of the Gulf. They thereby not only lowered the level of unemployment at home, but also helped fill the country's foreign exchange coffers with remittances. Nevertheless, the country continued to be heavily dependent on foreign aid (see table 9.5).[20]

The 1967 war dealt the economy a severe blow. The most serious consequence was the loss of the West Bank. In 1966 the region had contributed about 45 percent of Jordan's GNP; and although it accounted for only one-fourth of the kingdom's total cultivated area, it produced 65 percent of its vegetables, 60 percent of its fruits, and 30 percent of its cereals.[21] The loss of this territory also meant the loss of Jerusalem, the kingdom's major source of tourism revenue. Finally, the Israeli occupation of the area meant that the remittances of West Bankers working in the Gulf would no longer be channeled into the Jordanian economy.

The complement to the loss of territory was population gain: an additional 250,000 to 300,000 Palestinians who required emergency outlays for food and shelter took refuge in the East Bank. To exacerbate the situation, between 1968 and 1970 stepped-up *fidaʾiyyin* action against Israel led to Israeli retaliatory raids that disrupted agricultural production in the Jordan Valley and brought work on development projects near the cease-fire lines to a halt. Military expenditures rose to restore what had been destroyed and to attempt to keep military preparedness high. Further strain resulted from the United States' decision to cut

Table 9.4: Industrial Origin of Gross Domestic Product (Jordan)

Year	Public Admin. and Defense	Trade and Banking	Services	Ownership of Dwellings	Total GDP	Public Admin. and Defense as GDP %	Services as GDP %
1954	9.1	9.3	3.0	2.3	47.7	19	31
1955	9.7	9.3	3.3	2.3	43.0	23	35
1956	11.5	10.3	2.7	2.9	61.4	19	26
1957	13.3	12.0	3.7	3.1	61.9	21	26
1958	15.6	14.4	3.9	3.3	69.1	23	31
1959	15.0	18.8	7.8	6.3	85.2	28	39
1960	15.8	20.4	8.3	7.1	89.4	28	40
1961	16.7	25.6	8.6	3.0	110.9	15	34
1962	17.1	25.1	9.5	8.6	108.6	16	40
1963	17.6	27.8	10.4	9.4	117.7	15	40
1964	19.7	29.5	11.2	9.9	135.5	15	37
1965	21.4	33.5	12.8	10.7	151.0	14	38
1966	22.0	31.7	14.1	11.2	149.6	15	38
1967	26.0	42.5	15.2	11.9	177.1	15	39
1968	33.3	32.0	16.8	12.3	168.5	20	36
1969	36.3	42.6	18.3	12.8	198.3	18	37
1970	36.0	35.5	16.5	13.0	177.3	20	37

SOURCE: Odeh, *Economic Development of Jordan 1954–1971*, Appendix 2.
NOTE: In JD million at current factor cost. Percentages are rounded to nearest percent. JD1.00 = $2.80.

Table 9.5: Central Government Foreign Receipts of Unrequited Transfers, 1950–1968 (Jordan). In JD million.

Year	From U.K. Govt.		From UNRWA and other UN Agencies		From U.S. Govt.		From Arab Govts.		From Other Govts.		Total	
	Value	%	Value	%	Value	%	Value	%	Value	%	Value	%
1950	2.36	44	3.00	56	—	—	—	—	—	—	5.36	100
1951	3.55	51	3.36	49	—	—	—	—	—	—	6.91	100
1952	4.60	49	4.36	46	0.49	5	—	—	—	—	9.45	100
1953	6.43	52	4.86	40	0.97	8	—	—	—	—	12.26	100
1954	5.87	46	5.50	44	1.25	10	—	—	—	—	12.62	100
1955	8.04	52	4.66	30	2.73	18	—	—	—	—	15.43	100
1956	8.01	54	5.47	37	0.47	3	0.85	6	—	—	14.80	100
1957	1.75	10	4.90	29	6.73	40	3.51	21	—	—	16.89	100
1958	1.34	6	4.75	20	16.32	68	1.50	6	—	—	23.91	100
1959	2.80	11	5.40	21	17.32	68	—	—	—	—	25.52	100
1960	2.00	8	5.29	21	18.20	71	—	—	—	—	25.49	100
1961	2.36	10	5.15	21	17.05	69	—	—	—	—	24.56	100
1962	1.50	6	5.26	23	16.71	71	—	—	—	—	23.47	100
1963	1.50	7	5.51	24	15.51	69	—	—	—	—	22.52	100
1964	1.50	6	5.40	20	15.00	56	4.50	17	0.20	1	26.60	100
1965	1.40	5	6.00	22	12.00	45	7.30	27	0.10	1	26.80	100
1966	1.30	4	5.60	18	13.40	43	9.50	30	1.60	5	31.40	100
1967	1.50	3	4.80	9	7.60	15	37.60	73	0.10	...	51.60	100
1968	—	—	5.50	11	1.20	2	46.30	87	0.10	...	53.10	100
Total	57.81	13.5	94.77	22.1	162.95	38.0	111.06	25.9	2.10	0.5	428.69	100

SOURCE: Fakhoury, *An Analytic Study of Jordan's Balance of Payments, 1950–1968*, p. 75.
NOTE: Throughout the period the Jordanian dinar equaled $2.80.

off virtually all aid to Jordan because it had joined with Egypt in charging the United States with aiding Israel in the war.

The difficult fiscal situation was overcome largely thanks to ad hoc emergency grants totaling JD20.8 million ($58 million) from friendly countries. In addition, according to a decision of the Khartum conference that followed the war, Saudi Arabia, Kuwait, and Libya began to contribute £40 million ($96 million) annually as support for a confrontation state. However, even these substantial grants from Arab governments could not forestall an economic recession, and the civil war of 1970–71 cut short the 1968–69 recovery.[22]

The actual financial losses caused by the civil war have been estimated at JD16 million ($45 million) for both the public and private sectors. Subsequently, GNP dropped and Kuwait and Libya suspended their financial subsidies, which totaled more than JD23 million ($64 million) per year.[23] Iraq and Syria closed their borders and later their airspace, thereby severely limiting Jordan's sphere for agricultural and industrial exports. Not until after the 1973 war, but especially after the 1974 Rabat Arab summit conference during which Husayn acquiesced in the PLO's official designation as the sole, legitimate representative of the Palestinian people, did Jordan again find itself in the good political and economic graces of its fellow Arab states.

From 1973 to 1981 Jordan reaped the benefits of the oil boom. Increased liquidity in the Gulf drew expatriate workers in record numbers and led governments there to make available large amounts of financial assistance to their less well-endowed brother Arab states. Jordan witnessed a dramatic rise in remittances and became a primary candidate for financial assistance for development projects.

However, the post-1981 economic downturn precipitated by the drop in the price of oil and the continuing Iran-Iraq war has taken its toll on the Hashemite Kingdom. Austerity programs in the Gulf have led increasing numbers of expatriates to return to Jordan. Even for those who stay, higher costs of living have meant that expatriates have less money to send back to the kingdom. Likewise, Arab aid has dropped, cutting into Jordan's projected development plans and goals. The greatest threat to regime stability in the late 1980s appears to be the country's underdeveloped productive base—which was never given sufficient attention even in the boom years—and the growing numbers of unemployed.

POLITICAL DEVELOPMENT:
FROM TRANSJORDAN TO JORDAN

Having reviewed the basic features of the Jordanian economy and political system, the discussion will now turn to the post-1948 political
development of the country. Just before the proclamation of the All-
Palestine Government (APG) in October 1948 (for a discussion of the
founding and history of the APG, see chapter 2), Count Bernadotte, the
international mediator sent to Palestine by the UN, filed a report in
which he argued that since no sign had appeared of an Arab desire to
establish a government along lines similar to those of the Jewish state,
the Arab section of Palestine should be added to the East Bank of the
Jordan. Shortly thereafter, as the conference that proclaimed the APG
convened in Gaza, a Jordanian-sponsored alternative gathering, the
Amman conference, called upon King ʿAbdallah (as opposed to the Palestinian leader al-Hajj Amin al-Husayni) to protect the rights of the
Arabs of Palestine. Participants in the Amman conference rejected the
solutions (i.e., the APG) suggested by those Palestinian leaders who,
they claimed, had been responsible for the troubles that had befallen
the Palestinian people over the past thirty years. The conference concluded by investing ʿAbdallah with full authority to speak in the name
of the Arabs of Palestine.[24]

On December 1, 1948, another conference—the Jordanian- and Brit-
ish-sponsored Jericho conference of pro-Hashemite Palestinian notables—was convened. Conferees called for the unity of Jordan and Palestine and swore loyalty to ʿAbdallah as king of all Palestine. Prominent
among the Palestinians who sought Hashemite overlordship were some
of the wealthiest and best-known West Bank families. The list included large numbers of Nashashibis and other anti-Husayni partisans
who sought alliance with ʿAbdallah to outmaneuver and ultimately break
the alternative traditional Palestinian power center, al-Hajj Amin al-
Husayni and his allies.[25]

Meanwhile, the Jordanian government dissolved all Palestinian bodies that had been active during the mandate period or the 1948 war.
All functionaries appointed by the Arab Higher Committee were ordered to cease their activities. Bureaucratic responsibilities were turned
over to the military command. The West Bank population was directed
to obey the instructions and orders only of the military administration.

The military administration quickly gave way to a civil administration. On March 6, 1949, a royal decree appointed governors for the Jerusalem, Nablus, and Ramallah sectors as well as a civilian governor-general. The gradual integration of the West Bank governmental departments into their respective Jordanian ministries followed. On March 1, 1950, a royal decree forbade the use of the word "Palestine" in official documents. Henceforth, only the words "West Bank" were to be used. After the 1950 elections, a move was made to integrate the legal systems of the two banks. And, as of September 1, 1950, the Jordanian dinar was made the sole legal currency.

According to Jordan's 1949 electoral laws, Palestinians were guaranteed equal representation, but only in the lower house. The Municipal Elections Law restricted suffrage to those individuals who paid "a land or municipal tax at a rate of at least one dinar during the twelve consecutive months preceding the elections on the condition that if the property is held by more than one resident, each of the property holders pays his own share." In this way, only men with property, capital, or some taxable asset enjoyed suffrage.[26] The provision thereby effectively excluded from suffrage the vast majority of the refugees. Loyal Palestinians were rewarded with seats in the upper chamber. Not surprisingly they hailed from the most powerful West Bank families: the Nashashibis, the Tuqans, the Salahs, Dajanis, 'Abd al-Hadis, and Khalidis, the same families that dominated Palestinian representation in the cabinet.[27]

Amman also placed select Palestinians in senior posts concerned with West Bank problems. The ministries of agriculture, economy, education, development, and foreign affairs all counted Palestinians in senior administrative positions. Again, these bureaucrats were the pro-Hashemite Palestinians, members of the large landowning or sharifian families.[28] In general, Palestinians did not reach the most powerful cabinet positions: prime minister, deputy prime minister, minister of the interior, or minister of information.

Thus, integration, but not effective representation or power sharing, was the goal and Jerusalem, the seat of British administrative power and the leading Palestinian city under the mandate, was deprived of its former role after the annexation. By downgrading Jerusalem and its leadership, Amman anticipated that alternative leadership would crystallize in other urban centers. The intensification of local interests and political rivalries would then, the regime wagered, prevent the emergence of a truly all–West Bank Palestinian leadership.[29]

THE BEGINNINGS OF PALESTINIAN REORGANIZATION

As a backdrop to the discussion of political developments in Jordan on the national level, it is important to examine the nature of the organizations in which Palestinians participated in the wake of the *nakbah*. The 1950s on the West Bank have been described as the "years of hunger." Many of those who lived along the armistice lines depended for survival on regular "raids" into what had become Israel to get food—often from what had been their property. Those apprehended by the Jordanian army (known as the Arab Legion) as they recrossed the border were often tried for espionage. In the cities conditions were not much better. Those best able to provide for themselves and their families were government employees. For most, the basic struggle was simply to survive; political organizing or activity was a luxury few could afford.[30]

Immediately after the 1948–49 war attempts were made to revive several of the social associations that had operated in pre-1948 Palestine. For example, the Haifa Cultural Association sought to reorganize in Nablus as did the Jaffa Muslim Sport Club in Ramallah. However, regarded with suspicion by the authorities and forbidden to engage in politics, many such organizations disintegrated. Furthermore, rivalries among existing groups or fear for their position in the community sometimes prevented the emergence of new organizations.[31]

Virtually the only field in which the regime tolerated popular activity was that of refugee relief. UNRWA was a lifeline for Jordan: it provided shelter, food, educational facilities, and monetary support for one-third of the kingdom's residents. Within the camps, committees that had originally been set up to mediate conflicts came to play a key role in relief operations. The government viewed any actions that might alienate the refugees as potentially damaging to its negotiating position with UNRWA. At the same time, intent on maintaining good relations with the agency, the government stepped in to protect UN personnel when the camp committees went too far in attacking UNRWA. In general the committees that survived longest were those that demonstrated support for the government authorities and caused no problems for the Red Cross or UNRWA.[32]

Despite the restrictions and obstacles, organizing in various forms proceeded outside the camps as well. Charitable societies were one acceptable framework. However, there too, obtaining regime permission to found a society was often problematic, for no matter what the ostensible purpose or focus of the society, the fact that as a West Bank institution it was composed entirely of Palestinians and provided a place for their gathering usually meant that it would be perceived as a potential political threat.[33] And, in fact, no such organization could avoid becoming a forum for at least political discussion, if not activity. Given the absence of legal political parties, the existence of these societies, particularly the dates of their founding, take on added importance (see table 9.6). The clustering of foundings around 1956–1957, the period of the Nabulsi government, and in the post-1964 period, with the establishment of the PLO headquartered in Jerusalem, should be understood in the context of the political climate in Jordan during these periods, which will discussed in greater detail later.

Numerous other organizations were established on the West Bank

Table 9.6: Founding of Charitable Associations on the West Bank by District

Year	Jerusalem	Nablus	Hebron
1948	1		
1949			
1950	1	1	
1951			
1952	2		
1953		1	1
1954			
1955	1	1	
1956	4	2	
1957	3		
1958	2	1	1
1959		1	
1960	1	1	
1961		1	
1962		3	
1963	1	1	
1964	1		3
1965	20	3	7
1966	2	4	
1967			

SOURCE: *Dalil al-Jami'iyyat al-Khayriyyah f-il-Diffatayn al-Sharqiyyah w-al-Gharbiyyah.*

and then expanded to the East Bank. West Bank labor unions and professional associations for doctors, dentists, lawyers, engineers, pharmacists, veterinarians, and the like all eventually developed East Bank roots as well. The institutions were Jordanian, in that they had both East and West Bank members, but the West Bank members generally outnumbered the East Bankers and in elections for leadership slots the West Bankers usually gained more seats.[34]

In this context, it is important to stress that the sense of political identity among Palestinians has not been static. During the 1950s, because of Palestine's recent dismemberment and the resulting scattering and degradation of its people, some Palestinians felt ashamed of their identity. Having obtained Jordanian citizenship and Jordanian passports, many found it easier or more natural to identify themselves as Jordanians. The regime's policy of erasing all references to Palestine, by force if necessary, certainly also played a role. At the same time, throughout the Arab world many Arabs—Palestinians and others—identified with the larger Arab nation. This phenomenon was attributable both to the then relatively recent delineation of separate political entities in the region and to the surging popularity of Arab nationalist sentiment.

Those Jordanians, East and West Bankers alike, who sought change in the political system joined the various illegal political organizations—there was no other kind—that operated in the kingdom: the Communist party, the Arab Nationalist Movement, the Ba'th, Muslim Brethren, and others.[35] Palestinian participation in these groups at this stage must be viewed not as part of a Palestinian battle to assert a separate national identity, but rather as part of a larger multi-faceted anti-Western movement in the region, one of whose goals was the liberation of Palestine. Likewise, the program of these political movements should be understood not as anti-*Jordanian*, but as anti-regime: some opposed the Hashemites because of their long-standing association with and dependence upon the same Western powers who were responsible for the partition of Palestine and the creation of the state of Israel; others took a more extreme position, asserting that the Jordanian political entity itself was illegitimate because it had been carved out of the larger Arab nation by the British and the French.

Therefore, unlike the situation in Gaza, which appears to have produced the earliest widespread sense of strong Palestinian identity after 1948, in Jordan an autonomous Palestinian political identity and the drive to organize around it did not begin to manifest itself openly until the mid-1960s.

THE SEEDS OF CHANGE

To return to developments on the national level, on July 20, 1951, King ʿAbdallah was assassinated, bringing to an end his shaykh-like style of rule and paving the way for a younger leadership. Although the East Bankers continued to constitute the natural base of regime support, under Husayn, at least initially, the East Bank population was much less united in its backing of the regime than it had been under ʿAbdallah. Palestinian protests against UNRWA and Arab Legion policies subsided momentarily with Husayn's accession to the throne in May 1953. However, by autumn Palestinians had once again taken to the streets and continued their protests in the spring and summer of 1954. Palestinian concerns at this stage centered on the failure of the Arab Legion to respond to the pleas of the Palestinian-manned National Guard for reinforcements after Israel staged several particularly brutal border raids in October 1953 and March 1954.[36]

A reorientation of regime policy required more than refugee protest, however. It required an alliance of elements from the two banks.[37] Ideological political parties, although never officially licensed by the government, began to operate more or less openly in the 1950s and established important ties between East and West Bankers. As time went on, a coalition developed. Members of the former Palestinian ruling class who had continued to oppose the Hashemites and the annexation of the West Bank joined with the nascent industrial middle class and small peasant landholders who had been effectively squeezed out of access to power. By 1956 these groups, with the support of urban workers, unemployed agricultural laborers of the refugee camps, and independent intellectuals, were poised to challenge the regime and the Palestinian notables who supported it.[38]

The first domestic crisis of Husayn's reign was precipitated by his announcement that he intended to join the pro-Western Baghdad Pact proposed by the United States. His efforts to push its acceptance against the popular will triggered street demonstrations not only in the capital, but also in the small towns of the East Bank. The army was able to restore order but the king was forced to withdraw his support of the pact. With Arab nationalist and anti-Western sentiment led by Egypt on the rise, Husayn's regime, which still hosted a substantial British presence, appeared to be on tenuous ground. In March 1956, political pressures led the king to dismiss Glubb from the Arab Legion and replace him with a Jordanian general, ʿAli Abu Nuwar. Other British officers were subsequently replaced by Jordanians to complete the Arabization process.

The nationalist surge of the 1950s also forced the first free elections in Jordan. In the 1956 elections the electorate chose a nationalist government headed by Prime Minister Sulayman al-Nabulsi. Nabulsi, an Arab nationalist and an East Banker with distant West Bank roots, proceeded to conclude a military agreement with Syria and Egypt that placed the armed forces of all three under Egypt's command. He then struck a deal with Egypt, Syria, and Saudi Arabia in which they agreed to replace the British subsidy lost because of the dismissal of Glubb. Nabulsi himself frequently questioned the legitimacy of the existence of the Jordanian state as an independent political entity.[39]

Thus, a collision course was set between the Arab nationalist, pro-Egyptian policy of Nabulsi and the policy of the king. The conflict crystallized over the issue of the Eisenhower Doctrine.[40] Husayn favored adherence while Nabulsi and Abu Nuwar preferred Egypt's course of positive neutralism. Husayn finally forced Nabulsi to resign in early 1957. Abu Nuwar, one of the authors of a foiled coup attempt that followed, escaped to Syria.

Although Husayn survived the coup attempt, parliamentary democracy did not. Martial law was imposed and remained in effect for eighteen months. The military rounded up dissident elements; scores of army officers and civilian officials were dismissed and some were tried by military courts. The crackdown drove ideological parties underground as their leaders were either imprisoned or exiled. The government reimposed censorship on the press and on all publications, domestic or foreign.

Those within the Palestinian elite still loyal to the throne viewed the defeat of Nabulsi and his supporters with great relief. However, those among them who had joined the opposition were faced with two options: to accept continued "exile" and exclusion; or to forsake their ties to their countrymen and pursue their own interests through supporting the monarchy.[41] Many continue to struggle with this dilemma to the present.

It is clear from table 9.5 that the periods of nationalist political activity in Jordan have coincided with the periods of increased Arab/decreased Western financial assistance to the kingdom, notably 1956–57 and 1964–69. Only then was there any margin of freedom that allowed for the development of active, representative political bodies, whether nationalist political parties or specifically Palestinian institutions. Arab aid also rose substantially following the 1967 war, the only period during which Palestinian institutions operated openly in Jordan.

HUSAYN AND THE PLO

In terms of sheer numbers of Palestinians and geographic location Jordan, specifically the West Bank, was the most logical area to give rise to a Palestinian entity. At the same time, however, Jordan was the only Arab state to have granted its Palestinian residents citizenship. Some attribute the annexation and the granting of citizenship to 'Abdallah's longstanding ambitions to rule a larger kingdom. Others, while acknowledging the former argument, add that from the beginning 'Abdallah's kingdom had two purposes: to serve as a receptacle for those Palestinians who would be forced from Palestine to make room for the Jewish state; and to serve to prevent the emergence of any Arab or Palestinian nationalist movement in the country that might be anti-Western, as attested to by the primarily Western subsidies that have kept the country solvent.[42] Thus, the emergence of a separate Palestinian entity, whatever its form, posed a threat to both the basis (population and resources) and the raison d'être of the kingdom.

Therefore, when Ahmad al-Shuqayri set out to visit Arab capitals in 1964 to discuss the establishment of a Palestinian entity, winning the agreement of Jordan's Husayn carried greater weight than gaining legitimacy in the eyes of the other Arab regimes. Husayn's acquiescence in the establishment of the entity (the PLO) must then be understood in light of both Jordan's regional position at the time and the promises and guarantees Shuqayri provided concerning the nature and aims of the proposed entity.

In the first place, Husayn's concerns over Israel's announced intention to divert the Jordan River waters placed him in a position to seek rapprochement with Egypt and Syria, two countries that supported the idea of (and later sought to control) a Palestinian entity. Furthermore, given the establishment of the General Union of Palestine Students in 1959 and the General Union of Palestine Workers in 1963, in addition to the existing Arab Nationalist Movement's political apparatus and the young but growing Fateh organization, the eventual emergence of a Palestinian entity of some kind may have appeared inevitable. Husayn may have believed that by agreeing to its emergence under a traditional, conservative leader like Shuqayri (and according to a set of strict conditions which he, the king, set down), the entity could be better controlled than if it emerged elsewhere and under more radical sponsorship.

In order to convince Husayn to agree to the establishment of what would become the Palestine Liberation Organization, Shuqayri had to promise that the entity would not engage in organizing or arming Palestinians in Jordan. Upon his arrival in Amman in February 1964, following the first Arab League Council summit, Shuqayri clarified his intentions:

> The emanation of the Palestinian entity from Jerusalem does not seek to cut off the West Bank from the Hashemite Kingdom of Jordan; we seek the liberation of our violated homeland to the West of Jerusalem.[43]

He also promised Husayn that he would include in his speech at the first PNC meeting and in the Palestine National Covenant (Article 14) that the PLO had no territorial aims in the West Bank.[44] To strengthen his position with the king, Shuqayri included a number of Jordanian notables in the first meeting of the PNC and, when the PLO executive committee was formed according to the decision of the second PNC meeting (Cairo, May 1965), two Jordanian officers were asked to join the council (they resigned the following July).[45]

Husayn's stipulations combined with the long-suppressed Palestinian desire for national self-expression and action rendered confrontation inevitable. Friction first arose during the third Arab summit conference in September 1965. At the meeting, the PLO called for the mandatory conscription of all Palestinians in Lebanon and Jordan into the recently formed Palestine Liberation Army (PLA). Jordan flatly refused to draft Palestinians, and relations began to deteriorate. On January 2, 1966, the PLO and Husayn decided to confer officially and on April 1 announced an agreement that called for further study of the conscription request. The agreement did, however, open the door for military training of youth and accorded PLO officials a type of diplomatic immunity.[46]

Jordanian relations with Israel were another important factor in Jordanian-PLO friction. Throughout the 1950s and early 1960s Jordanian policy had been to avoid border incidents with Israel and subsequent harsh Israeli retaliatory raids by preventing Palestinian infiltration across the border. From mid-1965 on, however, border incidents and Israeli counter- and preemptive attacks grew more numerous. To curtail Palestinian activities, in the summer of 1966 the government closed all

PLO and affiliated offices. That move exacerbated Jordanian-Syrian tensions and led to border clashes between the two countries.

Relations between the PLO and Jordan hit a new low after the Israeli attack on the West Bank town of al-Samuᶜ on November 13, 1966. The following week, strikes and demonstrations broke out throughout the West Bank. Relations continued to deteriorate until February 4, 1967, when the government announced its intention to withdraw its recognition of the PLO. The PLO, Egypt, and Syria then launched an anti-Jordanian press campaign. Jordan responded by boycotting the Arab League meetings that Shuqayri attended. No attempt was made to repair relations until the eve of the 1967 war when Husayn traveled to Cairo to conclude a joint defense pact with Nasir and, in fact, returned to Amman on the same plane with the PLO chief.[47]

The events directly leading to the 1967 war and a recounting of the war itself are beyond the scope of this study, but the results of the war warrant examination. Most immediate and costly was Jordan's loss of territory and skilled labor, and the East Bank's "gain" of some 265,000 refugees (most of them 1948 refugees from the camps of the West Bank).[48] The war also marked a major turning point in the history of the Palestinian resistance movement (PRM). With the front-line Arab states defeated and in disarray, Palestinians in growing numbers decided to take the initiative in waging their struggle. Commando enlistment soared, especially after the battle of al-Karamah in March 1968 in which Palestinian fidaʾiyyin joined by Jordanian army troops inflicted heavy losses on Israeli forces that had crossed the Jordan River to destroy a fidaʾiyyin base. In a relatively short period of time, the PRM developed into a semiautonomous set of organizations operating in, and launching attacks on Israeli targets from, Jordan.

The fact that armed resistance could develop and operate openly in Jordan was a direct result of the war. There is no doubt that the 1967 disaster led many Palestinians to realize the importance of self-reliance in their struggle. Yet, clearly, many others had already reached that conclusion well before the war as witnessed by the rise of Fateh and other Palestinian resistance groups prior to 1967. In the past, however, the political and security climate had prohibited an open flowering of the movement. Jordan had cracked down on nationalist elements in the mid-1950s and during the 1966–67 period of conflict with the PLO. The strength and effectiveness of the Jordanian state's coercive apparatus on those occasions had enabled it to crush or suppress the political activists. However, the humiliating defeat dealt the Arabs in 1967 discredited the existing regimes and with them their modus operandi, which in the case of Jordan meant the supremacy of the military and the *mukhabarat* (internal security). The war threw the army and the state into disarray. Civilian support—tacit or overt—for regime methods was soundly shaken.

In contrast, commando legitimacy rose with each operation against Israel. Immediately after the war, Jordan embarked on a program to rebuild its shattered military. During the rebuilding process, support for the PRM, if only verbal, bought time and a certain amount of political legitimacy, which was then in dangerously low supply. The period of decline in the power of the state, brief as it was, afforded Palestinian institutions their greatest opportunity to develop and expand in Jordan.

Unfortunately for the PRM, however, the basis and position of nationalist elements in Jordan had gradually changed since the anti-Western surge of the 1950s. The huge amounts of Western financial assistance awarded since the late 1950s had enabled the bureaucracy nearly to quadruple in size. The government had gradually become the principal employer in the country, and the technocratic class that had developed had a vested interest in preserving its position and extending its power base. Potential regime supporters were wooed with jobs and grants. Newly founded institutions such as the Tribal Council and the Bureau of Agricultural Loans served as conduits for financial subsidies. In addition, retired military men were increasingly brought into the civil bureaucracy at all levels as the civilian and military bureaucracies were integrated under a single chief.[49] Thus, the nationalist East Bank/West Bank coalition of opposition parties, which had forced the political concessions of the 1950s, had slowly disintegrated. As a result, mobilized and active Palestinians were more isolated than before. This isolation paved the way for the September 1970 civil war.[50]

The September 1970 battles, often called the Jordanian civil war or Black September, drove the Palestinian armed resistance out of Amman to Jarash and ʿAjlun in the northwest. Casualities were substantial, especially in the refugee camps, where the fiercest resistance had been launched. Palestinian institutions suffered near-total destruction. The resistance had provided the protective shield the institutions needed to survive. By the time Jordanian forces finally drove the PRM from the country in July 1971, all Palestinian institutions had been "closed." Many resistance leaders were jailed. Others fled the country. Those who remained had either to abandon political activity or go underground.

Husayn's suppression of the PLO led Syria to close its border and airspace to Jordan. Kuwait and Libya cut off the aid that had been promised the Hashemite Kingdom by the 1967 Khartum summit. Nevertheless, internally, Husayn continued to command the loyalty of his traditional basis of support, the army, as well as the ever-expanding technocratic class, both of which groups contained substantial numbers of Palestinians.

RECOVERING FROM CIVIL WAR

Ironically, following the expulsion of the PRM in 1971, both Jordan and the PLO began, separately, to use the same slogan—"the unity of the Jordanian and Palestinian people"—but for very different reasons. For the Jordanian regime it was a continuation of the traditional policy of seeking to secure (or at least proclaim) the allegiance of the Palestinians of both banks to the Hashemite throne. For the PLO, however, the origins of the cry of unity were more complicated. In the first place, the expulsion from Jordan and the displacement and destruction the battle with the regime had caused left the organization extremely vulnerable. It could not afford to antagonize, much less fight, any regime. Instead, it needed to repair relations and consolidate support wherever possible. "Closing" its institutions and urging its people to work with Jordanians in a Jordanian framework was one step. For the left-leaning Palestinian groups—particularly the DF and PFLP—the move was a natural one: party ideology claimed the unity of the two peoples and the need to fight together for democracy and to liberate Palestine.

Finally, and just as important to both Palestinian and Hashemite concerns, was a political current that emerged in the occupied West Bank following Black September. Furious at the regime's war on the PRM some West Bankers, given their relatively recent occupied status, sought to secede from Jordan through the establishment of a Palestinian entity in the occupied territories. Jordan rejected such a move on the grounds that the West Bank was occupied Jordanian land, not the site of a future Palestinian state. And, although after 1973 the idea of an independent West Bank state became an established part of PLO thinking, prior to the 1973 war the resistance groups were still talking in terms of total, not partial, liberation of Palestine. The idea of establishing a state in only part of Palestine had not yet gained currency, and certainly not acceptance, in PLO circles.[51]

It is in the context of the West Bank separatist drive combined with the weakness of the Palestinian resistance that the United Arab Kingdom plan announced by King Husayn in March 1972 must be understood. With the Palestinian residents of the East Bank under close regime control since the civil war, the main battleground for the struggle over who represented the Palestinians became the West Bank. While the tug-of-war over West Bank and Gazan allegiance is an ongoing one, with each side scoring periodic successes and suffering occasional losses, in general Jordan relies upon its traditional Palestinian notable supporters, while the PLO has attempted to mobilize the more numerous Palestinians who are either anti-Hashemite or not tied to the regime. The United Arab Kingdom plan, announced in March 1972, proposed to transform the Hashemite Kingdom into two regions: the Palestine region (including the West Bank and any other Palestinian areas that wanted to join); and the Jordan region, the East Bank. In other respects it did not differ greatly from the pre-1967 version of the Hashemite Kingdom. According to the plan, the king was to remain head of state: legislative authority was to rest with him and with an assembly in which both regions would be equally represented. The plan then begins to resemble later "autonomy" proposals: the central executive's authority was to include international affairs, the economy, and internal security. Other matters were to be left to a local governor-general, supported by a regional cabinet and local assembly.

Meanwhile, the PLO was gradually reestablishing itself in a new base, Lebanon, and was making great strides to gain international recognition. The Arab League Council summit in Rabat in October 1974 finally accorded the PLO official status as the sole, legitimate representative of the Palestinians. This Arab recognition was followed in November 1974 by 'Arafat's famous appearance at the UN, after which the PLO was granted permanent observer status. Husayn was, once again, forced to accept setback, if not defeat. The 1976 West Bank municipal elections sponsored by the Israelis, in which candidates associated with the PLO scored solid victories, was clearly a defeat, not just for the Israelis, but also for the Jordanian regime.

Jordan then witnessed an "East Bank first" period during which West Bank subsidies (which Jordan had continued to pay even after 1967) were cut, the ratio of Palestinians in the Jordanian cabinet dropped to one-fourth, and some Palestinian government personnel were replaced by East Bankers. The first signs of an easing in tensions did not come until 1979, in response to the conclusion of the peace treaty between Egypt and Israel.[52] However, it was not until the aftermath of the Israeli invasion of Lebanon and the subsequent weakening and scattering of the PLO that the rapprochement was consolidated. In the shadow of the rebellion in Fateh and serious internal PLO dissension, the Palestine National Council was convened in Amman in November 1984. This was the first time that the PNC had met in Amman since the 1971 expulsion of the resistance, and King Husayn addressed the gathering. Shortly thereafter, Husayn and ʿArafat hammered out an accord—the February 11 agreement—to guide Palestinian-Jordanian coordination intended to lead to peace negotiations.

This PLO-Jordanian honeymoon, like those before it, was short lived. A break with the PLO was presaged by Jordanian moves in autumn 1985 toward rapprochement with the then PLO archenemy, Syria, after nearly six years of feuding. In early February 1986, after almost a year of feverish activity to work out a deal with the Americans whereby Palestinian participation in peace negotiations would be ensured, Husayn announced that cooperation was being suspended, and laid the blame at the feet of the PLO for failing to live up to its promises.

RENEWED COMPETITION FOR PALESTINIAN LOYALTY

The PLO denied Husayn's accusations. However, the accuracy of the king's charges is not as important as their consequences in Jordan, the occupied territories, and beyond. In Jordan all Fateh offices were closed, PLO bureaus were reduced to a bare minimum, and some PLO members were declared personae non gratae. The regime then involved itself in sponsoring another Fateh rebel, ʿAtallah ʿAtallah (Abu al-Zaʿim), in an attempt to split pro-ʿArafat ranks in Jordan, particularly among the PLA brigade stationed in the country.

Another significant political development that followed the breakdown of the February 11 accord was the publication of a new election law (plans for which had been announced in late 1985). Criticisms of the law were leveled from all sides.[53] Here only few of the provisions that have special import for Palestinians will be mentioned. Prior to the new law there were 120 seats in Parliament, with 60 set aside for each of the two banks. According to the 1986 law, the number of seats is to be increased to 142, with 71 for each bank. However, for the first time, the refugee camps are defined as electoral districts and of the 71 West Bank seats 11 are for East Bank refugee camps (ten camps and one heavily Palestinian area in Amman called al-Mahattah). Thus, the East Bank refugee camps are defined as West Bank electoral districts. Former Jordanian prime minister Ahmad ʿUbaydat was particularly critical of this aspect of the law, since, he argued, it implied an acceptance of the status quo and of the permanent nature of the camps, and further reinforced communal divisions in a country whose official line has been that there is no difference between the people of the two banks.[54]

Second, although few East Bank Palestinians entertained the idea, formerly there was no legal prohibition against their running for East Bank seats. The new law, however, explicitly states that they may not run for these seats. Finally, anyone—Palestinian or Transjordanian—who has belonged in the past to an outlawed political party (and in Jordan, there is no other kind) may not run for office. This effectively excludes the majority of politically active Jordanians, many of whom are Palestinians, thus leaving the field open to either inexperienced or solidly proregime elements.[55]

A lesser-known aspect of Jordanian-Palestinian competition, particularly over constituencies in the Gulf, is the series of "emigré conferences" sponsored by the regime. The first such conference was held in July 1985, the second in July 1986, and the third in July 1987; there are plans to hold a conference annually. Two obvious, official reasons may be surmised for holding such conferences: to give expatriate Jordanians the opportunity to visit Jordan and discuss their problems with the government so that it may become more responsive to expatriate concerns; and to stimulate interest among expatriates in investing in Jordan.

The interdependence or overlap of concerns between the expatriates and the government may be seen in the issues addressed in the conferences. At the 1985 conference the topics of the working papers included Jordanian stances on various political issues; development and investment opportunities; the state of the labor market; the problems of Jordanian expatriates; and the problems faced by expatriates on their return to Jordan.[56] In 1986, representatives from almost all the ministries were present at the conference (as was the king) and the one thousand attendees were given a chance to raise problems with the individual ministers. Primary among expatriate concerns were: the right of expatriates to vote; opening Jordanian schools in Kuwait (where the "Jordanian" community is counted at 400,000); problems of university acceptance for expatriate children; greater cooperation and assistance from embassies; and investment opportunities.[57]

However, it is clear that the conferences are also intended to assist Jordan in asserting "sovereignty" over the large Palestinian/Jordanian community in the Gulf states, particularly Kuwait, where many have lived all or most of their lives and have little or no sense of identification with Jordan, despite the fact that they hold Jordanian passports. While the first conference was convened in an atmosphere of PLO-Jordanian cooperation (following the conclusion of the February 11 accord), the second was held in the wake of the termination of that accord. While the PLO did not encourage people to go to the first conference, it accused those who attended the second of selling out the *qadiyyah* (cause);[58] ʿArafat called the conference nothing more than an attempt to steal Palestinian representation from the PLO.[59]

In assessing the role of these conferences the importance of increasing investment from abroad, something that is particularly pressing at this juncture, must not be underestimated. However, while the expatriate problems of where to educate children and how to reintegrate into the overburdened Jordanian job market upon one's return are relatively new, other expatriate problems have existed for a long time, and the Jordanian government has never before shown such an interest in serving its sons and daughters abroad. In Kuwait, for example, the Jordanian embassy had never been viewed as a gathering place; yet for the first emigré conference, nominations for representatives of the community were submitted to the embassy, which is also where voting for these representatives took place.[60] In what must be viewed as a related move, a few months before the February 1986 breakdown in Jordanian-PLO cooperation, the embassy set up a branch of the Jordanian Writers' Union in Kuwait. It has subsequently attempted to establish other alternative unions, notably a women's union.

The pressures to switch allegiances can be quite strong. The threat of losing one's passport is primary; concern for property in Jordan is another consideration. Nevertheless, the Jordanian play for the allegiance of its nationals in Kuwait has not yet met with a great deal of success. Prior to the second conference certain prominent "Jordanians" (who had before referred to themselves as leaders of the "Palestinian" community) did begin to speak of the large "Jordanian" community in Kuwait.[61] However, those who have opted for a Jordanian identity have demanded concessions from the government in exchange: special arrangements for their children to enroll in Jordanian universities and privileges in the fields of importing and property holding. Perhaps the most accurate characterization of the policy is that of the "carrot and stick."

A better publicized example of an economic play by Jordan for political allegiance conerns the proposed development plan for the occupied territories. While the November 1986 conference that discussed the plan and sought international funding support did not produce the results the regime had hoped for, it is, nonetheless, forging ahead. The intention is to allocate at least JD10 million ($28 million) annually for projects in the West Bank and Gaza. The stated goal is to promote economic development to increase employment opportunities and the famous "quality of life" in order to enable Palestinians to remain on the land.

While on the surface it is difficult from an Arab perspective to fault a program that seeks to support economic and infrastructural development among Palestinians under occupation, the timing and mechanics of the plan raise doubts about its noneconomic goals. In the first place, like the second development conference, the plan comes in the wake of the breakdown of Jordanian-PLO cooperation and the approval by Jordan of Israel's appointment of Palestinians (read pro-Jordanian Palestinians) to municipal posts on the West Bank. Moreover, while in the past money was channeled to the occupied territories through the Palestinian-Jordanian Joint Committee, the use of the development plan monies will be determined by the Jordanian government, with no PLO input. There is, therefore, the concern that the money will be used to reinforce support of pro-Jordanian West Bankers and to coopt others. Jordan's increasing role may also be seen in the reopening of the Cairo-Amman Bank (closed since 1967) and the requests submitted to the Israeli authorities to open branches of other banks as well as offices for the Jordanian national airline, Alia, on the West Bank.[62]

While improvements in the PLO-Jordanian relationship are unlikely—at least in the near future—to change Jordan's increasing involvement in the occupied territories, it should be noted that Husayn and ʿArafat did meet for discussions during the January 1987 Islamic summit in Kuwait, although ʿArafat was the only Arab leader Husayn did not meet at the airport on his arrival for the November 1987 Arab League Council summit. With both aware, no doubt to their continuing annoyance, that neither can go too far without the other, some form of reconciliation, however grudging and distasteful, would appear inevitable.

THE PROFESSIONAL UNIONS

The ban on political parties in the country and the failure to hold parliamentary elections in the post-1967 period until 1984 have left few avenues for overt expressions of political preferences. As a result, the professional unions in Jordan—unions of doctors, engineers, lawyers, dentists, pharmacists, journalists, writers, geologists, and agricultural engineers—have partially filled the political void.[63]

Most of these unions were founded in the 1950s, and the beginnings were difficult: professionals were few in number and their activities were limited. Only the doctors' and lawyers' unions had an activist record in the early period. The year 1967 marked a turning point. With no organized political parties in Jordan there was no group to take responsibility for formulating a response to the war. To fill the void, leaders of these unions along with some well-known national figures met and proclaimed the National Grouping (al-Tajammuʿ al-Watani) which also included representatives of trade unions. Baʿthis and Communists were prominent among its members. The king himself attended the first meeting, in which a national charter was drafted.

What came after the war, however, was the rise of the Palestinian resistance. The National Grouping consulted with the resistance and coordinated meetings, displays, and other activities that had not been allowed in the pre-1967 period. But soon political differences evolved in the grouping which paralyzed its work. To overcome the paralysis another organization was formed. Including representatives of the professional and labor unions, the Professional Grouping (al-Tajammuʿ al-Mihni) was in constant contact with the state regarding political matters. It met once a month throughout 1970 and until September 1971. At that point the regime put an end to its work on the grounds that its activities were political, not professional.

From 1971 until 1977 no coordinated trade or professional union work was permitted. However, Sadat's November 1977 trip to Jerusalem was a serious enough development to precipitate attempts to renew activity. A call was issued for a meeting of union leaders. Heads of the original six unions were joined by leaders of the journalists', geologists', veterinarians', and writers' unions and established the Council of Professional Unions (Majlis al-Niqabat al-Mihniyyah), which then began limited political work. In 1978, when Israel invaded Lebanon the council called for a meeting of trade unionists and political activists. About 200 people attended the meeting which sought to find a new formula or framework for national political work. The result was the founding of the General Secretariat of Patriotic and Popular Forces in Jordan. Members represented a broad spectrum of political tendencies: the Communist party, the Baʿth (both Syrian and Iraqi factions), Fateh, some Palestinian popular organizations, and some independents. It was headed by Shaykh ʿAbd al-Hamid al-Sayih (since 1984, speaker of the PNC). The General Secretariat operated for about four years: by 1982 political infighting had prevented it from devising a formula for joint political action and by 1983, further fractured by the split in the PLO, its activity was frozen.

Nevertheless, the Council of Professional Unions continued to function, participating in a limited way in national work. Among the council's activities were two visits to the prime minister's office after the May 1986 violence at Yarmuk University; drafting a memorandum outlining its objections to the 1986 election law; and seeking permission to have a march protesting the American raid on Libya (permission was denied and the council had to settle for writing a letter of protest).

The *mukhabarat* would no doubt like to control the unions further, but it is thwarted by several factors. In the first place, unlike the trade unions, the professional unions have constitutions that are not subject to the Ministry of Labor; therefore, the ministry cannot interfere at will. If the government were to attempt to interfere, it is precisely the members of these unions who have sufficient influence and economic clout to counter at least some government pressures. Average workers are not so fortunate. Given the unemployment situation in Jordan, if they are threatened with dismissal, they may have no employment alternative. It is far more difficult to threaten a professional engineer or lawyer who has his own practice or business.

As a result, the professional unions have the distinction of holding the only free and democratic elections in Jordan. The prominence of many of their members has forced the regime to keep its attempts at interference to a minimum and, on occasion, to heed their advice. Elections for leadership posts attract the attention of many beyond the unions' membership lists, for they are one gauge of the political pulse of the country. For that reason, at least in Amman, virtually everyone takes an interest in who is running and what political "party" he represents. Although the percentage varies depending on the union, Palestinian membership is generally in keeping with the community's size in the country. Some of the leaders of the professional unions are also members of the PNC, a fact that is not well received by the regime; but some of these same people see no contradiction between having a Palestinian political identity and being Jordanian citizens.

THE ISSUE OF COMMUNAL IDENTITY

Jordan is much more of a communal mosaic than most analyses portray it to be. While the discussion here will focus on the most frequently mentioned distinction—that between Palestinians and native East Bankers—other important divisions should not be overlooked. One that is rarely mentioned is that between north and south: while the situation is complex, in general, the southern Transjordanian tribes largely (but not uniformly) support the regime and the northern tribes are largely (though far from exclusively) antagonistic toward control by the southern tribes in alliance with a ruling family they consider to be foreigners (the Hashemites). For example, in the 1967–70 period the Palestinian resistance, particularly the Democratic Front, met with marked success in recruiting northern Transjordanians into its ranks. In many cases this enlistment was more an antiregime than a pro-Palestinian statement. The other communal distinctions are more frequently mentioned in the literature: the existence of a Christian minority, a small but politically influential Circassian community, and an even smaller Shishen minority.

Significant political divisions are also to be found among the Palestinians. Among the factors that determine one's sense of Palestinian identity or stance vis-à-vis the regime are: whether one is a refugee, whether one lives in a camp, when one came to the East Bank, and one's degree of economic success. Some Palestinians came to Transjordan well before the partition of Palestine. The majority prospered professionally, commercially, and largely identifies with the East Bank. Another group is the 1948 refugees—whether registered with UNRWA or not—who do not live in camps. Many have enjoyed a certain commercial and professional success. Others, as members of the government bureaucracy, have attained positions of responsibility and authority. Although most express a desire to regain Palestine, they nonetheless have investments in homes and businesses on the East Bank. Many are at least tacit if not open supporters of the regime. A third group comprises the noncamp residents who came to Jordan in 1967. They tend to be more militant in their Palestinianness, are closer to the camp dwellers, and have not achieved the economic success of the 1948 noncamp refugees. The fourth group comprises the 1948 and 1967 refugees who remain in the camps. They are the recipients of the majority of UNRWA assistance and remain the most disgruntled and, at least potentially, militant of the Palestinians residing in Jordan.[64]

The chapters on the mass organizations that follow chronicle how the regime has dealt over the years with sectoral expressions or attempts at expression of Palestinian identity, particularly during the pre-1970 period. However, in order to underline the complexity of the issue of communal identity in the 1980s as well as its salience for the regime, two cases that do not involve sectoral organizing will be detailed before proceding to the case studies.

The first is a rather classic example of regime suppression of attempts to rally Jordanians around their Palestinian identity.[65] It concerns the Committee for the Annual Palestinian Folklore Day, which was established in 1981 by Palestinian folklore specialist Nimr Sirhan in conjunction with the Nablus Charitable Society (Amman) and the General Union of Palestinian Writers and Journalists. The first celebration, scheduled for July 1, 1981, was announced and advertised by flyers distributed in Amman and Beirut. Permission for the celebration was granted by the mayor of Amman, and it was held in the Professional Unions' Complex in the Shmaysani district of Amman.

The turnout for the celebration was far greater than expected and, because of a lack of space inside, the gathering extended beyond the building, where spontaneous singing and dancing began among passersby who were not among the invited guests. The following day a press conference was held at the headquarters of the Jordanian Writers' Union. 'Abd al-Jawad Salih (deposed mayor of the West Bank town of al-Birah) of the PLO executive committee was in attendance and 'Abd al-Hamid Sayih spoke in the name of the committee. The committee's founding was officially proclaimed and July 1 was chosen for the yearly celebration. Immediately thereafter Sirhan was called in by the *mukhabarat*, who accused him of cursing the king and causing chaos at the event. After several days of questioning centering on who was behind the committee, Sirhan's passport was "withdrawn"[66] and he was dismissed from his job in the Ministry of Education.

The Israeli invasion of Lebanon in the summer of 1982 created a mood in the community that was far from conducive to any sort of celebration. Instead, the committee distributed leaflets urging people to volunteer to fight in Lebanon. Each day there were demonstrations outside the PLO office in Jabal al-Husayn. So great was the turnout that there were not enough buses for all who wanted to go. Moreover, many of those who wanted to volunteer did not have passports. Hence their chant: Fish 'anna jawazat! Wayn, wayn al-tashilat? (We have no passports! Where are the means to facilitate [our volunteering]?). Those who had passports and boarded the buses took with them food and clothing donated by local merchants and members of the community. (At the border the Syrians confiscated the food and clothing for their own use and turned back the buses, saying the fighters were not wanted in Lebanon.) The frustrated volunteers were blacklisted on their return to Jordan and their passports were withdrawn.

In 1983 the committee decided to apply again for permission for a series of celebrations planned to extend from July 1 to August 24. Permission was granted and the events drew even larger numbers than they had in 1981. Held in the same complex in Shmaysani the celebrations attracted crowds that overflowed into the streets. Police cars and armed jeeps were deployed around the complex to ensure that the festivities did not get out of hand. Other events were held at the headquarters of the Nablus Charitable Society in Amman and in Irbid at Yarmuk University and in the Irbid camp. By August 16 the regime's tolerance was spent and the final event, the cultural awards ceremony, was canceled.

Following the 1983 celebrations Sirhan was imprisoned for thirteen months on a variety of charges, including inciting people against the state. While he was in prison the committee, which he had worked to keep free of outside influence, was reorganized to include more progovernment members. Interestingly, the changes led the committee to be tied completely to the PLO. Sirhan, after his release from prison, was barred from returning to his job in the PLO's office of information and culture.

In 1985 following the conclusion of the February 11 accord between the PLO and King Husayn, the folklore celebration was held in the PLO office, but was canceled after three days. Not surprisingly, by summer 1986, with PLO-Jordanian relations at an all-time low after the breakdown in their year-long cooperation, Jordanian newspapers refused even to print the announcement of the event circulated by the committee.

The second example of regime handling of intercommunal relations concerns refugee camp youth centers.[67] As part of its services in the realm of social affairs, UNRWA had established separate youth centers for boys and girls in the refugee camps. The girls' focused on vocational training, especially sewing, while the offerings for boys were more diverse, including sports teams and a wide range of cultural and social programs. The only condition for membership in the centers was that one be a Palestinian refugee.

In 1970 UNRWA funding cuts deprived the centers of paid staff to direct activities. The center members were therefore forced to assume responsibility for running the programs, including some fund raising to cover minor expenses. Among their other activities the centers formed sports leagues, which began to organize yearly championship tournaments for soccer, basketball, volleyball, and boxing. In 1975 the camp teams decided to participate outside their leagues by competing with teams from Jordanian (East Bank) sports clubs.

The beginnings of what developed into a serious problem came in 1980, when the soccer team from al-Wahdat camp won the championship of the kingdom. Among the refugee camps, al-Wahdat has a special significance because of the heavy losses it suffered during Black September. It has, ever since, been a symbol of Palestinian resistance and defiance of the regime. Even West Bankers under occupation began to follow the fortunes of al-Wahdat's team with great enthusiasm. On the East Bank a special horn honk came to be associated with support for the camp's team.

With no legal political parties and no elections through which to express themselves politically Jordanians came to identify with soccer teams along communal lines: supporting al-Wahdat was a statement of Palestinianness, while rooting for a team from Ramtha, for example, was a declaration of East Bank loyalty. For many fans, Palestinian and Transjordanian alike, each time a refugee camp team locked horns with an East Bank squad, it was, on a very basic and emotional level, as if the civil war were being fought again. Violence among fans was a common occurrence: fights and brawls inevitably accompanied the matches.

In 1986, after bloody disturbances at a match involving al-Wahdat, the Ministry of Occupied Territories Affairs asked UNRWA to surrender its responsibility for the youth centers. The administrative councils of the camp centers were then dissolved and new councils (many of whose members are high-ranking government officials) formed under the auspices of the Jordanian Youth Centers. The names of the clubs were changed—al-Wahdat Youth Center is now called Nadi al-Diffatayn (the Two Banks Club)—and all are now to include both Palestinian and Jordanian youth.

To understand these two cases as but two examples of a Hashemite policy of suppressing Palestinian nationalism is to oversimplify, indeed to obscure, the basic issues. There is far more at work and at stake. First it is necessary to understand from which sectors threats to the regime may originate. A quick review of Jordanian history shows that serious threats to the throne have come from three sources: the army (1957), a broad coalition of East and West bankers (1955–56), and the Palestinians with some East Bank allies (1968–1971).

Since the coup attempt by ʿAli Abu Nuwar in 1957 the army has been Husayn's most constant and reliable source of support. Ensuring its loyalty has been one of the regime's top priorities. It is the threat of Palestinian separatism that is generally noted as the regime's greatest worry. Hence the refusal of the regime since the ouster of the PRM in 1971 to allow any specifically Palestinian institutions (with the exception of the PLO office) to operate in Jordan.

But the cases of the Folklore Committee and the camp sports centers cannot be explained as simple repression or denial of Palestinian identity in Jordan. If this were the case, the regime could have denied permission for the folklore celebrations or forced them to be held under a Jordanian banner; and the fierce communalism engendered by the sports competition could have been checked well before 1986, since it was clear to all as early as 1980 that al-Wahdat's team had become a symbol of Palestinian nationalism.

One possible explanation is that the regime realizes that it cannot erase the feelings of separate identity held by 60 to 70 percent of its citizens; thus, an occasional folklore celebration or soccer match, as long as it can be carefully controlled, allows for the release of pent-up nationalist frustrations. Sports in particular can divert young mens' energies from politics.

Another possible explanation lies in Jordan's relations with the PLO. As long as relations are good and the PLO is keen on preserving close ties, some minor concessions in the realm of national expression may be tolerated (although the PLO will be held responsible for the events and will therefore have a vested interest in maintaining order). The Folklore Committee case exemplifies this. On the other hand, when relations are poor, the regime may be expected to act quickly to quash any unnecessary Palestinian patriotic "zeal." This was certainly the case with al-Wahdat in 1986.

But neither of these answers is sufficient. The answer may be found in the third potential source of threat mentioned above—the possibility of a coalition of East and West Bankers.[68] The regime's greatest insurance against the emergence of such a coalition lies in maintaining a medium level of hostility or tension between Palestinians and Transjordanians. While both are citizens and have many of the same concerns—rising prices, unemployment, educating their children, greater political liberalization—unwritten policies of preferential recruitment into the army, sensitive government sectors and the like for East Bankers help keep the two communities divided. Occasional displays of Palestinian identity like the folklore festival, or outbreaks of communal violence at soccer matches, reinforce those elements from both banks who see cooperation as impossible or undesirable. These two groups have been nicknamed by some the "Palestinian and Jordanian Likud" because of their inflexibility and the exclusivist nature of their respective nationalisms. Just as important from the regime's point of view, communal tensions weaken the hand of the various illegal political parties which have, at least since 1971 (some even before), called and worked for unity among all Jordanians to fight for a change in the political system.

Thus, as long as the regime is certain of the loyalty of the army, the strength of its coercive apparatus, and the cooptation of large numbers of Palestinians through commercial or bureaucratic success, communal tensions and the ability to manipulate them constitute one of Husayn's greatest strengths. It seems highly unlikely that Palestinians alone can bring about major changes in the political system; indeed, many are unwilling to challenge the status quo. What is needed if political change is to be achieved and, therefore, what is most feared, is the kind of broad political coalition that united elements from both banks in the mid-1950s. Despite unofficial discrimination against them in the military and in some segments of the government bureaucracy, many Palestinians have been drawn into at least tacit support for the regime through economic success predicated upon Jordan's relatively unrestricted economic atmosphere.[69] Some continue to work through illegal political parties in anticipation of a future change in political atmosphere that will once again allow them to be openly active. But many others, Palestinians and Transjordanians alike, fearing the various penalties imposed for antiregime activity remain, for the time being, politically dormant.

[10]
Addressing Community Need: The FTUJ,
GUPWom, and PRCS

Jordan's population composition—60 to 70 percent Palestinian, one-third of whom were refugees, poor and crowded together in camps—rendered the country a likely recruiting base for Palestinian popular organizations. However, in Jordan the Palestinians were citizens and an increasingly integrated and integral part of the country. Moreover, the Hashemite regime, by nature, was suspicious of any organized groups—Palestinian or otherwise–but especially of those that provided a forum for political gathering and discussion. Backed financially by Western patrons like Britain and the United States who had their own reasons for "discouraging" political organizing, the regime succeeded in thwarting most attempts at overt political mobilization.

Nevertheless, in 1953 the regime was forced to acquiesce in the promulgation of a labor law that legalized trade union organizing. Unions were permitted to be established in certain nonpublic sector industries and as long as they were centrally controlled from Amman. No separate Palestinian identity for any labor union was allowed, even on the West Bank, despite the fact that the working class and its leadership in Jordan in the 1950s and 1960s were overwhelmingly Palestinian.

In the case of women, Palestinians had continued to operate charitable societies since the 1948 war, when they played a role in relief work. Palestinian women's involvement in these societies, as well as their participation in the outlawed political parties, continued through the 1950s and 1960s. Not until 1965 was a federation of the disparate Palestinian women's groups in the kingdom and beyond, the General Union of Palestinian Women (GUPWom), founded under PLO auspices in Jerusalem. Although the Jordanian regime never recognized the existence of a branch of the General Union of Palestinian Women in Jordan, the union grew quickly, focusing on the refugee camps where it offered services ranging from literacy classes to military training.

The situation of health care in the kingdom also presented unlimited possibilities for organizational development. While UNRWA provided limited medical care for the Palestinian refugees on its lists, some parts of Jordan, particularly the Ghur (Jordan Valley) and the more remote areas of the south, were without even the most basic medical facilities. Given its limited capabilities, the Jordanian Red Crescent Society was unable to respond to the needs of all citizens, and the state was unwilling or unable to commit resources sufficient to expand health care facilities. The need for primary health care among Palestinians was exacerbated after 1965 by the increasing numbers of those wounded in attacks by or against the Israelis. With the increased organizational and political freedom that emerged in Jordan as a result of the June 1967 "setback" (in Arabic the war is known as *al-naksah*), a small group of dedicated Palestinian doctors developed a network of hospitals and clinics in the camps and throughout the kingdom to serve the needs of all of Jordan's neglected sectors. Thus was born the Palestine Red Crescent Society (PRCS).

THE WORKERS

The beginnings of Arab Palestinian trade unionism date to the establishment of the Palestine Arab Workers Society (PAWS) in 1925. Haifa's port, iron and tobacco processing, and construction sector had spawned the development of an industrial working class and rendered it a natural headquarters. Although the PAWS functioned as a trade union *(niqabah)*, a mandate prohibition on such unions forced it to incorporate as a "society" *(jam'iyyah)*. Indeed, its activities extended beyond the workers to the community at large as it sponsored cultural and political symposia as well as sports teams for students.

The society's leadership developed a program that reflected a nationalist rather than a class orientation: the leftists and Communists who dotted the ranks of the PAWS joined for lack of an alternative. But the alliance was fragile. The PAWS's leadership regularly opted for compromise rather than confrontation over labor issues, and a struggle therefore gradually developed between the traditional leadership and some of the organization's leftist members. In 1945, disagreement over the issue of Palestinian representation at the World Labor Conference in London precipitated open confrontation. The leftists quit the PAWS to form a rival organization, the Conference of Arab Workers, which recruited primarily among petroleum workers and the port workers of Jaffa and Haifa. It also enjoyed the support of workers in Gaza and Jerusalem.

In the wake of the Palestine war, the part of Palestine occupied by the Arab Legion and the Iraqi army was placed under the control of a governor who closed the Conference of Arab Workers and imprisoned its leaders on the grounds that it was a Communist organization whose parent party had supported the Palestine partition plan. Similar steps were taken by the Egyptian military authorities who "administered" Gaza. In the meantime, the fall of Haifa, Jaffa, Lidd, and Ramlah to Jewish forces rendered their former Arab residents refugees. Many labor activists headed for Nablus, a secondary industrial city, where Husni Salih al-Khuffash headed the chapter of the PAWS. Here Palestinian trade unionists Zaki al-Shaykh Yasin, Diya' 'Abduh, Sa'di As'ad al-Din, Mustafa 'Asqalan, and Ruhi al-Khuffash as well as some younger activists resolved to revive the movement which had been fractured by the war. Despite the efforts of the military authorities, they firmly and successfully resisted early attempts to eliminate the society.[1]

As a first step in their reorganizing efforts, in early 1949 the trade unionists in Nablus invited cohorts from inside and outside Palestine to Nablus to attend a workers' conference to reconstitute a higher council for the PAWS. The Nablus leadership, twenty union members from Tulkarm, Jenin, and Jerusalem, as well as several who had fled from Jaffa and Lidd attended the meeting. The men voted Nablus the temporary headquarters of the Palestinian labor movement, resolved to organize both East Bank and West Bank workers, and elected Husni al-Khuffash proxy secretary-general since the former secretary-general was in London.

The first test of the revived PAWS was not long in coming. The 1949 Rhodes Armistice Agreements had stipulated the readjustment of Israel's borders. On the West Bank near Tulkarm, the Arab Legion, directed by British officers, conscripted Palestinian laborers to build a new road to take the place of the old road which fell on the Israeli side of the realigned borders. The army required village *mukhtars* to submit the names of all village residents for potential conscription and demanded monetary compensation from those unable to work. The trade unionists in Tulkarm appealed to the PAWS in Nablus for help in fighting the forced labor. Khuffash responded by visiting the area himself to investigate the problem. Following his visit, the PAWS initiated negotiations with the military authorities and won the workers the right to be paid for their labor.[2]

In 1950, the society struck against the Renault Mechanical Company and won its demands. PAWS headquarters then set to work to revive the branches in Jenin, Tulkarm, and Qalqiliyyah and established a new branch in Bayt Iba.[3] Former members of the Conference of Arab Workers began organizing among laborers in Bethlehem, Hebron, Ramallah, and Jerusalem.[4]

The depressed economic conditions prevailing on the West Bank in the early 1950s drove many Palestinians to immigrate to the East Bank. The resultant growth in the number of workers in Amman led the society to open a branch in the capital on February 18, 1951, but under the name of the Jordanian Arab Workers' Society. The government wasted no time in closing the society on the grounds that East Bank law did not permit the establishment of labor unions. In the meantime, after successful PAWS strikes against the Khalifah Mechanical Company, the governor of the Nablus area exiled Khuffash and another trade unionist for six months. However, popular reaction forced King 'Abdallah to rescind the order after only three months, and Khuffash returned to Nablus on February 2, 1951. Shortly thereafter, the government closed the PAWS's offices and confiscated all its assets.[5]

Regime opposition drove underground, but did not crush, the labor movement. Activists continued to work secretly under the auspices of other organizations (such as al-Nadi al-'Arabi) and held their meetings in private homes. Zaki al-Shaykh Yasin, another activist from Nablus, who served as head of the Federation of Trade Unions in Jordan (FTUJ) from 1958 to 1960, during this period held meetings in his home and paid organizing expenses out of his own pocket.[6]

In early January 1952, no doubt in deference to regime sensitivity to the use of the word "Palestine," the society changed its name to the Jordanian Arab Workers Society. Subsequently, there was a flurry of correspondence between Nablus and workers in Amman who finally opened an office in the Jordanian capital in February 1952.[7] To thwart anticipated regime opposition, the trade unionists contacted the International Labor Organization and complained about the government's refusal to permit free trade union activity. During an investigative visit by a representative of the International Labor Organization, Khuffash arranged several secret meetings for the investigator with nationalist workers. Pressure from the federation combined with the slightly more liberal policy of Prime Minister Fawzi al-Mulqi finally culminated in the promulgation of Jordanian Labor Law Number 35 of 1953, which legalized labor unions (although it outlawed their involvement in politics).[8]

Given the official green light, workers wasted no time in organizing. The first sectors to receive permission to found unions included the tobacco, construction, and Singer sewing machine workers (headed by Ba'this) and the tailors, shoe workers, and phosphate workers (led by Communists).[9] On July 25, 1954, the FTUJ was officially registered, led by Zaydan Yunis, a dedicated labor activist of modest origins from Jaffa who was a liberal, but an independent.[10] New unions sprang up quickly, and by mid-1956 thirty-nine unions counted more than fifty branches throughout the kingdom. Membership jumped from 465 in 1954–55 to 9,128 in 1956, although the growth slowed markedly in the next few years. By 1958–59, the ranks had risen to only 9,832,[11] presumably owing to the restrictions imposed by the government against virtually all organizations in the wake of the attempted coup of 1957.

Despite the union's name, the working class in Jordan—both the East and West banks—was overwhelmingly Palestinian. However, many of the Palestinians who were active in the movement were members of the Communist party and considered themselves part of the Jordanian working class.[12] Whatever their own sense of identity, the leadership of the labor movement in Jordan remained almost exclusively the preserve of workers of Palestinian origin until after the 1970 civil war.[13]

The goals of the FTUJ closely resembled those of the PAWS, its predecessor. They emphasized workers' rights as well as their social and economic interests.[14] When compared with the goals stated in the GUPW constitution, the absence of political content from the Jordanian federation's constitution is striking. In Jordan, especially on the West Bank, Palestinians were on home turf and were therefore in a position to push for wage and labor law concessions. More important, the regime permitted nothing further, nothing vaguely political, and at times worked to undermine the union's position.

To increase effective monitoring and control there were attempts by some in the government to transfer authority for trade union registration and supervision from the Ministry of Social Affairs to the Ministry of the Interior.[15] The government also attempted to prevent labor leaders from attending conferences as proven by a letter from the FTUJ to the Ministry of Social Affairs and Labor dated September 30, 1967, in which the union complained of government interference and attempts to prevent its members from traveling.[16]

Despite government interference to discourage political activity, the overwhelmingly Palestinian composition of the working class meant that the union could hardly avoid the Palestine question. The workers had opposed the Jordanian annexation of the West Bank but had been unable to prevent it. By the time the issue of Jordan's joining the Baghdad Pact arose (1955), the workers' suit had improved. Strengthened by an increasingly anti-Western ally, Egypt's President Nasir, the workers participated—albeit in an unofficial capacity—in demonstrations and strikes against the proposed pact. Union headquarters often hosted meetings to plan antipact demonstrations. Another opportunity for workers to express their national sentiment came during the 1956 Suez War when, in near public support for Egypt, they formed committees to back the Egyptian position.[17]

The FTUJ's boldest political move came in 1956 when it called for a boycott of American vessels after U.S. dockworkers announced their intention to boycott Egyptian ships following Nasir's closure of the Suez Canal to Israeli shipping. This time, however, in the regime's view, the union had exceeded the bounds of acceptable political involvement and it forbade the boycott. Verbal blustering could be tolerated, but Jordan depended too heavily upon food imports from the U.S. to permit a real boycott. Following the incident, the government rounded up major union figures, in particular, the Communists. In general, however, the atmosphere under the Nabulsi government (October 1956–April 1957) encouraged trade union expansion as well as its participation in the national movement.[18] The unrest that followed the dismissal of the Nabulsi government and the subsequent imposition of martial law (which was lifted only to be reimposed in 1958) brought the period of expansion and activism to a grinding halt.

In addition to the political constraints, the regime's stipulation that the headquarters of the federation be in Amman—despite Nablus' natural claim—worked against labor union development. Permission for any kind of activity, even a simple party or exhibition, had first to be obtained from Amman. At times, the distance from Amman worked in the favor of the West Bank unions, because they operated in a completely Palestinian environment. In general, however, the government thwarted attempts to assert greater independence from the center.[19] According to one list, of twenty-eight unions registered through July 1956, only six had headquarters on the West Bank and of those, three were not members of the federation. Of those headquartered on the East Bank, only two had West Bank branches.[20] Another source, listing unions established through September 1955, named only three of twenty-five unions as having West Bank headquarters. Of those with East Bank headquarters, only three had West Bank branches.[21]

The FTUJ and the General Union of Palestine Workers

The political differences between Jordan and Egypt, the competition over the same constituency, as well as some personality clashes rendered the initial GUPW-FTUJ relationship a rocky one.[22] The FTUJ had been in operation for nine years before exiled Husni al-Khuffash pushed from Cairo for the establishment of the GUPW. Khuffash had left Jordan for political asylum first in Syria and then in Egypt following the events of April 1957 and claims in his memoirs that the Jordanian federation tried to block the establishment of the GUPW.

In March 1964 FTUJ president Wajih Manku, not a government man, but one who had been encouraged by the government to run for office,[23] had proclaimed his federation's willingness to assist in the establishment of a union of Palestinian workers. But the FTUJ's subsequent actions contradicted Manku's words. One incident involved the July 1964 IFATU educational symposium in Gaza that was to be convened in order to draft a GUPW constitution and set goals and principles. Despite an April 1964 GUPW announcement of its willingness to cooperate with the FTUJ and its promise not to attempt to organize Palestinian workers in Jordan, the FTUJ delegation to the symposium strongly criticized the young GUPW for damaging the Palestinian workers' movement. The FTUJ sent a letter to the IFATU in which it stated that it did not recognize the GUPW and suggested the form the GUPW should take in order to receive FTUJ recognition. It accused the GUPW of poisoning the prevailing friendly relations between Egypt and Jordan and, Khuffash claims, the FTUJ urged the trade unions in Gaza not to join the GUPW.[24]

Shuqayri had invited several Palestinian worker representatives from Jordan—Muhammad Jawhar (who was later appointed by the Jordanian government as the first "observer" in the FTUJ, a position from which he later moved to become the first "government man" to preside over the union),[25] FTUJ president Wajih Manku, and Sami Kharuf—to the first meeting of the PNC (late May 1964), at which the PLO was established. Several other activists (Communists) were invited, but the Jordanian regime prevented them from attending.[26] Later, in April 1965, Muhammad Jawhar made an uninvited appearance at the first conference of the GUPW (in Gaza) and, according to Khuffash, worked to undermine the conference.[27] On the other hand, Wajih Manku, an invited guest, warmly greeted the establishment of the GUPW in his address, and announced, presumably on behalf of the FTUJ, solidarity and intention to cooperate with the GUPW. He stressed that they were all "soldiers of sacrifice waiting the hour of uprising in order to regain their usurped right to Palestine."[28]

The records of the second conference of the GUPW (April 1967) make only passing references to Jordan. The delegates condemned the Hashemite regime several times; however, the record of activities mentions a trip made by Khuffash to Jerusalem in order to confer with the PLO's

DPO and after which he visited the FTUJ chapters in Amman, Zarqa', and Nablus.[29] Given the regime's closing of the PLO offices in 1966 it is likely that relations between the two remained strained.

In the wake of the 1967 war, the government was forced to loosen slightly its reins of political control. As a result of the greater freedom and the resultant rise in power of the PRM, the GUPW consulted the FTUJ about forming a united council to coordinate the national struggle.[30] In Cairo, on July 23, 1969 in conjunction with members of the PLO's DPO, the two unions reached an agreement and on August 4, 1969 they announced the formation of the Arab Palestinian Office for Supporting the Steadfastness of Workers in the Occupied Territories.[31] The office included four representatives from each of the two unions and one representative from the DPO.

While the labor movement certainly benefited from the surge in organizational freedom that accompanied the rising power of the PRM, the record of its overall achievements during the 1968–1970 period is mixed. In terms of solving workers' problems, the resistance served to distract and fragment more than assist. It led workers in Jordan to attempt to solve their problems through the *fasa'il* and their auxiliary organizations. For example, if a worker had a problem, rather than seeking to solve it through his particular trade union, he would often go to the "workers' bureau" of the *tanzim* of his choice: in other words, instead of going to the Union of Bank Employees, he would go to Fateh or the Democratic Front. This situation resulted in large part because of the general weakness of the unions.[32]

During the 1970 civil war, the FTUJ called for reconciliation between the PRM and the government so that the *fida'iyyin* might maintain their bases in the country. As a result of its stand, following the defeat and expulsion of the resistance, the regime dissolved the union's executive committee and appointed a new one. Adjustments were also made in the union's constitution in order to guarantee the government easier access and greater influence. Throughout the labor movement the government pushed for leadership positions candidates more sympathetic to Hashemite interests—primarily, but not exclusively, East Bankers, who had entered the work force in greater numbers in the 1960s.[33]

Post-1970 Developments

The history of the Jordanian labor movement since 1970 has been one of a constant struggle on the part of the unions to hold off or thwart government attempts at encroachment.[34] The first significant post-1970 development was the gradual introduction of foreign workers into the labor market to take the place of Jordanians and to break what little power some unions enjoyed. A notable case was that of the textile workers' union, which was controlled by the Jordanian Communist party and which had been very active in demanding improved working conditions. In 1972 the union struck the Jordan Textile Company. Muhammad Jawhar, who had left his post as head of the FTUJ in 1971, was brought in by the government to settle the matter. As a result of his efforts, members of the union were dismissed and Filipino and other foreign workers were brought in to take their place. Although there is no law in Jordan forbidding the organizing of foreign workers, there is a decision of the Ministry of Labor (established in 1975) to that effect that serves the same purpose.

Other measures taken to weaken the labor movement included the revision of the FTUJ constitution and the Labor Law, both of which gave the regime sweeping new interventionary powers. According to the structure of the FTUJ, each union was represented in the federation's central council according to the size of its membership. Before 1972 a union could have as many as, but not more than, six members on the council. According to the new amendment that number was upped to twelve. Since some of the larger unions already cooperated with the government and other unions, with assistance, could doctor their membership lists so as to appear to have more members, the number of representatives on the central council who would be supportive of the regime increased dramatically. The revision of the Labor Law empowered the cabinet to issue decrees to dissolve unions and gave the Ministry of Social Affairs (under whose jurisdiction the trade unions fell) the right to redivide and reorganize unions.

The labor movement was given a reprieve of sorts in 1973. Increasing regional tensions, the situation of "no peace, no war," and their culmination in the 1973 war led to a reemergence of nationalist forces in Jordan, nearly dead or dormant since the expulsion of the PRM. The revival of these forces led to increased worker activity as well.

Two institutional developments confirmed the renewed importance of the labor movement. In 1974 a special bureau was opened by the *mukhabarat* to monitor the workers. In 1975 a separate Ministry of Labor was established. As the number of strikes for improved labor and living conditions increased, the regime, under pressure from management, pushed in 1976 for another amendment to the Labor Law. The new provision empowered the minister of labor to reorganize unions without even consulting the FTUJ; the opportunity was used to crush the influence of the Communists.

When these measures did not work to the regime's satisfaction, more direct forms of influence were used. In some cases potential candidates were "persuaded" not to run. Trade union activists were also routinely imprisoned and the number of dismissals of activists from their jobs increased.[35] In one case, individuals who constituted an entire election list were held in a room until elections were over; it was announced that the list had withdrawn from the election. When there were problems at the Jordan Ceramic Factory, the *mukhabarat* came and closed the facility. The workers were then given the choice of burning their union membership cards or going to jail.

By the mid-1980s the government had gained control of most unions. In conditions of high unemployment in the country and greatly diminished opportunities in the Gulf, the most effective threat against activist workers is dismissal. Employers have no trouble replacing these employees, and at a lower wage. The specter of loss of job simply for attending a union meeting is more than many Jordanians are willing to risk for a trade union movement which to date has been weak and largely ineffective.

Thus, the workers' movement in Jordan has never played a powerful role in the country's political life. Despite the arrival in the 1950s of seasoned Palestinian trade unionists and their integration into the leadership structure, the labor movement's successes have been few. Part of the problem lies in the absence of a pre-1948 labor union tradition on the East Bank. Further exacerbating the problem is the continued strength of traditional and family ties, which tend to obscure class awareness. In addition, a large percentage of the labor force is employed in sectors where the regime has outlawed union organizing. In the public sector, employment is conditional upon clearance from the *mukhabarat*, something a worker with an activist past is unlikely to receive. Most important, however, has been the on-going active regime opposition to effective and independent labor organizing.[36]

THE WOMEN

Ignorance, poverty, and sickness—these were listed by 'Isam 'Abd al-Hadi, a leading figure in the Palestinian women's movement, as the three major enemies of women. She hastened to add, however, that even if Palestinian women succeed in overcoming these adversaries, another problem, the lack of a *bayt* (home) remains.[37] Palestinian women have and continue today to struggle for rights not just as women but also for political rights as Palestinians.[38]

Women's involvement in the Palestinian national movement dates to the early days of the British mandate.[39] In 1921, Palestinian women organized a march to the home of the British high commissioner in Jerusalem during which they voiced their demands that the economic pressures on Palestinian peasants be eased, further land sales to Jewish immigrants be prevented, the immigration of Jews to Palestine be halted, political prisoners be released, and the Balfour Declaration be canceled.

In 1929, growing women's organizing led to the founding of the Arab Women's Society (AWS), which subsequently changed its name to the Palestinian Arab Women's Society, headquartered in Jerusalem. Between 1936 and 1948, women established some 200 societies throughout Palestine to deal with such problems as illiteracy, child care, the blind, and the handicapped. At the same time, women regularly participated in marches and demonstrations, and sent cables to mandate officials to protest official policy. Thus, from the beginning, the Palestinian women's movement combined humanitarian and political work in the service of the national cause. Beginning in 1947, with partition and armed conflict looming, the women's societies opened centers to teach civil defense—the use of weaponry and first aid.[40]

During the war and immediately thereafter, women's activity focused on humanitarian concerns. Schools and churches as well as society headquarters were converted into centers to care for children and the wounded. Women helped establish hospitals and clinics, both permanent and temporary facilities, to address the tremendous need for medical care. These societies continued to assist the Red Cross until UNRWA assumed responsibility for providing refugee relief.[41]

Some societies on the West Bank continued to operate after the war. However, with the annexation of the territory to Jordan in 1950, the adjective "Palestinian" had to be dropped from the name of the Women's Society and political considerations forced activity to retreat to the social and humanitarian realm. The Arab Women's Society continued to exist as a federation of societies based in West Bank towns and villages that assisted the Jordanian government in providing basic services to those in need, but it withdrew from direct involvement in the national cause. Women's activity remained Palestinian in content, if not in name, in the sense that on the West Bank, it served the needs of Palestinians. However, with almost all the societies located in cities or large towns, activity where it was most desperately needed—in rural areas and the refugee camps—was minimal.[42]

In the 1950s and early 1960s, women committed to political work joined one of the illegal political parties: the Communist party, the Ba'th, the Arab Nationalist Movement, and, somewhat later, Palestinian underground organizations like Fateh. But their numbers were very small. In 1964, the establishment of the PLO sparked a resurgence of interest among women in organizing. During 1965, the government licensed fifteen new women's societies, although a number of them had begun to operate unofficially well before their registration dates.[43]

The first step toward organizing a unified structure to include all the Palestinian women's organizations that had been established across the diaspora was taken in a February 1965 meeting held in the office of the AWS in Jerusalem. The meeting, convened in response to a call from the AWS president Zulaykha al-Shihabi, assembled representatives from women's organizations in Jerusalem, Nablus, Bethlehem, al-Birah, Tulkarm, and Jenin. The delegates agreed upon a structure for a preparatory committee for a federation that would include representatives of Palestinian women's groups throughout the Arab world.

The committee, which comprised Palestinian representatives from Jordan, Gaza, Kuwait, Syria, and Egypt, met in the headquarters of the AWS in Jerusalem on March 18, in order to review the steps necessary for holding a conference of Palestinian women. The delegates elected Zulaykha al-Shihabi president and Samirah Abu Ghazalah secretary. They then called for a meeting to be held in July 1965 in Jerusalem to unite the diverse organizations in a single federation, the General Union of Palestinian Women. The preparatory committee drafted a constitution, an agenda for the conference, a plan for a budget, and recommendations for topics to be studied. Invitations to the conference were extended to well-known women from all over the world.[44]

With the assistance of the PLO's DPO, the conference opened the morning of July 15, 1965 in Jerusalem. Among the notable recommendations of the conference were that the union be recognized as the only legitimate agency to represent Palestinian women; that the PLO consider the GUPWom one of its popular bases; and that the PLO executive guarantee women's representation of all forms and in all fields.[45] The rest of the resolutions did not differ substantially from the overwhelmingly political recommendations published by the other popular organizations.

On July 20, 1965, the conference elected an administrative council, the agency responsible for the day-to-day operation of the union. Among its members were the following Palestinians living in Jordan where, according to the constitution, the union had its seat (if no official branch): president, 'Isam 'Abd al-Hadi; vice-president, Faridah Irshid; secretary, Samihah Qabj Khalil; secretary of external relations, Aminah al-Husayni; secretary of internal relations, Nuhayl 'Uwaydah; treasurer, Lidiya al-A'raj.[46]

Since its founding, the union's fate has been closely tied to that of the PLO.[47] For example, its constitution stipulates that the permanent headquarters of the GUPWom be located in the country that hosts the principle PLO office. At the time of the founding of the union that was Jordan. When the Jordanian regime closed the PLO office in 1966, it closed the GUPWom office as well, and GUPWom activities in the country were forced underground. At that point, the Egypt branch assumed the responsibilities of the general secretariat. In 1969, with the rise of the PRM in Jordan the DPO decided to transfer the union's general secretariat authority from Cairo to Amman, the new PLO seat, but the Egypt branch refused to surrender its authority.

Despite the disruption caused by the war and the organizational disorder in the upper levels of the union hierarchy, ground-level activity continued to expand in Jordan. Although a branch of the GUPWom never officially operated in Jordan—the union was never licensed, only the presence of its headquarters was recognized by the government—chapters of the union gradually sprang up throughout the kingdom, from the refugee camps to the cities of Amman, Salt, Irbid, Aqaba, and Karak.

Membership dues, the amount of which varied from town to town, and contributions sustained the union financially, although the Palestine National Fund supplied regular subsidies. In addition, the union raised money through the displays, festivals, and plays it sponsored and from regular bazzaars. It used its income to open vocational training centers, literacy programs, and military training sessions for women. Among its other services, the union carried out a social census and sponsored educational sessions ranging in topic from health care and women's issues to the latest developments in the national struggle. In general, the programs had two goals: to raise women's standard of living through education or training to secure additional income, and to prepare women for a more active role in the national struggle.[48]

During the 1967–1971 period, the union participated widely in international conferences and symposia and thereby played an important informational role. The GUPWom's official organ, al-Tha'irah al-Fi-

lastiniyyah (The Palestinian Revolutionary), which featured articles on cultural topics, recent developments in the national struggle, and issues of particular interest to women, was also produced in Amman. At the same time, the revival and preservation of Palestinian cultural heritage received special attention. Embroidery production, the cornerstone of the program, developed on a wide scale as a means of identity affirmation and greater economic independence.

The development of the woman's role in the national movement cannot be divorced from the expansion of her role in the commando organizations. Although some women had joined outlawed political parties prior to 1967, the rise of the resistance movement in the wake of the 1967 war and particularly after the battle of Karamah in March 1968 sparked an increase in women's participation. Several commando organizations set up separate women's offices. In many cases the women with prior political and often military experience became the union's most active members. By 1969 military training had become a precondition for joining the union. Military camps operated for three months in the summer. Some camps were open—girls and women went during the day and returned home at night—while others were closed—girls, often from Lebanon or Syria, stayed for an extended period. For those who could not attend the military camps, the union offered local training sessions.

According to personal accounts, the often-mentioned dichotomy between camp and noncamp dweller did not limit the ability of the union to operate in the refugee camps during this period. Women who had participated in the pre-1948 women's movement were generally from wealthy families of urban backgrounds. This continued to be the case in the 1950s and early 1960s. After the rise of the commando organizations, the character of the women's movement began to change.[49] The movement by the GUPWom into the camps to include previously excluded village women helped transform the union into a more widely based organization. Many of the new activists came from middle- or lower-middle-class families or from the camps themselves. In this way, the GUPWom narrowed the socioeconomic gap between the leadership and the women whose energies they sought to enlist. Whatever distance remained was largely overcome by the patriotic surge that followed the beginning of military operations carried out by Palestinian *fida'iyyin*.[50]

In August 1969 the union leadership held a meeting to select an administrative council for the unofficial "branch" that had come to operate in Jordan. The general secretariat in Amman focused its efforts on the kingdom, but at the same time, at the request of the DPO, encouraged the formation of branches in Kuwait, Iraq, and Syria. But the clouds of Black September were gathering. Following the "events" of September 1970, only four of the seven members of the general secretariat remained in Amman. The other branches refused to acknowledge the remaining members as constituting a quorum of union leadership, and the union once again found itself in a state of organizational limbo, a situation that lasted until the union was completely reorganized in Beirut in 1974.[51]

Toward A New Framework

Following the ouster of the PRM in 1971, no separate Palestinian unions operated in Jordan.[52] Most of the GUPWom's nonpolitical activities were adopted and continued by charitable or other women's societies. The Society for Family Care, established in 1969, has been particularly successful in reaching women in the refugee camps. The Society of Arab Women in Jordan, founded in November 1970, also stepped in where the GUPWom had been forced to abandon activities. In other cases, the government, the Quakers, or the Mennonites assumed responsibility for ongoing projects.

For those women who preferred to continue to work in a strictly Palestinian setting, even if the work was largely devoid of overt political content, several options remained. The first was the numerous charitable societies associated with a particular Palestinian city or district which had been founded prior to 1970. Others were founded in the post-1970 period, among them: the Nablus Charitable Society (1972), the Bayt Dajan Charitable Society (1973), the Bayt Iksa Charitable Society (1978), the Friends of Jerusalem Society (1978), and the Ramallah Charitable Society (1980). Another option was to become involved in UNRWA schools, either in a teaching or volunteer capacity. Finally, within the camps, women could join or advise youth clubs, which sponsor musical and dance troupes.

The Palestinian focus of this discussion should not obscure the fact that women's activity in Jordan had always included cooperation and coordination between East Bank and West Bank women. Given the fate of Palestinian institutions in 1970, many women accepted that in the future any type of activity in Jordan would have to take place within a joint Palestinian-Jordanian framework. For those women who were determined to stay involved politically, secret activity through the remnants of the political parties that had composed the crushed national movement—the Communists, the DF, Fateh, the PFLP, and the Ba'th—was the only option. Each of these parties, to varying degrees, represented a forum for joint Palestinian-Jordanian participation.

It was not until 1974, with the UN's proclamation of International Women's Year, that a group of Jordanian women—of both East Bank and West Bank origin—met and formed a preparatory committee to celebrate the year. The committee began a concentrated campaign of symposia and memoranda to the government requesting the establishment of a women's union. Approval came in August and the first conference of the Women's Union in Jordan (WUJ) was held in November 1974.

The union stressed the need throughout the kingdom to open branches that would have the freedom to develop their own programs and budgets based on local needs. Branches were founded in Salt, Madaba, Karak, Irbid, Ramtha, Ribbah, and Zarqa'. The number of union members quickly expanded from 50 founders to 3,500, of whom 1,500 belonged to the central branch in Amman. Activities included training in sewing, knitting, embroidery, typing, and the like; literacy classes; operating nursery schools, kindergartens, and children's centers; and holding symposia and various types of social and cultural gatherings. Centers offering these classes and services were set up in many of the refugee camps as well as in some of the smaller and poorer Jordanian towns.[53]

The WUJ leadership included women from a broad range of political affiliations—the Communist party, the DF, the PFLP, Fateh, and some independents—all of whom had a nationalist inclination and who sought to further Palestinian-Jordanian cooperation. The political bent of the union led it to take a real interest in women's concerns. Its efforts to study and improve women's economic, legal, and social status in the kingdom meant WUJ involvement in a variety of political issues, both domestic and foreign, primary among them the Palestine question.

Any activity aimed at lobbying for changes in regime policy, whether in the economy, employment conditions, or the Palestine problem set the union on a potential collision course with the government. An early sign that a confrontation was approaching was the accusation by the Ministry of Development (under whose jurisdiction the WUJ fell) that in international conferences (where the union was particularly outspoken on the Palestine question) the WUJ "took positions antagonistic toward the country." The regime's first concrete move against the union came when the ministry terminated the WUJ's project in the Karak area (the funding for which had already been approved by the Ministry of Labor and the Industrial Development Bank) designed to improve rural women's work and earning opportunities through the establishment of a dairy and a traditional handicraft center.[54]

On February 18, 1981 the union leadership received a letter from the Ministry of the Interior ordering the closure of the union on the grounds that the WUJ had violated its constitution. Union members were shocked. After a lengthy study it became clear that the closure order was not issued for the reasons given. Rather, it was an attempt by the Ministry of Development to restrict the WUJ and bring its activities under the auspices of another women's organization, the General Jordanian Women's Union (GJWU), which the ministry had been working to establish and which was founded just a few days prior to the closure of the WUJ. Two prominent lawyers, Ibrahim Bakr and Faris al-Nabulsi, contributed their time to take the issue to the high court in order to have the closure order rescinded.[55] They succeeded; but the Ministry of the Interior continued to obstruct the union's work and finally froze its activity.[56]

The effective closure of the WUJ and its replacement by an organization closely tied to the regime left Jordanian women with no single, independent framework in which to work. The GJWU has not attempted to reach out to rural or poor women. It has no branches outside the capital and its only center is in downtown Amman, beyond the reach of even the poor of the capital.[57] It is essentially a federation of the various women's organizations, but has no separate program of its own. A woman unaffiliated with a member society may apply for membership as an individual, but she must be approved, something unlikely for women with activist pasts.[58] An indication of the way the GJWU has been viewed outside Jordan is that, unlike the WUJ, it has not been recognized by the General Arab Women's Union.

Jordanian women, Palestinians and East Bankers alike, are thus left little scope for effective action on women's issues. Occasionally, a crisis will move—or, more importantly, allow—them to mobilize. For example, during the 1982 invasion, women representatives of various political parties and organizations gathered at the PLO headquarters and, along with other women activists, founded the Women's Agencies in Jordan, which set up a committee to collect donations of everything from food and clothing to blood, all to be sent to Lebanon. They also called for sit-ins at the Red Cross office to protest U.S. support for Israel and, in 1986, to protest the U.S. bombing of Libya. In all cases, the regime ordered in police to break up the sit-ins.[59]

The regime has been quite successful in closing activist unions and establishing close control over the work of the GJWU. Departicipation appears to be the goal.[60] Certainly the prevailing conservative climate in the country (in large part encouraged by the government), which censures women for many activities outside the home, has made achieving departicipation even easier. Politicized women continue their activities in secret in anticipation of the time they feel sure will come, when greater opportunities for organizing and mobilizing women will emerge.

THE PALESTINE RED CRESCENT SOCIETY

As a country overburdened with refugees and underendowed with natural wealth, Jordan did not possess financial resources sufficient to develop a country-wide network of medical facilities. UNRWA health services alleviated the problem, at least among the refugee camp residents, but were in no way adequate for larger community needs: a refugee camp was usually visited two or three times a week by a single doctor who could offer only limited medicines and minimal services. At the same time, the cost of health care in the few hospitals the kingdom had was prohibitive for refugees[61] as well as for many of Jordan's other East Bank and West Bank poor. The problem of insufficient services grew more acute with the rise of the PRM, which needed additional medical facilities to care for wounded *fidaʾiyyin*.

A small group of Palestinian doctors who worked with the refugees first conceived of the idea of special health facilities for Palestinians. In the beginning, headquartered in Salt, the operation which later became known as the Palestine Red Crescent Society called itself Fateh Medical Services. The three main personalities involved in the operation at the time were Fathi ʿArafat, ʿUmar Saltawi, and Mahmud Hijazi.

After 1967, hospitals counted increasing numbers of men who had been wounded during Israeli raids on the Jordan Valley or in *fidaʾiyyin* operations against Israeli targets. Jordan had no blood bank at the time and given the increased need for blood the Fateh doctors approached some women, who as part of their work with charitable organizations regularly visited the sick and wounded in local hospitals, and asked them to organize a program of regular blood donation. Fateh then bought the facilities needed for a blood bank and established it on the grounds of the Salt hospital.[62]

Although run by Fateh, the facilities offered treatment to Palestinians and Jordanians alike. Services were available free of charge; however, as a sign of appreciation or payment, women sometimes brought embroidery to the medical services' office. Their offerings marked the beginning of the PRCS program for the production, display, and marketing of embroidery as a means of securing additional income and reviving and preserving Palestinian cultural heritage.[63]

Since the group's only facilities (a simple office and a few beds) were in Salt, the doctors asked volunteers to look into the possibility of expanding by renting a building in Amman. After finding a suitable building the medical services staff set about recruiting volunteers and soliciting contributions. Seeking to develop services both horizontally and vertically, they contacted Palestinian and Jordanian specialists in the fields of health, social work, information, administration, and planning. Many came to serve as both paid and volunteer staff.[64] No sooner had the Amman center been established than it opened a pharmacy, a social center, and an information and administration office.

News of the existence of the medical services spread by word of mouth and soon the office had more volunteers and medicine than it could use. Fateh's first popular clinic was built in Marka camp (on the outskirts of Amman) with the assistance of boys and girls from the camp. (After receiving training from medical personnel, these young people helped to fill the need for medical support cadres.) The large quantities of pharmaceuticals contributed from a variety of sources led the doctor activists to open additional clinics—with government permission—throughout the kingdom, so as not to waste the medicine.[65]

Doctors who volunteered were posted to around-the-clock duty at the clinics. In many places, especially in the south and the Jordan Valley, no medical facilities had existed prior to the opening of the clinics: doctors had simply not wanted to go there. However, given the surge of enthusiasm and pride in the PRM, for Fateh, for "the cause," young doctors were willing to volunteer a year of service in the out-of-the-way posts in exchange for only food and housing.

The medical services established its first nursing school in 1968 in the Abna' al-Shuhada' school in Amman. Students graduated into staff jobs at the first Fateh hospital in the capital. In the same year, a school that trained first aid officers was opened in the al-Husayn camp in Amman. In 1969, the first institute for health and social counselors began operations in the capital. In addition to the hospitals, special convalescent centers were opened, and the organization initiated its Social Affairs (Shu'un) Section by setting up permanent and temporary displays of traditional Palestinian handicrafts.

The frequent shelling of the camps and their hospitals taught the

Fateh medical personnel the need to build an underground shelter with a small operating room in each of their centers. The first of these was designed by engineer Yasir ʿArafat and was added to the facilities in Salt. The second was built in Irbid, where the Palestinians faced daily shelling, an experience which also taught them that each hospital had to be self-sufficent in both personnel and supplies.[66]

As the amount and scope of the work increased, the leadership decided to organize committees to avoid oversights or duplication of efforts. It was at this point, in 1968, that the group elected to change its name to the Palestine Red Crescent Society. Fateh members sought official permission to found and operate the society but were told by the government that Jordan was their country and, therefore, that no permission was needed.[67] In 1969, the PNC designated the PRCS the health institution of the PLO. In September of the same year, thanks to the efforts of Mahmud Hijazi, the International Red Cross granted the PRCS observer status.

The rapid expansion of services and the increase in the number of wounded demanded a larger hospital. A three-story building in the Jabal ʿAmman area was rented and PRCS members and volunteers set about to prepare it for use. They contacted Arab and international organizations from which they sought proper furnishings and equipment for the hospital, named Karamah after the March 1968 battle. Gradually, the PRCS began to receive contributions from all over the world in the form of equipment, supplies, and volunteers. Some countries designated a certain number of places in their university medical faculties for Palestinians. Other Arab Red Crescent societies as well as the Red Cross in such countries as the USSR, the People's Republic of China, Bulgaria, Yugoslavia, East Germany, Czechoslovakia, and North Korea donated blood, blankets, medicine, and ambulances.

The PRCS's meteoric rise to prominence contrasted sharply with the record of its Jordanian counterpart, the Jordanian National Red Crescent Society. Founded on December 12, 1947, throughout the years the JNRCS's work was confined to limited relief work, the distribution of food and clothing to needy families, and monitoring cases of families separated by the Arab-Israeli conflict, including prisoners and the missing. On the surface, the PRCS-JNRCS relations were good; in reality, however, the PRCS's swift development created friction between the two even through the PRCS took care to consult regularly with the Jordanian Ministry of Health.[68]

The rapid growth of the PRCS alongside the PRM created fear among some in Jordan that the far-flung PRCS clinics were being used to recruit *fida'iyyin*. PRCS members flatly deny the charge. Some bedouin did join the *fida'iyyin*, but it was because they were grateful for the services it provided. Fateh even had a camel-riding unit composed of bedouin. It was the Jordanian army—not East Bankers who had benefited from the medical services—that inflicted the damage on PRCS facilities during Black September.[69]

During the civil war, the army looted and destroyed four hospitals, eighteen clinics, seven dental clinics, twenty-four ambulances, numerous pharmacies, and a training center for health care assistants. Losses have been estimated at close to JD500,00 ($1.4 million).[70] With the resistance's retreat to Jarash, a new hospital was established, but when the PRM was finally ousted from Jordan in July 1971, the remaining PRCS facilities were closed and the medical personnel moved on to new headquarters in Lebanon. The Jordanian government made no attempt to revive any of the clinics or hospitals in its name.

Health care in the camps remains inadequate; what is available outside is often prohibitively expensive or, in the case of emergencies, too far away. The lack of facilities or limited access to what facilities do exist remain serious problems in the Hashemite Kingdom, which, ironically, in the mid-1980s is unable to accommodate all of those graduates of medical faculties who are seeking a hospital in which to intern.

[11]
Mobilizing in Education

As we have seen in the case of the workers, the Hashemite Kingdom regarded labor organizing with great suspicion. Even after a visit from the International Labor Organization effectively forced the government's acquiescence in the legalization of unions, the regime reserved the right to restrict the organizing privilege to certain sectors. The government outlawed organizing among teachers on the grounds that the labor law did not apply to public sector workers. Only in UNRWA, in which solely Palestinian employees served a completely Palestinian constituency outside the realm of the government, did teachers effectively exercise the right to form unions. On the other hand, those who were to be educated, the students, posed a threat of a different nature. Because of their traditional interest and involvement in politics, their attempts to organize on any basis, Palestinian or Jordanian, were even more closely monitored and regularly thwarted than were teachers' activities.

THE TEACHERS

In July 1954, the Union of UNRWA Teachers in Jordan was founded with headquarters in Jerusalem and chapters in Jericho, Amman, Bethlehem, Karamah, Hebron, Tulkarm, Nablus, Jenin, and Qalqiliyyah. On April 10, 1955, the Union of Teachers in the Hashemite Kingdom of Jordan followed suit. Headquartered in Amman, it opened branches in Irbid, Nablus, Jerusalem, Hebron, Karak, and Ma'an. Shortly thereafter, on October 16, 1955 another teachers' guild, the Union of Catholic School Teachers in the Hashemite Kingdom of Jordan was born with headquarters in Amman but no regional branches. None of the unions joined the FTUJ and the Union of Teachers in the Hashemite Kingdom was laid to rest by a decision of the prime minister on January 14, 1956 on the grounds that government employees were not permitted to form unions.[1]

The UNRWA teachers' union lived in a legal limbo, neither outlawed nor licensed by either the Jordanian government or by UNRWA. Despite the lack of official licensing, political conditions, especially during the prime ministership of Sulayman al-Nabulsi, enabled the union to grow. At the end of 1957, after the imposition of martial law and the outlawing of all union activity, UNRWA replaced the union with "employees' committees," weakened replicas of their predecessors, and led according to agency design by senior staff, most of whom were not teachers and therefore felt little urgency to press for teachers' demands. Nonetheless, owing to their large numbers, the teachers gradually regrouped and regained their former power in spite of the UNRWA-imposed committee structure.[2]

The catalyst for the establishment of the General Union of Palestinian Teachers did not come until after the 1967 war. In 1968 UNRWA attempted to implement a new system called "reclassification of teachers," which contained several disturbing elements. Unlike its treatment of its other employees, according to the new system UNRWA intended to set teachers' wages according to the school level they instructed rather than according to experience. The agency decided that university degrees would no longer be recognized, university graduates would be ineligible to receive teaching appointments, and teachers would no longer receive permanent appointments. A ceiling was placed on promotions and UNRWA decreed that children would be promoted automatically from one grade to the next regardless of achievement.[3]

In addition to the administrative changes, UNRWA attempted to institute curriculum changes. After a review of textbooks, it decided to delete or replace such words as *tahrir* (liberation), *fida'i* (literally, one who sacrifices oneself, the word used by Palestinians for their fighters), and others. Palestinian history as a course was canceled, and the Arabic names of Palestinian towns and villages on maps used in geography classes gave way to their Hebrew counterparts.[4]

Negative reaction first erupted in Syria, where the UNRWA employees completely rejected the new system. In early 1968, UNRWA teachers in Lebanon followed suit and called a strike which lasted a month. During the course of the strike, representatives from each school were selected and together were called the "teachers' delegation," but the delegation eventually brought the strike to an end. A new leadership was then formed which attempted another strike. However, the teachers were unable to take a united stand; the work stoppage remained partial and ended in failure.[5]

In Jordan, the teachers reacted to the proposed changes by forming a committee which met with UNRWA and government officials, but which came away from the meetings empty handed. The five-member committee, elected from representatives of all UNRWA schools on the East Bank, comprised Husayn al-Ajrab, president, along with ʿAbdallah Musa, ʿUmar Saʿid Ismaʿil, Jumʿah Naji, and Ahmad Luhaydi. To emphasize their rejection of the new system the committee voted to call a two-day teachers' strike, the first in Jordan since 1956, beginning May 14, 1968. The two-day strike, which coincided with the anniversary of the establishment of the State of Israel, aimed at pressuring UNRWA. The teachers opted for a strike of limited duration because the end of the school year was at hand and they wanted to avoid penalizing the children for teacher militancy.[6]

Although the strike was limited to the East Bank, it affected UNRWA teachers elsewhere. East Bank representatives made direct contacts with teachers in Lebanon, Syria, and the West Bank who chose delegates to join their counterparts in Jordan in a larger teachers' council which then warned the UN that failure to respond to their demands would precipitate an open strike.

During the summer that followed, the teachers held meetings with UNRWA representatives in Beirut but, despite promises to the contrary, the agency's position did not change. At the same time, the teachers continued to organize and expand contacts so that they returned for the new year in a far stronger position. With their demands still unaddressed, on September 20 they proclaimed an open strike that included UNRWA schools in Jordan, Syria, and Lebanon. The Arab Teachers Federation (ATF) quickly responded by lending its support as did several Arab newspapers. After only one week, the agency opened negotiations with the teachers' council. The talks lasted three weeks and won for the striking educators 80 percent of their demands.

The PLO's DPO had been monitoring the conflict between UNRWA and the teachers. After the strike succeeded, Faruq al-Qaddumi, then head of the DPO, contacted the teachers' committee and worked with interested teachers to draft a constitution and bylaws for the General Union of Palestinian Teachers, which was proclaimed on January 1, 1969. Thus, the impetus for founding the GUPT came from above, although the basis for the union was clearly in place. The structural elaboration of the union followed.[7]

Shortly after the formation of the GUPT, the Communist party pushed for the establishment of the General Union of Jordanian Teachers. Several of the leaders of the Jordanian union, notably Radwan Khuraz and Dr. ʿUmar al-Shaykh, were Palestinians. The Jordanian government backed the GUJT, to the degree it backed any union, because of its

Jordanian rather than Palestinian focus. The Jordanian government never officially licensed or recognized the GUPT, but the union did enjoy a de facto recognition in the form of Jordanian government ministries' cooperation with it.[8]

At the end of July 1969, the DPO contacted some of the UNRWA teachers in Jordan and requested them to attend a conference for Arab teachers in Alexandria, Egypt in order to gain GUPT entry into the Arab Teachers Federation. The GUPT did gain membership in the ATF, but not without a battle. Controversy arose over the issue of membership for both the GUPT and the GUJT. Both sought to join, yet given their overlapping constituencies, the ATF could admit only one. The fact that the Jordanian government had selected Palestinians to represent the GUJT exacerbated the situation. Had the Jordanian union sent East Bank delegates both unions might have joined. Instead, the conference voted in favor of the GUPT and not the GUJT. In any case, the conflict's significance soon disappeared since with the expulsion of the Palestinian resistance from Jordan in 1971 both unions collapsed.[9]

In the meantime, after the delegation's return to Jordan, the DPO named a GUPT general secretary and requested that the members of the Alexandria delegation enlist in the union's general secretariat. Although some declined, the others began their work by appointing preparatory committees in a number of countries with concentrations of Palestinian teachers. These committees were responsible for coordinating elections for local branches.[10] By the end of 1969, the general secretariat had formed preparatory committees in Syria, Jordan, and Kuwait; in early 1970, committees were appointed in Iraq, Egypt, Algeria, and Morocco.[11]

On the ground level in Jordan, each school elected a committee. The committees, in turn, selected regional delegates who nominated countrywide representatives. Active GUPT members came only from UNRWA schools. Palestinians teaching in government schools were allowed to join, but according to Jordanian government policy, could not serve in leadership positions.

The development of the GUPT branch in Jordan was cut short by the 1970–71 civil war. Despite its short life it could boast numerous achievements. It established and equipped, although never had the opportunity to operate, the Abna' al-Shuhada' School. Like its sister organizations, it sponsored numerous displays to highlight or promote Palestinian heritage. The branch took a special interest in encouraging and displaying children's artwork, and initiated literacy programs directed primarily at women. Held in the Jabal al-Husayn area, the literacy sessions lasted three months and employed a simplified curriculum aimed at teaching the basics of reading and writing.

From 1969 to 1971, the UNRWA teachers' committee took a backseat to the GUPT. According to one representative, the work of the committee (work for teachers' labor demands) all but stopped. When the resistance left Jordan, the GUPT leadership fled to Syria. In its first meeting following the 1971 exit of the resistance, the PNC called for an end to separate Palestinian institutions in Jordan—more a confirmation of the reality than a new development. Immediately thereafter, the name of the GUPT branch reverted to the UNRWA teachers' committee. The committee has continued to serve as the GUPT affiliate in Jordan, although it is no longer a branch in name.[12]

In 1972, UNRWA teachers reinvigorated the committee system and again concentrated on addressing work-related demands.[13] Although the GUPT leaders had fled, middle-level members remained and continued to work secretly. Through these unofficial members in Jordan, the teachers' committee works to implement GUPT policies. When the GUPT holds a conference, members of the UNRWA committee attend: the 1984 GUPT conference in Aden hosted twenty UNRWA teachers from the East and West banks. The GUPT executive committee has five members from Jordan, but their names are not officially known. The degree to which these unofficial GUPT members are free to participate in union activities outside the country depends upon the state of PLO-Jordanian relations.[14]

The most basic difference between the days of open GUPT activity and the post-1970 period is that since 1970 any activities and demands must be completely labor oriented. Not even a hint of the political is tolerated. The teachers are certain that any attempt on their part to extend their activity to the political realm would result in a clampdown on the UNRWA committees. The committees have not even tried to celebrate Palestinian national days, for fear of thereby being forced to celebrate Jordanian national days as well.

Even so, the teachers have little if any leverage, and UNRWA is often able to ignore their demands for improvements or reforms by arguing that it is suffering financial problems. Strikes are out of the question, for the government cannot afford to jeopardize its relationship with UNRWA, one of its financial lifelines. A strike in this sector would be viewed as a security issue and would be suppressed immediately.

Until 1979, if complaints arose, a working team, composed of teachers from all areas of UNRWA operation, would discuss common problems, and agreement with the agency would be reached through a memorandum of understanding. After 1979, however, UNRWA insisted than any further changes had to be based on a comprehensive study comparing conditions in the private and government sectors. At first the teachers rejected such a study. Finally, with the participation of the International Civil Service Commission a complete study was carried out. Its findings ruled in favor of the teachers and it made numerous recommendations. To date, UNRWA has not taken steps to implement the recommendations. The major problems were and continue to be low salaries and the issue of termination benefits.

Labor-related demands of teachers in Jordan appear unlikely to be addressed in the near future. Even during the days of the PRM's protective support, political concerns overwhelmed issues like wages and working conditions. Even with the departure of the resistance and a return to a concentration on nonpolitical issues, the government continues to forbid effective teacher organizing. Teachers constitute perhaps the largest professional sector in the kingdom and their work conditions are among the poorest. If allowed, they would likely become vocal in expressing their demands for improvement. More serious from the regime's point of view, the potential influence of each teacher must be multiplied by thirty, forty, or fifty—depending upon how many children he or she teaches.

THE STUDENTS

As we have seen with the other popular organizations, the Palestinians' status in Jordan as full citizens renders difficult, and in many cases erroneous or artificial, discussions of them as separate from other Jordanians. While the history of Jordanian student activity outside the Hashemite Kingdom may be divided into separate East Bank and West Bank components, the same is not true inside, and it is the history of the movement inside on which this discussion focuses.[15]

Prior to 1962, the absence of universities in Jordan meant that the kingdom, at least internally, was free of student organizing on the university level. This did not mean that secondary students or students in training institutes were quiescent. Given the constraints of the time— the prohibition against unions as well as political parties—students who wanted to take an activist role usually participated secretly in one of the illegal political parties.

In 1953 (the same year that labor organizing was legalized in Jordan) with encouragement and support from the Communists and the Baʿthis, Jordanian students convened their first conference. Held in Amman despite regime opposition, the Conference of Jordanian Students discussed a variety of student concerns and elected a leadership composed of independents and those associated with the Communist and Baʿth parties. Among the recommendations and resolutions of the conference were: the right of students to form a union; free education for all; and the establishment of a national university.

This conference was the beginning of wider student activity. Following it most of the governorates of both banks held public conferences and elected local student committees. These committees played an important role in leading the student struggle and in organizing marches and demonstrations against the regime and its connection to U.S. and British policies in the region. (The president of the 1953 conference was killed during a demonstration in Amman.)[16] Among the demands were the dismissal of the British officers serving in the country, mass mobilization, and arming the people as a response to recurring Israeli raids. Throughout the nationalist surge of the mid-1950s the students were in the forefront of organized political activity; however, the major focus of their activity was political, as strictly educational or academic demands took a backseat.

After the events of 1957, student activists took their place alongside others in Jordanian jails. Thus ended the period of open and organized student work. The students were stripped of their right to an elected student union to represent them and oversee their interests. Nevertheless, they remained one of the most active groups, always in the forefront of marches and demonstrations related to the Palestine question. For example, in 1963 the students marched, demanding that Jordan join the announced union of Syria, Egypt, and Iraq. Their slogan was: La dirasah wa-la tadris, illa bi-wihdah maʿa al-Raʾis (No study or instruction unless there is unity with the President [ʿAbd al-Nasir]). Tens of students were killed or wounded in these demonstrations. Again in 1966 following the Israeli raid on the Hebron district town of al-Samuʿ, students took to the streets demanding arms to confront Israeli raids.

During the 1957–1967 period, it was outside of Jordan that the greatest development took place in open student organizing on the university level. In late 1959, following the founding of the General Union of Palestine Students, the General Union of Jordanian Students was also founded in Cairo. It was the GUPS, not the GUJS, that the majority of Palestinians from Jordan joined; the GUJS was primarily for native East Bankers. The GUJS closely followed the GUPS and in fact called itself a base of the Palestinian revolution. It took slogans and programs from the GUPS and after 1964, its funding came primarily from the PLO.[17]

However, as happened in the GUPS, the predominance of Ba'this in the GUJS's executive committee in the early 1960s led it into head-on confrontation with the Egyptian regime after the dissolution of the Egyptian-Syrian union. The government expelled the members of the executive committee and closed the GUJS headquarters. With the center crushed, the various chapters of the union in other parts of the Arab world and Europe were forced to operate independently. In the meantime, in 1961–62, another union was established by Jordanian students studying in Eastern Europe, the Jordanian Students Union. (Both the GUJS and the JSU considered themselves offshoots of the 1953 Amman conference.) The GUJS was given new life in Damascus in 1963 only to witness further fracturing in 1966 as a result of the feud between the Syrian and Iraqi Ba'th. Inside the country, it appears that with the help of the DPO, headquartered in Jerusalem (1964–66), the GUPS tried to establish a secret branch in Jordan. Organizers managed to open three chapters—in Jerusalem, Ramallah, and at Jordan University in Amman. However, as they were forced to operate secretly, their activity seems to have been negligible.[18]

The June 1967 war served as a new impetus to student activity. The regime's ignominious defeat forced it to ease its controls and allow a margin of liberalization in order to placate its many critics. The first and most spontaneous form of student expression of discontent took the form of enlisting in one of the numerous Palestinian resistance organizations. Not until February 1968 did a student organization emerge, the Student Struggle Front, at Jordan University; shortly thereafter, both the General Union of Jordanian Students and the Jordanian Students Union began operating openly in the country. However, the general political climate in Jordan and the increasing popularity of the resistance led the student organizations to concentrate on political rather than academic or educational issues. Palestinian political issues took priority; the national democratic struggle for Jordan was overlooked. Activities were limited to organizing marches, issuing communiqués of solidarity with the resistance, and confronting attempts by the regime and the school administration to obstruct their work.

In 1969 and 1970, given the increasing importance of the resistance to the balance of power in the country, the student movement enjoyed its greatest freedom. Greater numbers of students participated, and their participation was more open and effective. They became a force with which the government, university, and school administrations had to reckon. But if the strength of the resistance was the students' greatest asset, it was at the same time a liability. All activity was governed by the vision of the resistance and its constituent *fasaʾil*. This splintered the student movement ideologically and precluded effective coordination: there was the Student Struggle Front (which was founded by friends and members of the Popular Front for the Liberation of Palestine, but after the founding of the Democratic Front it leaned in the direction of that organization and in 1977 changed its name to the National Union of Jordanian Students); the General Union of Jordanian Students; the Jordanian Students Union; the Union of Students of the Two Banks (the USTB, which was launched by Fateh); and thirteen student offices belonging to the *fasaʾil*. Numerous attempts were made to unify student ranks, but to no avail. Neither they, nor any other sector, were able to overcome the political differences that divided the PRM's constituent groups.

A Case Study in Student Activism: The USTB

One student organization that did operate openly in Jordan, albeit for only two years, was the Union of Students of the Two Banks (the East and West Banks) which, as the name indicates, counted both Palestinian and Jordanian members. Owing to the government's ban on student organizations, students had looked to the existing political parties to fill the gap. While each party had its own student group, or, more accurately, its own office for students, the offices had no autonomy, no right of independent decision making.

The impetus to form the USTB came from student members of Fateh, who observed a gradual attrition among the *tanzim*'s Jordanian members. Fateh recruited a committee to study the problem, and it concluded that the organization's program was too particularistic, too Palestinian, to stimulate enthusiasm among Jordanian members. Thus, in 1968, under the slogan of the unity of the two banks, some of the Fateh students formed the USTB. Unlike the other student unions, the group tried to place primary emphasis on students' everyday needs and academic concerns rather than on political issues relating to the national struggle.[19]

The USTB had chapters throughout Jordan, from Irbid to Aqaba. Although the union began among university students, it extended its activity to secondary and preparatory students as well.[20] Administratively, it was divided into two regions: the northern region, with headquarters in Irbid; and the southern region, with headquarters in Amman. In the northern area alone there were some 5,000 members, more than half of them Palestinians.

In Irbid, the leadership felt a strong obligation to deal with student concerns rather than focusing on politics, and it suffered as a result. The Ikhwan tried to control it while the Ba'th and Communists boycotted it because they operated their own student offices. Despite the obstacles, the union not only survived but even managed to assert its independence from Fateh, something that gained for it a de facto if not de jure legitimacy from the authorities.

In the north, the union raised its own money for activities by sponsoring plays, showing films, and soliciting donations from charitable societies. It established a Needy Students Fund which helped to buy school supplies for poor students, and it rented a house to provide lodging for students who came from the countryside to Irbid for high school. With the assistance of the GUPT, it opened a night school for the illiterate. On the political side, the union sponsored lectures and symposia. Spurred on by the formation of the Husayn Youth Movement, in the summer of 1969 the union ran a three-month summer training camp near Salt. Thousands of students from Jordan and beyond who represented the entire spectrum of political factions participated in the camp.

Owing to its location in the capital and thus its proximity to the Palestinian political leadership, the southern area concentrated much more heavily on political activities. It had its cultural, social, and informational side, but was concerned only marginally with students' educational demands. Though the union never joined the GUPS, it did send observer representatives from its general secretariat to GUPS conferences. Primarily in the south, but also in the north, the union depended for its existence upon the protective support of the PLO.

With the exit of the Palestinian resistance from the country in 1971, the union collapsed. Some of its leaders were jailed. Subsequent attempts to revive it in a slightly altered form succeeded in part, but the union was effectively laid to rest in 1974. Despite its short life and limited accomplishments, the USTB stands out among student unions for its notable concern (at least in the northern region) for student needs rather than solely for political stances.

The Need for a New Framework

The exit of the PRM from Jordan in July 1971 meant the end of the protective shield it had offered to a wide range of popular organizing, whether attached to it in name or not. Many were imprisoned for their part, actual or assumed, in the resistance; others fled to Syria and Lebanon. Student organizations on all levels were shut down and political activity was forced underground.[21] The regime and university administration then tried to involve the students in more harmless activities like school trips and parties, while at the same time continuing to round up and detain activist elements.

In early 1972, Jordan University students took to the streets to protest an increase in tuition; but it was not until 1973–74 that sufficient pressure had built up to lead the regime to agree to the formation of the Union of Jordan University Students. While partisans of the DF, the Communist party, and some elements in Fateh believed that this new union should be used to the degree possible to address student needs, others—including the Iraqi Ba'th, the GUJS leadership outside, and some members of Fateh—called for a complete boycott because they saw the union as a means by which the regime could discover which students were members of the secret student organizations.

The former group succeeded in gaining control of the union and in 1974–75 was able to win some academic concessions as well as greater freedom for itself in the university: a headquarters for the union on campus; permission to publish a student magazine, 50 percent of the funding for which was to come from the university; funding for the union from the university; the participation of student representatives from the union on university committees responsible for loans and grants; and the right to establish relations and coordination with Arab and foreign universities. It organized numerous student meetings, most notably a large demonstration on November 23, 1974 in support of both the Rabat decision (regarding the representative status of the PLO) and the uprisings in the occupied territories.

When the government and the university administration were unable to rein in the union or place their supporters in leadership posts, the university issued an order dissolving the union on the pretext that its constitution needed amending. The students protested the move, but to no avail. The activity of the GUJS and the JSU continued throughout vocational institutes, secondary schools, and Jordan and

Yarmuk universities, but all in secret. They were forced to operate through the academic societies (jam'iyyat 'ilmiyyah) attached to each university faculty. In 1975–76 these same student forces managed to reach leadership positions in most of the societies and then strove to increase coordination among the societies to overcome the lack of any other form of open student organizing.

To the degree possible these societies did play an important role. Their "wall magazines" were transformed into political podiums expressing the various political positions of the students. The societies also organized a wide range of political, cultural, and artistic activities inside the university: on March 1, 1976 there was a march in solidarity with the students of the West Bank; on March 30, 1976, the Day of the Land, there was a large festival with more than two hundred students in attendance calling for solidarity with the Palestinians and supporting their right to self-determination; at the same time a "Palestine fund" was established to collect contributions to support students and institutions in the occupied territories. Similar solidarity marches were organized by secondary students and students in vocational institutes. In some cases the students tried to leave their school grounds and take their demonstrations into the streets. These attempts were stopped by the police and the army. Participants were detained; many had their passports withdrawn.

In July 1977 the National Union of Jordanian Students was founded and served to reshape Jordanian student politics both internally and abroad. The NUJS attracted most of the GUJS members in Jordan, as well as the membership of many of the chapters abroad. While there were many differences between the two, the most basic was that the GUJS's program was more like that of a political party, with a high political content, while the NUJS exhibited more concern for students' academic and educational demands.

Meanwhile the students continued to push for the right to have a legal and recognized representative union. Protests erupted at the end of 1977 and in the spring of 1978. The academic year 1978–79 saw a marked increase in student activism in the fields of both political and educational demands, particularly at the two universities. More than fifty were arrested, thirty expelled, and tens more were called in for questioning by the mukhabarat. The students were not dissuaded. They continued their marches, symposia, and sit-ins. The period was characterized by close cooperation between Palestinian and Jordanian students, despite attempts by the authorities to split student ranks. Indeed

East Bankers accounted for more than half of the twenty-two students expelled as a result of the student uprisings of late April 1979, which were in part demonstrations against the signing of the Camp David accords. In addition, several were killed and a number were wounded. The situation in the universities has not changed greatly in the 1980s. The general economic slowdown in the Arab world and the consequent increase in unemployment in Jordan combined with rising tuition costs have, if anything, exacerbated students' concerns. They have also added to student frustrations with the fact that they are effectively prevented from even voicing their discontent, much less organizing to seek solutions. The government's response has been the same. No student organizing is allowed: those suspected of belonging or known to belong to any of the outlawed political parties are called in by the *mukhabarat* for frequent interrogation sessions. If their activities are regarded as too dangerous, they may be expelled from school. This punishment is particularly devastating because there is no appeal, a student may never reregister, and the expulsion order is usually issued just before the student is scheduled to graduate or complete a semester. The appointment of professors is also contingent upon receiving clearance from internal security, and dismissal is also used as a political weapon against faculty.

By the end of 1981, the government had expelled some five hundred students from Yarmuk University, which, probably because of the larger number of less-privileged students enrolled there, had assumed the role of leader of student activism in the country. The first major outburst at Yarmuk came in February 1984, when several thousand students joined in demonstrations that won both curriculum modifications and the reinstatement of some five hundred of their colleagues.

By late 1985 pressures were again building. Student concern over rising tuition, dissatisfaction with the academic program (including the government's failure to completely Arabize classes), and the lack of any meaningful student organization were becoming intolerable. At the same time, student political frustrations rose as Israel bombed the PLO headquarters in Tunis with impunity, Jordanian-PLO cooperation disintegrated, Fateh offices in the Hashemite Kingdom were closed, and a Day of the Land sit-in was held despite regime opposition, as was a sit-in to protest the U.S. bombing of Libya. The last two events resulted in the arrest of a number of students. The combination of academic, economic, and political frustrations led to a sit-in which began on May 11, grew in size, and was finally put down by the state's armed bedouin guards on May 15.[22] At least three students were killed, and many others, wounded, filled Irbid's hospitals or sought refuge with professors or friends on campus.

In the wake of the most violent measures taken against student activism to date, the science faculties were severed from Yarmuk University and incorporated into the new Technology University several kilometers away, on the road to Ramtha. President 'Adnan Badran was dismissed and replaced by a technocrat, Muhammad Hamdan. However, from the regime's perspective the uprising's most disturbing aspects (because of their long-term implications) remained unaddressed: the student participants (estimated at between three and five thousand or about one-third to one-half of the regular matriculating students) represented the entire political spectrum, as Ikhwan members made common cause with Communists. Perhaps even more worrisome for the regime, East Banker and West Banker were struggling, not at cross-purposes, but together.

PART III
Conclusions

[12]
Diversity in Diaspora

National dispersion and occupation, uncertain employment and residency, and the potential of political repression or even physical assault have all characterized the post-1948 Palestinian experience. In the late Ottoman period and then more fully under the British mandate, social and political institutions had gradually evolved which, in the absence of the clash with Zionism over the Jewish National Home, would have led the country to independence and formed the basic political infrastructure of a Palestinian state. Instead, however, Palestinian political development was brutally interrupted; and the period following the *nakbah* required, not just a reassembling of the pieces of the shattered sociopolitical structure of the community, but a new framework capable of mobilizing a once unified, now scattered people to reassert their identity and national rights.

Despite the obstacles, economic conditions and political imperatives led Palestinians in increasing numbers and in changing frameworks in the 1950s and 1960s to join together on the basis of their shared identity rooted in physical displacement and political disenfranchisement. The popular organizations examined in this study developed out of needs and efforts from within the respective communities and, later, from initiatives of the PLO leadership. The goal was to mobilize all members of the diaspora communities to serve the national cause.

The institutions discussed in detail in previous chapters evolved with the aim of preparing broad sectors of the Palestinian population to enter the political struggle as a support and a complement to the military struggle. As the bridge between the vast majority of Palestinians and the "revolution," they were to assume responsibility for creating experienced, capable, and politically aware cadres to lead the political work.[1] In this regard the successes of the popular organizations have been limited. Some have served to recruit *fida'iyyin* and to politicize and provide basic military training to other members of the communities. Depending upon the country, they have helped alleviate the difficult economic, legal, and social conditions in which Palestinians live. They have established consumer cooperatives, vocational institutes, and health and child care centers. They have raised their voices in a variety of international circles and have worked to preserve and revive Palestinian culture.

The history and varying records of accomplishment of these organizations have been detailed in the case studies. Before concluding, it is useful to summarize the major problems they have encountered. The fact of living in diaspora conditions with no sovereign state in which safely and continuously to base activities has been the most serious hindrance to more effective operation of the organizations. The difficulties encountered in traveling from one country to another, communicating between countries, and formulating policies relevant for a people living in diverse social, economic, political, and legal conditions has also complicated and often obstructed Palestinian organizing efforts. As a result some analysts have charged the unions with a preoccupation with conferences and meetings in which they have only an observer role, and with having failed to attend to the needs of the national struggle.[2]

Equally serious is that the popular organizations have suffered from a lack of trained political cadres. Those with experience have often migrated to the Gulf states which, with the exception of Kuwait, have severely restricted Palestinian organizing. Another problem, the leadership's dependence upon the *tanzimat* rather than on the popular unions' membership, has led to the development of a relatively narrow power base which inclines the hierarchy to concern itself more with the interests of their respective *tanzimat* than with those of the union per se. In several instances an obvious gap has developed between leadership and cadres.

The passivity of the members of some unions and during certain periods reflects the weakness of the organizational structures. The failure of the leadership to formulate clear regional and local policies combined with the conflicts that may arise between *tanzim* loyalties and union loyalties has produced a lack of internal cohesion. In a situation where a member's responsibilities may begin and end with paying dues, voting in elections, and celebrating national events, joining a popular union offers no advantages. Indeed, in some countries it may be a political liability.

Another more basic problem exists. Following the 1973 October war, a major split developed in Palestinian political thinking between those who sought a peaceful or negotiated solution and those who believed that armed struggle remained the only road to Palestine. The tendency to seek a peaceful solution combined with the greater bureaucratization of the PLO as it expanded in Lebanon led to a lessening of enthusiasm for the revolution among some of the popular sectors that had formerly participated directly in the armed struggle. In its new headquarters in Lebanon the PLO developed into a bureaucratic quasi-government and the commando groups increasingly resembled regular armed forces rather than the bands of the "people's war" of 1965–1970. Political battles between the *fasa'il* for control of the popular organizations in some cases became more important than the role and activity of the organizations themselves. In certain communities, the result has been popular demobilization. Having noted all the internal faults and errors of these organizations, the most serious limiting factor continues to be the degree of political pressure or repression to which the national movement has been exposed—a factor over which Palestinians have little control.

Despite the harsh criticisms that observers sometimes level at the popular organizations, they did play a pioneering role in the reemergence of a Palestinian national movement and its organizational manifestation, the PLO. The PSU and the GUPS in particular graduated the leadership cadres of the post-1968 PLO. Despite subsequent periods of stagnation, the emergence and elaboration of a national political framework so shortly after the destruction and dispersal of 1947–49 represented a major achievement. The organizational structures remain in place and continue their informational, social, and limited political roles. Changes in regional conditions may spark their reactivation in the future.

A REEXAMINATION OF THE MARGINALITY FRAMEWORK

Chapter 1 suggested that the concept most central to understanding the position of Palestinian diaspora communities in host societies and their mobilization through the elaboration of separate institutional infrastructures is that of marginality. The study has used the term "marginality" to refer to a condition of lack of integration into the political or productive economic structure of the host state. The central argument of the study has been that the greater the degree of economic or political marginality of the Palestinian community to the host society, the greater the likelihood that independent Palestinian institutions may emerge. The emergence of a social or political movement involves three major elements: motive, opportunity, and resources.

The element of motive has a long history in the Palestinian case.

The failure of the British to reconcile competing Zionist and Arab claims to Palestine led them to submit the problem to the United Nations in 1947. The UN finally voted in November 1947 to partition the small British mandate between its Arab and Jewish communities. The massive population displacement that followed the passage of the partition resolution and the increasing military confrontations that ensued led to the expulsion or flight of more than 700,000 Arab Palestinians from their homes. By 1950, the establishment of the State of Israel, the Jordanian annexation of the West Bank, and the Egyptian military occupation of the Gaza Strip combined to exile the word "Palestine" from the political map. However, the disappearance of the word did not mean the end of a Palestinian identity. Indeed, the identity that had begun to be forged at the end of World War I had been further shaped by the experience of the national struggle against Jewish immigration and the application of the Jewish National Home principle in Palestine under the British mandate. The defeat and dispersal of 1947–49 laid the basis for further developments in modern Palestinian political identity. The desire to regain the lost homeland, and the concomitant inability to be absorbed economically or politically by some states or to assert a separate historical experience in others, led to the further evolution of a distinct Palestinian identity that motivated those who shared it to reorganize on its basis.

Feelings of shared identity as a motive constitute a necessary, but not a sufficient cause for Palestinian reorganization. The other necessary elements were opportunity and resources. Opportunity is a function of political freedom to form independent Palestinian organizations. Resources include such elements as preexisting organizational structures and leadership, the availability of people to join, financial means to operate offices, and the like. This study has concentrated on opportunity as the key element. The evidence strongly suggests that the degree of economic or political marginality of the Palestinian community determines in large part the presence or absence of opportunity. The less integral or more marginal the community, the wider the field for organizing allowed by a host state.

The tables on the following pages summarize the components of the concepts of marginality and opportunity. Opportunity has two basic elements: the strength of state coercive power and the degree to which the state is willing to use that power to repress a given group or movement—national or expatriate. The greater the threat posed to the internal stability or external security of the state by the group's organization, and the fewer the benefits on any other level—regional or internal

Table 12.1: Marginality Framework

Country	Internal Political Marginality	Internal Economic Marginality	State Coercive Power
Egypt	High	High	High
Kuwait	Medium	Medium	Medium
Jordan	Low	Low	Pre–1967, high; 1967–1970, low but increasing; post-1971, high.

Determinants of Political Marginality	Determinants of Economic Marginality	Determinants of State Coercive Force
1. Palestinians as % of host state population	1. Palestinians as % of host state population	1. General level of organizing permitted in country
2. % of Palestinians granted citizenship	2. Palestinian place in the work force; economic structure of the Palestinian community	2. Existence of political parties or pressure groups
3. Palestinian representation in bureaucracy	3. Nature of host state economic system	3. Confrontation state?
4. Indirect forms of pressure available: presence in media, schools, etc.		4. Nature of regime
		5. Government censorship of media
		6. Reputation of police or intelligence service

Table 12.2: Determinants of Political Marginality

Country	Palestinian % of Population	% of Palestinians Granted Citizenship	Palestinian Representation in Bureaucracy	Indirect Forms of Pressure
Egypt	.01%	Negligible	Negligible	Student coalitions with sympathetic sectors of Egyptian population
Kuwait	15–20%	Negligible	Substantial; were critical in bureaucratic development	Representation in the media, university, and the professions
Jordan	Pre-1967, 50–66%; Post-1967, at least 50% (not including occupied West Bank)	Almost 100%	Proportional	Sheer size of Palestinian population; concentrations in refugee camps; support from other Arab regimes

Table 12.3: Determinants of Economic Marginality

Country	Palestinians as % of Population	Palestinian Place in Host State Productive Structure	Nature of Host State Economic System
Egypt	.01%	Found in all sectors; no sector of monopoly or particular power	Large agricultural-industrial base post-1974 growing free market orientation
Kuwait	Increasing in 1960s and 1970s to 15–20%	Found in all sectors but only in partnerships; expatriate ownership not permitted	Monoproduct, oil exporter; consumption and import oriented; labor importer
Jordan	Pre-1967, 66%; post-1967, at least 50%	Importance of West Bank capital and human skills; labor force predominantly Palestinian, importance of Palestinian remittances from the Gulf; large Palestinian representation in the professions	Foreign aid dependent; small productive base; concentration in service and "security" sector; labor exporter

Table 12.4: Determinants of State Coercive Power

Country	Con-frontation State‡	Media Censorship	Political Party Activity	Nature of Regime	Reputation of Police or Intelligence	Trade Union and Other Organizing Permitted
Egypt	Yes	Heavy under Nasir; some freedom under Sadat; greater freedom under Mubarak	Only gov't sponsored through early 1970s; gradual emergence of opposition parties since mid 1970s	Authoritarian/military; increasing moves toward greater liberalization under Mubarak	Pre-1970, effective and repressive; degree of repression gradually easing	Elaborate but controlled
Kuwait	No	Moderate/light until 1986; post-1986 greater censorship	National Assembly but no parties; parliamentary blocs emerge periodically	Amirate with vocal National Assembly	Effective, not omnipresent	Variety of Kuwaiti societies and federations
Jordan	Yes	Heavy	Minimal—heavy repression	Monarchy/military bureaucracy	Effective and repressive	Numerous societies; heavy governmental control

stature or legitimacy—that may accrue to the state as a by-product of
the development of the organization, the more likely the regime will
be to use its coercive apparatus to repress separate institutional development.

The evidence suggests that the regime's willingness to exercise
repression is based on the degree of economic or political marginality
of the Palestinian community to the country's productive structure.
As the tables indicate, numerous elements factor into an analysis of a
community's marginality or integration. Furthermore, the factors are
not static. Economic and political developments, both domestic and
external, may alter the marginality of the community. They may also
affect the strength of state coercive power or a state's willingness to
use force against Palestinian organizing efforts. The factors are not easily quantifiable and for that reason, table 12.1 does not attempt to rate
them beyond the high-medium-low distinctions. A more detailed
breakdown would exceed the divisions suggested by the evidence. The
four tables represent a preliminary attempt to design a new framework
for understanding Palestinian–host state relations, not definitive sum-
maries of the political, economic, and security infrastructures of the
host countries.

Each of the case study countries belongs to a category of Arab states
in which Palestinians came to reside after the partition of Palestine.
Many criteria may be chosen according to which to classify and analyze the Palestinian communities. This study has chosen the legal status of Palestinians as the signpost, with the assumption that their legal
status is the surface manifestation of deeper socioeconomic and political conditions in the host states. Such a categorization does not imply
that the treatment or living conditions of Palestinians has been uniform in each of the countries of the same category.

Using legal status as a basis for classification, Egypt represents the
category of countries of first refuge whose members did not enfranchise
the vast majority of Palestinians, although they did issue travel documents. Syria, Iraq, and Lebanon belong in the same category. Kuwait
exemplifies the peninsular Gulf states to which Palestinians migrated
for economic reasons. These states did not offer citizenship or travel
documents (with a few exceptions), nor the prospect of permanent residence. They imported the valuable human capital that the skilled and
educated Palestinians offered to their state-building efforts. Finally, Jordan stands alone in the category of Arab countries that annexed a part
of Palestine and granted citizenship to its residents.

A brief review of each of the case studies in light of these tables reveals the following. Egypt was not faced with a de facto influx of large numbers of refugees in the 1947–49 period. It kept immigration from Gaza to a minimum and those refugees that it did receive it later tried to send back to Gaza. Most of those the government allowed to stay possessed financial resources sufficient to support themselves and their families. Egypt enfranchised only a few, mostly pre-1948 residents or wealthy newcomers, and, at least initially, Egyptian law forbade the new refugees to work. The regime argued that the refugee situation would be of short duration and that to enfranchise the Palestinians would undermine efforts aimed at securing their return or compensation, but a more plausible source of the policy lay in an Egyptian unwillingness to absorb additional numbers of the poor and discontented in a period of economic deterioration and political instability.

Although the 1952 revolution did not lead to an immediate change in Egypt's international or regional position vis-à-vis the Palestinians, Nasir's Arab nationalism, positive neutralism, and revolutionary socialism catapulted him to leadership of the anti-Western Arab camp. Palestinians took note as the political pendulum began to swing in their favor. Although Egypt's Palestinians were few in number (only about 15,000 in 1960), scattered throughout the country, and socioeconomically diverse, it was in Egypt that Palestinians achieved the first major breakthrough in the realm of open, separate reorganizing.

During the Nasir period, much of Egypt's influence with other Arab regimes as well as its popularity with the Arab masses in general depended upon its efforts in pursuit of Arab unity, anti-Westernism, and the liberation of Palestine. Given such a small indigenous Palestinian community, allowing or encouraging the emergence of Palestinian institutions carried great symbolic value and few political liabilities as long as Egyptian intelligence continued to monitor their activities closely. Egypt's generous, almost open-door education policy for Palestinians, as well as the 1962 presidential decree calling for equal employment opportunities for resident Palestinians in the Egyptian bureaucracy, was an extension of the same policy.

Palestinian institutions, especially the GUPS, strove to maintain independence of political thought and action, and refused to allow outside forces to dictate policy. During the early 1960s, no problems arose since the GUPS and the Egyptian regime pursued basically compatible policies. However, when their respective interests diverged, the government called the shots and not the Palestinians (e.g., Sadat's expulsion of Palestinian students in 1977). Thus, the fact that the Egyptian stage produced the GUPS and the GUPW—or at least helped orchestrate them—owed to the small numbers of Palestinians permanently residing in the country and to the strength and efficiency of Egyptian internal security, which was capable of suppressing elements that strayed too far from the regime's line.

In Kuwait, the legal structure, which distinguishes between citizen and noncitizen in virtually every facet of life and renders the acquisition of citizenship all but impossible, underlines the marginality of non-Kuwaitis. The citizenship law that serves as the basis of the structure was issued in 1959. At that time, expatriates still constituted a minority, but given Kuwait's oil wealth and potential, the drafters of the law probably sought to prevent large-scale enfranchisement that the country would be unable to support when the oil wealth ran out. Palestinians in Kuwait were never accorded refugee status as they were in other Arab states and therefore enjoy no special privileges. However, the size of the Palestinian community in Kuwait and, even more important, the role it has played in the development of the bureaucracy, educational system, the economy, and the media have invested it with unquantifiable, but significant power that its formal legal status belies. Only Palestinians have been allowed to form separate unions (although they are not offically licensed)—a clear sign of their influence and the extent to which the Kuwaiti population supports them and their cause.

At the same time, Kuwait's distance from the battlefield has meant that an armed Palestinian presence was unlikely to emerge there. As long as the expression of Palestinian identity posed no threat to the country's stability, tolerance or even support for the popular organizations was the natural response. Only when domestic or regional issues exacerbated internal divisions in which Palestinians, although not enfranchised, might have made alliance with a particular Kuwaiti faction against the regime did the government move against the Palestinians. The Kuwaiti government has always had less tolerance for the Palestinian left—the DF and the PFLP—than for the more conservative Fateh. Thus, Kuwait may be seen as a median case: its large Palestinian community is an integral part of the economy and bureaucracy, but the community's legal status combined with its conservative orientation and Kuwait's distance from the battlefield have afforded it considerable freedom to organize.

Unlike any other host state, Jordan pursued deliberately inclusionary policies vis-à-vis the Palestinians. ʿAbdallah formally annexed the West Bank in 1950 and granted its inhabitants Jordanian citizenship. He had long had ambitions to rule a larger Arab kingdom and adding a part of

Palestine to his realm put him a step closer to realizing his dream. The annexation also meant the addition of valuable human and capital resources that Transjordan lacked. After the annexation and enfranchisement, assertions of Palestinian identity—whether institutional or otherwise—effectively threatened the integrity of the regime. And, despite their citizenship, the vast majority of West Bankers did not enjoy genuine equality with East Bankers in the government bureaucracy, the military, or in the economic realm.

Furthermore, 'Abdallah and Husayn after him depended upon British and American aid for the country's survival. The price tag on the aid packages included the pursuance of pro-Western regional policies, a path that was anathema to most Palestinians, since they held the British responsible for the partition of Palestine. They later regarded Americans with equal suspicion as heirs to British policies and designs. A collision course developed between Jordan's financial lifeline and the political aspirations of the majority of its population. Internal nationalist fervor combined with support from Egypt forced Husayn to back down from his intention to join the Baghdad Pact. For a brief period, Egypt sent the kingdom financial aid. However, when internal dissent threatened the regime, Husayn dismissed Jordan's short-lived Arab nationalist cabinet and declared martial law. Arab aid dwindled while U.S. aid soared.

Husayn's acquiescence in the formation of a Palestinian entity in 1964 came only after Shuqayri promised that the entity would not threaten the integrity of Jordan. Husayn's desire to seek rapprochement with Nasir in view of Israel's announced intention to divert the Jordan River waters undoubtedly also rendered him more amenable to accepting the Palestine Liberation Organization. However, when the PLO exceeded the bounds that Husayn found tolerable, the king closed its offices in 1966. Only after the military defeat and economic disaster caused by the 1967 war was there a decline in his ability, both economically and from the standpoint of internal legitimacy, to support the kind of policies he had practiced before the war. In the wake of the war, the United States cut its aid to Jordan, and the Arab states, much less likely to support the regime's Palestinian policy, began to send compensatory aid. Yet, once its military and internal security apparatus had sufficiently healed, it precipitated military confrontation with the PRM and finally, in July 1971, drove the resistance from the country. As a result, all independent Palestinian institutions were either closed or destroyed.

During the brief period of their ascendancy, Palestinian institutions in Jordan enjoyed more mass support and participation than anywhere else, with the possible exception of post-1971 Lebanon. However, any expression of Palestinian separatism in Jordan, by definition, questions the legitimacy of the broader Jordanian entity. Some argue that given the kingdom's continued dependence on Western aid, Jordan is unlikely to allow the emergence of a national movement actively supportive of Palestinian rights that might precipitate confrontation with the West's reliable and most highly paid ally in the region, Israel. Therefore, despite the large number of Palestinians in Jordan, many of whom are poor camp residents and in need of various forms of economic and social assistance beyond UNRWA's limited capabilities, separate Palestinian institutional development in the Hashemite Kingdom has been—with the exception of the short periods mentioned— meager at best and subject to very close monitoring and control. Barring any radical changes, this situation will persist in the future.

APPLYING THE MARGINALITY FRAMEWORK TO SYRIA AND LEBANON

Before concluding it is useful to examine briefly the basic characteristics of the Palestinian communities in Lebanon and Syria in order to test the applicability of the concept of marginality to Palestinian communities beyond the three countries examined in detail in this study.[3]

Lebanon

The influx of refugees posed potentially more severe problems in Lebanon than in any other Arab host state. Refugee numbers were estimated at 140,000 in 1952 (10 percent of the population). Given Lebanon's already high population density, limited natural resources, and limited economic absorptive capacity, the prospect of the extended presence of such relatively large numbers of newcomers alarmed many Lebanese. Lebanon already counted among its population a large number of well-educated and skilled workers. Its bureaucracy and industry were not in need of an infusion of expertise from outside. Indeed, during the 1950s Lebanon was suffering from substantial unemployment and, as a result, the employment of non-Lebanese in the government was prohibited.

In addition, the delicate confessional balance between Muslims and Christians, which had been worked out in 1943 as the basis of formal intercommunal political relations (the National Pact) was threatened by the large influx. While some of the Palestinians who took refuge in Lebanon were Christians, the vast majority was Muslim. Thus, granting citizenship to large numbers of Palestinians was out of the question on both economic and political grounds.

As noncitizens the Palestinians had no political rights in Lebanon. Legal employment required obtaining a work permit, which was beyond the reach of many Palestinians, forcing them to work illegally and for low wages in what was already an exploitative unskilled labor market. Life in the camps of Lebanon was closely and, according to camp residents, oppressively regulated by Lebanese internal security (al-maktab al-thani). While Palestinian students with Jordanian passports took an active role in political life at the universities (primarily the American University of Beirut), any organizing—labor or political—among the indigenous Palestinian population was quashed by the security forces.

The Palestinians remained economically and politically marginal in Lebanon, but during the 1950s and 1960s the Lebanese state was still intact and able to suppress any organizing attempts. However, even at this time forces were at work there that eventually led to the disintegration of the state. If one accepts the principle that no country willingly concedes sovereignty over its territory to a foreign force, the Cairo agreement concluded between the Palestinian resistance movement and the Lebanese government in 1969, which transferred authority over and responsibility for the Palestinian refugee camps to the PRM, should be viewed as a symptom of the waning power of the central government. This agreement formalized the marginality of the Palestinians and thus laid the basis for the development of separate and independent Palestinian institutions. Since their arrival the Palestinians had been outsiders to the Lebanese system. The new political leeway to organize combined with the gradual decline or disintegration of the Lebanese state both enabled and forced the Palestinians to develop their own political, legal, and social institutions. While the development was slow at first, it was spurred on by the expulsion of the resistance from Jordan and then by the complete collapse of the Lebanese state in the 1975–76 civil war. This period witnessed the flowering of a Palestinian social, economic, and political infrastructure. Indeed, post–civil war Beirut became for the Palestinians the closest thing they had had to a political and cultural capital since pre-1948 Jerusalem. The 1982 Israeli invasion of Lebanon brought that period to an abrupt and violent end as virtually all of the Palestinians' political and social institutions were destroyed and the PLO's military was banished from Beirut to all parts of the Arab world.

Thus, in terms of the framework and the countries already examined, despite the tremendous difference in the numbers of Palestinians and the different socioeconomic and political dynamics that were at work, the communities in Lebanon and Egypt exhibit certain important similarities. In both countries the Palestinians were absolutely marginal: in Egypt, although they were employed through the mid-1950s and 1960s on the same basis as Egyptians, they were marginal because of their small numbers, which led them to have virtually no economic or political impact; in Lebanon their large numbers, the already overcrowded state of the labor market, and the potential threat the Palestinians posed to the country's political balance led the government to devise highly restrictive and exclusionary policies to regulate all aspects of Palestinian life. Because of the organizing opportunity the marginality of the communities allowed by Egypt in the 1950s and 1960s and in Lebanon in the 1970s, they have both been responsible for creating conditions conducive to some of the most important developments in the history of the national movement.

As noted before, these developments are also a function of the strength or weakness of the state. The Egyptian state was quite strong during most of the period examined, but the Palestinians posed little threat. In Lebanon, on the other hand, the Palestinians, despite their marginality, posed such a threat that they were very carefully watched and their attempts to political activity suppressed. It was not until the state began to collapse that the Palestinians were able to mobilize in Lebanon. In the 1980s, as various Lebanese militias, from the Phalangists to Amal, have taken their turn at attempting to assert control, breaking the power of the Palestinians has been a primary goal. Accordingly, one may expect that a reconstituted Lebanese state with an effective internal coercive apparatus would exert all efforts to dismantle what exists or may be rebuilt of Palestinian institutions in Lebanon, just as the pre-1969 state prevented their development.

Syria

Syria alone among the Arab host states was suffering neither from unemployment nor from limited natural resources at the time of the 1948 influx of 90,000 to 100,000 Palestinian refugees. During the 1950s when the issue of resettlement of the refugees was raised, the fertile and underpopulated Jazirah region along the Euphrates River was considered.

Although Syria did not grant citizenship to the Palestinian newcomers, in terms of their treatment domestically, their failure to hold citizenship made little difference. In the 1950s a series of laws was passed that placed Palestinians on a virtually equal footing with Syrians in the critical areas of employment, commercial activity, and education. There is also a special wing of the Syrian Ba'th party, Sa'iqah, for Palestinians; and Syria is the only Arab state that drafts noncitizen Palestinians into its army.

Consequently, Palestinians have been able to integrate into the Syrian economy and social structure to a greater degree than they have in any other Arab country, with the exception of Jordan. As a result, the case of Syria most closely resembles that of Jordan. Far from being marginal to the host state economic and political structure, the Palestinians have become virtually an indivisible part of it. Their integration combined with the highly repressive nature of the regime, particularly since 1970, has meant that the field for development of Palestinian institutions in Syria has been quite narrow, regime proclamations of support for "the cause" notwithstanding.

In virtually all cases there are Syrian equivalents of the Palestinian mass organizations (Syrian workers' unions and women's federations), although their activity, too, is restricted. Membership in the Ba'th party has increasingly become, for Syrian and Palestinian alike, the sine qua non for appointments and promotions, particularly in the government. Thus many of those who have been active and powerful in the Palestinian organizations in Syria have participated as members of Sa'iqah, which is effectively an arm of the Syrian regime.

In the period following the split in the PLO, Syria has witnessed a marked development in the activities of Palestinian women, primarily through the DF, which has come to fill the gap left by the forced departure of mainstream Fateh from open activity in Syria. As economic conditions in Syria have deteriorated, anti-Palestinian grumblings have grown louder. If the deterioration continues, one may expect to see the beginnings of discrimination against Palestinians. If the marginality framework is correct, there should be attempts at greater institutional expressions of separate political identity among Palestinians as a result. The degree to which these attempts can succeed will depend on how the economic crisis affects the degree to which the regime's coercive apparatus remains capable of repressing them.

TOWARD THE FUTURE

The case studies demonstrate that the marginality framework understood in terms of motive, opportunity, and resources explains in general terms the degree of Palestinian institutional development in Arab host states. But the future of the Palestinian struggle for self-determination, the most basic motive for the establishment of the institutions, cannot be predicted with any certainty, for it hinges on a vast range of factors, many of them external to the communities. This study has shown that within a very short time of the dispersal and disruption of its society and institutions, a scattered Palestinian people reasserted its collective identity first in Arab, and then in international circles. Wherever a political opening appeared, Palestinians worked to reorganize and mobilize.

The institutions examined in this study played a key role in the post-1948 reemergence of the Palestinian national movement and its drive for the establishment of a national political entity. Although the devastating effects of the 1982 Israeli invasion of Lebanon and the uprooting of the PLO from its headquarters in Beirut continue to be felt throughout the diaspora, in most cases the popular organizations have regrouped and continue to function within the political limits imposed by the host countries. The restoration of PLO unity during the April 1987 meeting of the PNC in Algiers was an indispensable step along the road to the reinvigoration of the national movement. When regional and Palestinian conditions permit, the popular organizations may once again rise to the prominence they have enjoyed in the past as crucial building blocks of a sovereign Palestinian state.

Notes

1. Diaspora, State-Building, and Arab Domestic Politics

1. As quoted in Hurewitz, *Struggle for Palestine*, p. 220.

2. The expression is taken from the subtitle of the book by Ann Mosely Lesch, *Arab Politics in Palestine 1917–1939: The Frustration of a Nationalist Movement* (Ithaca, N.Y.: Cornell University Press, 1979).

3. For a review of the "state of the art" in analyses of the development of the modern state and its role see Peter B. Evans, Dietrich Rueschemeyer, and Theda Skocpol, eds., *Bringing the State Back In* (New York: Cambridge University Press, 1985).

4. Charles Tilly, "War Making and State Making as Organized Crime," in *ibid.*, p. 175.

5. See Charles Tilly, ed., *The Formation of Nation States in Western Europe* (Princeton, N.J.: Princeton University Press, 1975).

6. The phenomenon of sectorally based organizing, or corporatism, has been most carefully studied in the Latin American and southern European context. See Philippe Schmitter, "Still the Century of Corporatism?" *Review of Politics* 36(1): 85–131.

7. Figures on original population as well as number of refugees vary widely. See UNRWA, *UNRWA: A Brief History 1950–1982*, pp. 2–6; and *Al-Filastiniyyun f-il-Watan al-ʿArabi*, pp. 89–95.

8. The issue of expulsion versus flight has been among the most controversial in Palestinian and modern Israeli history. For works on the subject using recently declassified Israeli archival material see: Tom Segev, *1949: The First Israelis* (New York: Free Press, 1986); Simha Flapan, *The Birth of Israel: Myths and Realities* (New York: Pantheon Books, 1987); Benny Morris, "Operation Dani and the Palestinian Exodus from Lydda and Ramle in 1948," *Middle East Journal* (winter 1986), 40(1):82–110 and "The Harvest of 1948 and the Creation of the Palestinian Refugee Problem," *Middle East Journal* (autumn 1986), 40(4):671–686. See also Nafez Nazzal, *The Palestinian Exodus from Galilee, 1948* (Beirut: Institute for Palestine Studies, 1978).

9. For a list of Palestinian villages, those destroyed or emptied and those that remain, see Shukri ʿArraf, *Al-Qaryah al-ʿArabiyyah al-Filastiniyyah* (Jerusalem: Arab Studies Society, 1985), pp. 163–279.

10. Several other words are also used to describe the Palestinians' condition: *manfa* (exile) and *tasharrud* (banishment).

11. Turki, *The Disinherited*, p. 8.

12. See Rothschild, *Ethnopolitics*, and Clifford Geertz, "The Integrative Revolution: Primordial Sentiments and Civil Politics in the New States," in Geertz, ed., *Old Societies and New States*, pp. 108–128, 153–157.

13. See Khoury, *Urban Notables and Arab Nationalism*.

14. For a detailed description of the early development of nationalist sentiment in Palestine see Muslih, *The Origins of Palestinian Nationalism*.

15. Dov Ronen, *The Quest for Self-Determination*, p. 53.

16. See Jeffrey A. Ross, "The Mobilization of Collective Identity: An Analytical Overview," in Ross and Cottrell, eds., *Mobilization of Collective Identity*, pp. 9–10. He contends that a group's identity is exogenously defined and coercively enforced by the dominant group.

17. While the 1948 camps and, later, post-1967 camps were in many cases established far from urban areas, the gradual growth of these major urban areas (Damascus, Beirut, and Amman in particular) eventually led to the camps' engulfment by these centers. At the very least it has lessened their isolation.

18. Other Palestinian organizations of a similar nature with branches across the diaspora are: the General Union of Palestinian Writers and Journalists, the General Union of Palestinian Doctors and Pharmacists, the General Union of Palestine Artists, the General Union of Palestinian Engineers, and the General Union of Palestinian Lawyers and Jurists. Another institution, SAMED (the Palestinian Martyrs' Works Society), was a large employer and sponsor of economic projects in Lebanon, and to a lesser extent in Syria.

19. The two classic works on the PLO—Quandt, Jabber, and Lesch, *The Politics of Palestinian Nationalism* and Cobban, *The Palestinian Liberation Organization*—as well as many lesser books and articles devote very little attention to the 1948–1964 period.

20. Fateh is an acronym in reverse for *Harakat al-Tahrir al-Watani al-Filastini* (the Palestinian National Liberation Movement). The movement was the first purely Palestinian national group to emerge after 1948. It was first conceived by such notable members of the Cairo students' union as Yasir ʿArafat and Salah Khalaf. It distinguished itself in Palestinian circles for its military operations against Israel; its leaders assumed control of the PLO in 1969 and have held control until the present.

The Baʿth was the product of the 1952 union of two parties, the original Baʿth (renaissance) party and the Arab Socialist party. Founded by Arab ideologues Michel ʿAflaq and Salah al-Din Bitar, its slogan was "one Arab nation with an eternal mission." It combined elements of Marxist dialectics and socialism with its call for Arab unity and liberation. With two regionally distinct and feuding branches, the Baʿth is the government party in Syria and Iraq.

The Arab Nationalist Movement (ANM) was born at the American University in Beirut and developed a wide range of semisecret cells in Lebanon, Syria, and Jordan. Arab unity was its primary focus and when Nasir and the Syrian Baʿth parted ways, the ANM stepped in as the Egyptian president's most loyal supporter. Its eclectic ideology evolved to produce the Popular Front for the Liberation of Palestine.

21. Tilly, *From Mobilization to Revolution*, pp. 54–56, 62–63, 71–73.

22. See Germani, *Marginality*, for a discussion of the various aspects of marginality.

23. *Ibid.*, p. 10.

2. The Long Road Back: The Evolution of a Palestinian Entity

1. For a more detailed description of the opposing positions see Shuʿaybi, *Al-Kiyaniyyah al-Filastiniyyah*, pp. 20–29 for Transjordan and pp. 37–39 for Egypt.

2. "ʿUmum Filastin, Hukumat," in *Al-Mawsuʿah al-Filastiniyyah* [All-Palestine Government in The Palestine Encyclopaedia] (Damascus: Palestine Encyclopaedia Authority, 1984), 3:342.

3. To write about the APG requires gathering bits and pieces of information from a variety of sources. One excellent source is Shuʿaybi, pp. 18–22. Another, although the larger work itself has many shortcomings, is to be found in *Al-Mawsuʿah al-Filastiniyyah*, 3:342–344. Original Arabic sources that touch on the topic include: Muhammad ʿIzzah Darwazah, *Al-Qadiyyah al-Filastiniyyah fi Mukhtalif Marahiliha* [The Palestine Problem in Its Various Stages] (Sidon: Al-Maktabah al-ʿAsriyyah, 1951), 2 vols.; Khayriyyah Qasimiyyah, ed., *ʿAwni ʿAbd al-Hadi: Awraq Khassah* [Personal Papers of ʿAwni ʿAbd al-Hadi] (Beirut: PLO Research Center, 1974); ʿAbdallah al-Tall, *Karithat Filastin* [The Palestine Disaster, Memoirs of ʿAbdallah al-Tall] (Cairo: Dar al-Qalam, 1959).

4. Shuʿaybi, p. 21.

5. "Muʾtamar Ghazzah" [The Gaza Conference] in *Al-Mawsuʿah al-Filastiniyyah*, 3:389.

6. Articles on, as opposed to sentence references to or descriptions of, the Amman, Nablus, and Jericho conferences may be found in *Al-Mawsuʿah al-Filastiniyyah*, 4:377–379.

7. Astal, "Al-Wadʿ al-Qanuni li-Qitaʿ Ghazzah tahta al-Idarah al-Misriyyah," pp. 9–10.

8. *Al-Filastiniyyin f-il-Watan al-ʿArabi*, p. 579.

9. *Ibid.*, p. 578.

10. *Qararat Majlis Jamiʿat al-Duwal al-ʿArabiyyah al-Khassah bi-Qadiyyat Filastin*, p. 75.

11. For a complete list of Arab League resolutions on the Palestine question see *ibid*.

12. In her study *The Palestinian Liberation Organization*, Cobban cites Salah Khalaf as dating the founding of Fateh to October 1959 and Hani al-Hassan as dating "the final unification of the Fateh core" to 1962 (p. 23). However, based on interviews with other Fateh leaders, including Khalil al-Wazir (Abu Jihad), and the organization's early publications cited in Fawwaz Hamid al-Sharqawi, "Harakat al-Tahrir al-Watani al-Filastini 'Fateh' 1965–1971," master's thesis in political science, Cairo University, 1974, Shuʿaybi places the beginnings of Fateh in late 1957 (p. 52). The discrepancy may be a result of each interviewee's idea of what constitutes the "beginning" or the "founding" of the movement.

13. Shuʿaybi, pp. 73–74.

14. For additional information on the PANU see "Al-Idarah al-Misriyyah li-Qitaʿ Ghazzah," *Al-Mawsuʿah al-Filastiniyyah*, 1:132.

15. Shuʿaybi, p. 74.

16. *Ibid.*, p. 75.

17. For a more detailed discussion of the various meetings see *ibid.*, pp. 87–94.

18. For a concise discussion of the transformation from pre-1967 PLO to commando leadership see Hamid, "What Is the PLO?" pp. 98–101.

19. For this reason, some of the organizations with limited popular support enjoy seemingly disproportionate representation. Owing to financial backing, their military units have been of consequence even though their political or ideological appeal among the majority of Palestinians is limited. Examples include Sa'iqah, the Arab Liberation Front, and the Popular Front for the Liberation of Palestine-General Command.

20. Although governed by the PLO Department of Popular Organizations (Da'irat al-Munazzamat al-Sha'biyyah), Palestinians use a variety of names to refer to these institutions: *munazzamat sha'biyyah, munazzamat jamahiriyyah,* and *ittihadat sha'biyyah.* They are generally translated as mass or popular organizations or unions.

21. Kadi, *Basic Political Documents,* pp. 122–123.

22. Original constitutions were not available and one assumes that the constitutions have been subject to modification over the years. However, the basic goals of the unions from their beginnings should be reflected in the more recent documents. The documents used were the following: *Al-Nizam al-Asasi l-il-Ittihad al-'Amm li-Talabat Filastin; Al-Nizam al-Dakhili l-il-Ittihad al-'Amm li-'Ummal Filastin; Al-Nizam al-Asasi l-il-Ittihad al-'Amm l-il-Mar'ah al-Filastiniyyah;* and *Al-Nizam al-Asasi w-al-Dakhili.*

23. *Al-Nizam al-Asasi* (PRCS).

24. Rubenberg, *The Palestine Liberation Organization,* p. 42.

3. The Powerful Patron

1. Mitchell, *The Society of the Muslim Brothers,* p. 55.

2. *Ibid.,* p. 75.

3. See Bishri, *Al-Harakah al-Siyasiyyah fi Misr, 1945–1952,* pp. 255–268.

4. Kazziha, *Palestine in the Arab Dilemma,* pp. 93–94.

5. Issawi, *Egypt in Revolution,* p. 57.

6. *Ibid.,* p. 37.

7. Gamal 'Abd al-Nasir, "Philosophy of the Revolution, 1952," in Nasir, *Nasir Speaks: Basic Documents,* E. S. Farag (London: Morsett Press, 1972), pp. 18, 49.

8. This section is a summary of the book *Al-Lajnah al-'Ulya li-Shu'un al-Muhajirin al-Filastiniyyin.* The presentation here follows the order of the book as closely as possible.

9. Hala Sakakini, *Jerusalem and I: A Personal Record* (Jerusalem: Commercial Press, 1987), p. 124.

10. The Arab League Council issued a decree in its 16th session, September 14, 1952, in which it urged Arab governments to take the measures necessary to allow separated Palestinian family members to reunite in the country in which the head of the family resided. The book of the Higher Committee for Palestinian Immigrant Affairs mentions a decree of 1950 to this effect, which I am unable to locate among league decisions. The book also argues that the refugees were returned to Gaza in fulfillment of this Arab League decision. Even if there had been a decision to this effect in 1950, the timing is wrong. By the

book's own admission, the Egyptian cabinet's decision to return the refugees to Gaza came in 1949. A further problem is that the numbers of those who came, left, and were assisted simply do not tally. Unfortunately, this is the only book available on the period. Like other periods and places, accurate and consistent demographic figures for Palestinians in Egypt remain elusive.

11. *Al-Lajnah al-ʿUlyah li-Shuʾun al-Muhajirin*, p. 20.

12. Interview with Mr. Raghib Qiddis, who worked in the assistance distribution program, December 27, 1983.

13. Interview with Khadijah ʿArafat, head of Social Affairs section of the PRCS Egypt branch, December 28, 1983.

14. *Al-Filastiniyyun f-il-Watan al-ʿArabi*, p. 125.

15. Interview with Fakhri Sarraj, director of the PLO office in Cairo, November 21, 1983.

16. Shaʿth, "High-Level Palestinian Manpower," p. 81. Dr. Shaʿth is a former member of the GUPS and a leading member of the Palestinian community in Cairo.

17. Interviews with Ahmad Sidqi al-Dajani, longtime member of the PNC, November 15, 1983; Fakhri Sarraj, November 21, 1983; and Fuʾad Ibrahim ʿAbbas, longtime resident of Egypt and member of the General Union of Palestinian Writers and Journalists, December 20, 1983.

18. In Arabic, "al-aradi al-filastiniyyah al-khadiʿah li-riqabat al-quwwat al-musallahah al-misriyyah," Abu Niml, *Qitaʿ Ghazzah, 1948–1967*, p. 47.

19. *Ibid.*, p. 47.

20. Nutting, *Nasser*, p. 363.

21. Abu Niml, p. 43.

22. Khulusi, *Al-Tanmiyah al-Iqtisadiyyah fi Qitaʿ Ghazzah Filastin, 1948–1961*, pp. 51, 53.

23. *Ibid.*, pp. 42–43.

24. *Al-Filastiniyyun f-il-Watan al-ʿArabi*, p. 152.

25. *Ibid.*, pp. 269–270.

26. Abu Niml, p. 294.

27. *Ibid.*

28. *Ibid.*, p. 262.

29. Astal, "Al-Wadʿ al-Qanuni li-Qitaʿ Ghazzah tahta al-Idarah al-Misriyyah," p. 13 and p. 24, note 55.

30. In 1964, after the APG had been put to rest, the Egyptian Passport, Emigration, and Nationality Directorate began issuing travel documents to Gazans. See Astal, p. 23, note 36.

31. In Arabic, "Mamnuʿ al-ʿamal bi-ujr aw bi-dun ujr," from interview with Fuʾad Ibrahim ʿAbbas, December 20, 1983.

32. *Al-Jaridah al-Rasmiyyah*, no. 146, July 2, 1960.

33. Astal, p. 23, note 36.

34. Interview with ʿAbbas. Unfortunately, more accurate figures on the Palestinian presence in Egypt are not available.

35. Interview with Yusra al-Kayyali, a 1948 Palestinian refugee to Egypt, November 19, 1983.

36. *Al-Waqaʾiʿ al-Misriyyah*, no. 58, July 22, 1954.

37. *Al-Waqaʾiʿ al-Misriyyah*, no. 74, September 16, 1954.

38. *Al-Waqaʾiʿ al-Misriyyah*, no. 84, October 24, 1954.

39. Interview with ʿAbbas.

40. *Al-Jaridah al-Rasmiyyah*, no. 58, March 10, 1962.

41. Interview with Sarraj, August 14, 1984.

42. *Qitaʿ Ghazzah*, p. 73.

43. *Ibid.*, p. 23.

44. *Ibid.*, p. 73.

45. *Ibid.*, p. 31.

46. See Jackson, *Middle East Mission;* and Touval, *The Peace Brokers.*

47. For a discussion of the economic reasons behind the dissolution of the union see Petran, *Syria*, pp. 135–145.

48. Kerr, *The Arab Cold War*, p. 11.

49. Shuʿaybi, *Al-Kiyaniyyah al-Filastiniyyah, 1947–1977*, pp. 101–102.

50. *Ibid.*, p. 101.

51. Cobban, *The Palestinian Liberation Organization*, pp. 45–46.

52. Nutting, p. 462.

53. Elmessiri, *The Palestinian Wedding*, pp. 89–93. Al-Qadisiyyah is a site in Iraq where in 637 A.D. a small Arab force routed the Persian army.

54. Interview with PLO official in Cairo, November 1983.

55. From an interview with the Egyptian military governor-general of Gaza in Cairo, General ʿAdil Muhammad Mahmud, December 1, 1983.

56. Sarraj interview.

57. Baron, *Les Palestiniens Un Peuple*, pp. 351–353. See also Fahmy, *Negotiating for Peace in the Middle East*, pp. 96–101.

58. For details of the Egyptian press's treatment of the Palestinians and the Palestine question see Karem Yehya, "The Image of the Palestinians in Egypt, 1982–1985," 45–63.

59. Law Number 104 of 1985 (Amendment to Law Number 15 of 1963), *Al-Jaridah al-Rasmiyyah*, no. 28, July 4, 1985.

4. GUPS: The Political Training Ground

1. Interview with ʿAbd al-Muhsin Abu Mayzir, official spokesman of the Palestine National Salvation Front and former PSU member, Damascus, September 11, 1986. Amin al-Husayni studied at al-Azhar, Dar al-Daʿwa w-al-Irshad, and the Faculty of Arts and Sciences at the Egyptian University. See Hut, *Al-Qiyadat w-al-Muʾassasat al-Siyasiyyah fi Filastin, 1917–1948*, pp. 201–202.

2. *Tarikh al-Harakah al-Tullabiyyah al-Filastiniyyah*, p. 4.

3. Musa, "Hawla Tajribat al-Ittihad al-ʿAmm li-Talabat Filastin."

4. Interview with ʿAbd al-Fattah Sharif, former employee of the APG and longtime resident of Egypt, February 15, 1984.

5. *Al-Harakah al-Tullabiyyah al-Filastiniyyah*, pp. 4–5.

6. The Arab League Council issued several recommendations concerning Palestinian students. On March 21, 1949, the general secretariat authorized the appropriation of LE2,000 ($5,600) for needy students. Later, on September 23, 1952, additional assistance was requested for Palestinian students in Egyptian universities. A December 11, 1954 decision approved the funds requested in 1952 on the conditions that the student demonstrated need and did not receive money from UNRWA. For the texts of the resolutions see *Qararat Majlis Jamiʿat al-Duwal al-ʿArabiyyah al-Khassah bi-Qadiyyat Filastin.*

7. Abu Iyad (Salah Khalaf) with Eric Rouleau, *My Home, My Land*, p. 19.

8. Alan Hart, *Arafat: Terrorist or Peacemaker?*, p. 104.

9. Abu Iyad, p. 19.

10. Interview with Fakhri Sarraj, director of the PLO office in Cairo, November 21, 1983.

11. Interview with Muhammad Subayh, former president of the GUPS, November 26, 1983.

12. Interview with Sa'id Kamal, former ANM member of the Palestinian student organization in Iraq and the GUPS in Cairo, November 28, 1983.

13. Hart, pp. 86–87.

14. Abu Iyad, p. 20.

15. Interview with Subayh; and with Zuhayr al-Khatib, former president of the GUPS, March 10 and 11, 1984.

16. Abu Iyad, p. 21.

17. *Ibid.*

18. *Ibid.*, p. 22.

19. *Ibid.*, p. 23.

20. For the complete story see Husayni, *Muwajahat al-Nashat al-Sahyuni 'ala al-Sa'id al-Tullabi.*

21. Abu Iyad, p. 23.

22. Hart, pp. 90–91.

23. *Al-Harakah al-Tullabiyyah al-Filastiniyyah*, p. 6.

24. On March 8, 1969 Colonel 'Abd al-Wahhab al-Shawwaf, brigade commander of Mosul, headed a revolt coordinated with UAR arms and other support. 'Abd al-Karim Qasim, who had himself seized power in a July 1958 coup, received advance warning of the uprising and brutally suppressed it.

25. Kamal interview.

26. *Al-Harakah al-Tullabiyyah al-Filastiniyyah*, p. 6.

27. *Ibid.*

28. The Egyptian military authorities in Gaza, which had no universities at the time, permitted no student organizing on the secondary school level.

29. Kamal interview.

30. Much of the general description that follows of the content of GUPS national conferences is taken from Musa.

31. The list was given by Subayh during an interview.

32. *Al-Harakah al-Tullabiyyah al-Filastiniyyah*, pp. 15–16.

33. Kamal interview.

34. *Ibid.*

35. Musa, p. 182.

36. Subayh interview.

37. Musa, p. 182.

38. The word *inshiqaq* has, since 1983, been used to refer to the split within Fateh and, more broadly, within the PLO. 'Arafat's supporters called the rebels *munshaqqin*, while anti-'Arafat forces termed his loyalists *munharifin* (deviationists).

39. Musa, p. 182.

40. Kamal interview.

41. Khatib interview.

42. *Al-Kitab al-Sanawi l-il-Qadiyyah al-Filastiniyyah, 1964* (1966), p. 105.

43. Kamal interview.

44. *Ibid.*

45. Musa, p. 186.

46. *Al-Harakah al-Tullabiyyah al-Filastiniyyah*, p. 21.

47. Musa, p. 183.

48. Kamal interview; and interview with Ghazi Fakhri Murar, former GUPS official, January 10, 1984.

49. Sharif al-Husayni, "Al-Mu'tamar al-Watani al-Sadis l-il-Ittihad al-'Amm li-Talabat Filastin," pp. 307–309.

50. *Al-Harakah al-Tullabiyyah al-Filastiniyyah*, p. 30.

51. Subayh interview.

52. Interview with 'Azzam al-Ahmad, former member of the Iraq branch of the GUPS, May 8, 1984.

53. Murar interview.

54. Interview with former member of the Asyut chapter of the Egypt branch of the GUPS identified only as Jabir, July 5, 1984.

55. In addition, King Hasan of Morocco, President Bourguiba of Tunisia, King Sa'ud of Saudi Arabia, and President Nasir of Egypt all contributed regularly. After the independence of the United Arab Emirates, Shaykh Zayid made yearly contributions. After the founding of the PLO, the GUPS was given JD12,000 ($33,600) per year, thus making it the wealthiest of the Palestinian popular organizations. From Kamal interview.

56. Khatib interview.

57. No membership lists were available for examination. Those interviewed provided figures from memory and experience. 'Abd al-Fattah Sharif claimed that during the early 1950s, prior to the PSU's admission to the IUS, it counted some 500 members. According to Muhammad Subayh, Sa'id Kamal, and Zuhdi al-Qudrah (PLO representative in Cairo and former Cairo GUPS member), in 1959, the entire GUPS counted more than 2,000 students. No estimate was available for the percentage of the 2,000 in Egypt. A former member of the Asyut chapter declared that by 1969, the branch in Egypt counted 6,000 members out of a total Palestinian student population (GUPS members or not) of 30,000. Fakhri Sarraj and Zuhdi al-Qudrah stated that there were 12,000 Palestinian students in Cairo in 1970, but that not all were GUPS members.

58. Jabir interview.

59. Murar interview.

60. Dajani, *The Institutionalization of Palestinian Identity in Egypt*, p. 44.

61. Abdallah, *The Student Movement and National Politics in Egypt*, pp. 150, 152.

62. See Abdallah, pp. 149–175.

63. *Ibid.*, p. 176.

64. El-Rayyes and Nahas, *Guerrillas For Palestine*, p. 94.

65. Hinnebusch, *Egyptian Politics Under Sadat*, p. 51.

66. Shoukri, *Egypt: Portrait of a President, 1971–1981*, pp. 101–111.

67. Hirst and Beeson, *Sadat*, p. 128.

68. El-Rayyes and Nahas, p. 94.

69. From a discussion with Dr. 'Abd al-Mun'im Sa'id 'Ali, of the Al-Ahram Center for Strategic Studies. Dr. Sa'id 'Ali was a participant in the student movement in the late 1960s and early 1970s.

70. El-Rayyes and Nahas, p. 95.

71. Dajani, p. 46.

72. Baker, *Egypt's Uncertain Revolution Under Nasser and Sadat*, p. 167.

73. Hinnebusch, p. 244.

74. Interview with Zaynab al-Ghunaymi, a member of the Egypt branch of the GUPS during this period and a member of the GUPWom administrative council, September 13, 1986.

75. Ghunaymi interview.

76. Dajani, p. 46.

77. Abu Kashif, "Al-Hawiyyah al-Wataniyyah l-il-Filastiniyyin fi Misr," p. 282.

5. The Search for Community: The GUPW, GUPWom, PRCS, and GUPT

1. *Mudhakkirat Husni Salih al-Khuffash*, p. 68. (Hereafter cited as *Khuffash Memoirs*.)

2. *Khuffash Memoirs*, p. 68.

3. Interview with Naji al-Kawni, August 4, 1986.

4. From an interview with 'Awni Battash, former general secretary of the GUPW in Kuwait and current director of the PLO office in Kuwait, March 7, 1984.

5. *Khuffash Memoirs*, pp. 71–72.

6. Kawni interview.

7. Interview with Yunis al-Katari, member of the PLO Department of the Occupied Homeland and now active with the Egypt branch of the GUPW, November 21, 1983.

8. *Khuffash Memoirs*, p. 72.

9. *Ibid.*, p. 81.

10. Kawni interview.

11. *Khuffash Memoirs*, p. 84.

12. Kawni interview.

13. *Khuffash Memoirs*, p. 85.

14. Kawni interview.

15. Interview with Palestinian writer and historian 'Abd al-Qadir Yasin, December 24, 1983.

16. *Al-Mu'tamar al-Awwal l-il-Ittihad al-'Amm li-'Ummal Filastin*, pp. 152–159.

17. *Ibid.*, pp. 150–151.

18. Yasin interview.

19. *Al-Mu'tamar al-Awwal*, pp. 95–100.

20. *Khuffash Memoirs*, p. 98.

21. *Al-Kitab al-Sanawi l-il-Qadiyyah al-Filastiniyyah, 1967*, pp. 119–120.

22. *Qararat al-Mu'tamar al-Thani, 1967*, pp. 302–303.

23. The union had called for these economic measures at the sixth meeting of the PNC in 1969. See *Al-Kitab al-Sanawi l-il-Qadiyyah al-Filastiniyyah, 1969*, pp. 82–83.

24. *Qararat al-Mu'tamar al-Thani, 1967*, pp. 249–252.

25. Kawni interview.

26. *Qararat al-Mu'tamar al-Thani, 1967*, pp. 245–248.

27. Interview with ʿAdil ʿAtiyyah, current secretary of the GUPW, December 24, 1983.

28. *Watha²iq al-Mu²tamar al-Khamis, 8–10 Junyu 1974*, pp. 39–53.

29. *Ibid.*, p. 79.

30. ʿAtiyyah interview.

31. These sentiments were expressed by most of the Palestinians interviewed during the research period (September 1983–February 1984). See also Yehya, "The Image of the Palestinians in Egypt, 1982–1985."

32. ʿAtiyyah interview.

33. Interviews with Samirah Abu Ghazalah, October 17 and November 28, 1983.

34. *Al-Nizam al-Asasi li-Rabitat al-Mar²ah al-Filastiniyyah.*

35. Abu Ghazalah interview, November 28, 1983.

36. Abu Ghazalah interview, October 17, 1983.

37. Interview with Arab ʿAbd al-Hadi, former member of the Egypt branch of the GUPWom, January 11, 1984.

38. Dajani, *The Institutionalization of Palestinian Identity in Egypt*, p. 59.

39. Interview with Zaynab al-Ghunaymi, a member of the Egypt branch of the GUPS who participated in the center's activities and who is currently a member of the administrative council of the GUPWom, September 13, 1986.

40. Dajani, p. 74.

41. Interview with Yusra Shihab al-Din, former member of the Egypt branch of the GUPWom and former director of the GUPWom's student dormitory in Cairo, February 5, 1984.

42. Ghunaymi interview.

43. ʿAbd al-Hadi interview.

44. Abu Ghazalah interview, January 12, 1984.

45. Based on two interviews with women who were active in the Alexandria chapter, Fa²iqah Muhammad ʿAli and a woman identified only as Alexandra, February 9, 1984.

46. Interview with ʿAblah al-Dajani, member of the Egypt branch of the GUPWom, October 30, 1983.

47. ʿAbd al-Hadi interview and interview with Maysun Shaʿth, member of the Egypt branch of the GUPWom, December 14, 1983.

48. ʿAbd al-Hadi interview.

49. ʿAbd al-Hadi and Abu Ghazalah interviews.

50. Interview with Fayha² ʿAbd al-Hadi, member of the Egypt branch of the GUPWom, July 31, 1986.

51. Dajani, p. 61.

52. Fayha² ʿAbd al-Hadi interview.

53. The information for this section derives from an interview with Musa Abu al-ʿAmrayn, assistant general secretary of the Egypt branch of the GUPT, August 4, 1986.

54. This is no longer the case. Palestinians must now pay for health care in hard currency, a factor that has led to an increase in PRCS services in the country and to the development of a social insurance program.

55. Interview with Nahidah al-Husayni, a founder of the Egypt branch of the PRCS, January 10, 1984.

56. From interviews with Fathi ʿArafat, a founder of the PRCS in Jordan and

current head of the society, October 8, 1983; and interview with Nahidah al-Husayni.

57. Husayni interview and interview with Hind Abu Saʿud, a founder of the Egypt branch of the PRCS, December 22, 1983.

58. Abu Saʿud interview.

59. Interview with Inʿam ʿArafat, December 10, 1983.

60. Dajani, p. 71.

61. ʿAli Ibrahim, "Jamʿiyyat al-Hilal al-Ahmar fi Misr: Takhtit yatalaʾim maʿa al-Ihtiyajat" [The PRCS in Egypt: Planning Appropriate for Needs], Balsam [Nicosia, the official magazine of the PRCS] (November 1984–January 1985), nos. 113–115, p. 89.

62. Dajani, p. 72.

63. Ibid., p. 73.

64. Ibrahim, p. 89.

65. Dajani, pp. 75–76.

66. Interview with Amal al-Amirkani, PRCS Public Relations Division, July 30, 1986.

67. Dajani, p. 79.

68. Ibrahim, p. 89.

69. Amirkani interview.

70. Interview with Khadijah ʿArafat, head of the Social Affairs Section of the Cairo PRCS, December 28, 1983.

71. ʿArafat interview.

72. Abu Saʿud interview.

6. Opportunity in Exile

1. Kanafani, " ʿAsharat Amtar Faqat" [Only Ten Meters], from the short story collection ʿAlam Laysa Lana [A World Not for Us] in Kanafani, Al-Athar al-Kamilah, vol. 2. The translation is mine.

2. Hudson, Arab Politics, p. 187.

3. Ismael, Kuwait, ch. 3.

4. Kanafani, Rijal f-il-Shams [Men in the Sun], in Kanafani, Al-Athar al-Kamilah, pp. 112–113.

5. Ghabra, Palestinians in Kuwait, pp. 66–70; also my interview with Khalid Abu Khalid, a Palestinian poet who went to Kuwait by the "underground railroad," September 9, 1986.

6. Sabah, Al-Hijrah ila al-Kuwayt min ʿAm 1957 ila 1975 pp. 157–163.

7. Information on immigration into Kuwait in this section is taken from two interviews (October 6 and 8, 1986) with Hani al-Qaddumi, who served as the first director of the Bureau of Passports and Residence, 1948–1961.

8. Qaddumi interview.

9. Interview with Saʿdallah Hijazi, a Palestinian businessman from Jaffa who came to Kuwait in 1951, October 10, 1986.

10. Qaddumi interview; Ghabra, pp. 19–21.

11. Interview with Ahmad Shihab al-Din, a member of the first delegation of Palestinian teachers to Kuwait in 1936, October 9, 1986.

12. For more details on the early development of Kuwait see Khususi, Dir-

asat fi Tarikh al-Kuwayt al-Ijtimaʿi w-al-Iqtisadi f-il-ʿAsr al-Hadith, pp. 109–121.

13. *Al-Kuwayt al-Yawm*, no. 253, 1959, Appendix.

14. Qaddumi interview. The difference between holding a passport and being a citizen is significant. Qaddumi himself, although director of passports, had no travel papers until at one point he decided to travel to Basra and went to Shaykh ʿAbdallah Mubarak for a *laissez-passer*. The shaykh was shocked that he had no travel document and had him issued a Kuwaiti passport. After independence Qaddumi was granted Kuwaiti citizenship for his many years of service.

15. Sabah; Statistics taken from charts on pages 55, 56, 62, 63, 76, and 77. Statistics are official Kuwaiti government figures. No census has been conducted since 1975.

16. Law Number 38 of 1964 (private sector) established the conditions for employing foreign workers and organized their immigration. It lists requirements for obtaining work permits as well as grounds for their cancellation, requirements for employing foreigners, and duration of employment. See Hadawi, *Al-Jinsiyyah wa-Markaz al-Ajanib wa-Ahkamihim f-il-Qanun al-Kuwayti*, p. 273.

17. Qaddumi interview.

18. From a discussion with Shafeeq Ghabra, December 20, 1986.

19. Hadawi, p. 275.

20. *Ibid.*, p. 256.

21. ʿAtiyyah, *Qanun al-ʿAmal f-il-Qitaʿ al-Ahli*. Law Number 38 of 1964 (Article 72) concerning work in the private sector. The right of Kuwaitis to form unions is guaranteed by Article 28 of Law Number 18 of 1960. Article 73 of Law Number 38 of 1964 forbids unions to engage in political, religious, or sectarian activities.

22. Smith, *Palestine and the Palestinians, 1876–1983*, p. 139. While on the surface the regulations may appear restrictive, it has been suggested they in fact constituted a reform of earlier laws that had discouraged the emergence of expatriate businesses. As a result of the new regulations, in the mid-1960s Palestinians and other expatriates began to enter the Kuwaiti private sector in greater numbers. See Ghabra, p. 44.

23. Ismael, p. 119.

24. "Summary of the Final Report on the Economic and Social Situation and Potential of the Palestinian Arab People in the Region of Western Asia," pp. 26–29.

25. Sabah, p. 146.

26. Hasan, *Al-Filastiniyyun f-il-Kuwayt*, p. 11, note.
He states that the figure was confirmed by Ahmad al-Duʿayj, chief of the Kuwait Planning Council. It should also be noted that in the Kuwaiti statistics of 1965 and 1970, Palestinians and Jordanians were listed under the same heading.

27. Sabah, p. 146.

28. Ministry of Planning, Kuwait, *Statistical Abstract, 1976*, table 17, p. 31. Post-1975 statistics do not differentiate non-Kuwaitis according to country of origin.

29. Hasan, p. 13.

30. Sabah, p. 324.

31. Hasan, p. 21.

32. 'Abd al-Rahman, "Muqaddimah Awaliyyah Nahwa Tartib wa-Tathwir al-Bayt al-Filastini f-il-Kuwayt," p. 10.

33. Interview with Siham Abu Ghazalah and Siham al-Dabbagh, officers of the GUPWom (Kuwait), March 5, 1984.

34. For a full discussion of the role of the Palestinian family in Kuwait see Ghabra, chs. 5, 6, and 8.

35. Hasan, p. 37.

36. 'Abd al-Rahman, "Al-Awda' al-Ta'limiyyah l-il-Jaliyah al-Filastiniyyah f-il-Kuwayt," p. 5.

37. Hasan, pp. 96–97.

38. 'Abd al-Rahman, "Al-Awda' al-Ta'limiyyah," p. 12 and table 9.

39. Hasan, p. 97.

40. Ibid., p. 99.

41. Ibid., pp. 99–100.

42. 'Abd al-Rahman, "Al-Awda' al-Ta'limiyyah," table 10.

43. Ibid., p. 13.

44. Interview with Salwa Abu Khadra, founder of the private school Dar al-Hanan, March 14, 1984; see also Hasan, p. 112.

45. 'Abd al-Rahman, "Al-Awda' al-Ta'limiyyah," pp. 13–14.

46. For more details see Layla Ahmad, "Riyah al-Ummiyyah Tahubbu 'ala al-Filastiniyyin f-il-Kuwayt" [The Winds of Illiteracy Blow on the Palestinians in Kuwait], al-Watan, April 12, 1984.

47. Interview with Salih al-Kiswani, president of the Kuwait branch of the GUPS, September 27, 1986.

48. Ghabra, p. 105.

49. Iqbal Taha, "Al-Filastiniyyun f-il-Kuwayt wa-Mashakil al-Iqamat" [Palestinians in Kuwait and Residency Problems], al-Anba', March 24, 1985.

50. Freedom of the press was curtailed in July 1986 when, concomitant with the dissolution of the National Assembly, press censorship was imposed.

51. Salim Za'nun, quoted by Khawlah Nazzal in "Al-'Alaqat al-Kuwaytiyyah al-Filastiniyyah, 1" [Kuwaiti-Palestinian Relations, part 1], al-Watan, March 3, 1986.

52. 'Abd al-Rahman, "Al-Nashat al-Siyasi al-Filastini f-il-Kuwayt," p. 4.

53. Discussion with Dr. Basim Sirhan, professor of sociology, Kuwait University, February 23, 1984.

53. I was told at the PLO office in Cairo (dominated by Fateh loyalists) in February 1984 that it was unclear whether the community in Kuwait would remain loyal or go over to the rebels. A prominent Palestinian supporter of Abu Musa in Kuwait confirmed this in October 1986.

55. Both Palestinians and Kuwaitis have expressed these sentiments in interviews.

56. Khayr al-Din Abu al-Jubayn, quoted by Nazzal in "Kuwaiti-Palestinian Relations, 1" (see note 51).

57. 'Abd al-Rahman, "Al-Nashat al-Siyasi al-Filastini f-il-Kuwayt," pp. 3–4.

58. In July 1978 'Ali Yasin, director of the PLO office in Kuwait, was assas-

sinated. Although it was widely believed that Iraq was responsible, it was never proven. In June 1980, there was an unsuccessful attempt on the life of his successor, ʿAwni Battash.

59. "Report: the first annual Conference of Palestinian Popular Organizations, December 18, 1977–January 29, 1978. Kuwait. Xerox.

60. A Kalashnikov is the Russian AK-47 rifle, a symbol of the Palestinian armed struggle.

7. Workers and Women

1. Smith, *Palestine and the Palestinians*, pp. 137–138.

2. For more on the development of the labor movement in Kuwait see ʿAjami, *Al-Harakah al-ʿUmmaliyyah w-al-Niqabiyyah f-il-Kuwayt.*

3. Interview with ʿAli Qubʿah, former member of the Kuwait branch of the GUPW and an ANM labor organizer, June 7, 1984.

4. Interview with ʿAwni Battash, former general secretary of the Kuwait branch of the GUPW and current director of the Kuwait PLO office, March 7, 1984.

5. Qubʿah's and Battash's accounts are not completely complementary and in some cases are contradictory.

6. Battash interview.

7. ʿAbd al-Rahman, "Al-Ittihadat w-al-Tajammuʿat al-Shaʿbiyyah al-Filastiniyyah f-il-Kuwayt," pp. 4–5.

8. Battash interview.

9. *Mudhakkirat Husni Salih al-Khuffash*, pp. 79–80.

10. The main sources for the history of the labor movement during this period include the memoirs of Khuffash, the unpublished article of ʿAbd al-Rahman, "Al-Ittihad at w-al-Jamʿiyyat" (for which it is likely that ʿAwni Battash was interviewed), my interview with Battash, my interview with ʿAli Qubʿah, and the record of the first GUPW conference.

11. *Al-Muʾtamar al-Awwal l-il-Ittihad al-ʿAmm li-ʿUmmal Filastin*, p. 13.

12. Battash interview and interview with Palestinian historian ʿAbd al-Qadir Yasin, December 24, 1983.

13. A further problem arises over the timing of Khuffash's visit to Kuwait. Battash and ʿAbd al-Rahman mention that Khuffash came to Kuwait in February 1963 to discuss the idea of a general union. In his memoirs, Khuffash mentions a June 1964 trip to Kuwait (when he found that nothing had been done). In addition, the record of the first conference reports a July 1965 visit to Kuwait. None of the sources discusses the trips noted by the others. In fact, they may all have taken place. Both oral and written sources suffer from the possibility of error or poor memory. The written sources may be victims of an inaccurate typesetter or a careless editor.

14. *Al-Muʾtamar al-Awwal*, p. 13.

15. *Ibid.*, pp. 142–143, 150–151.

16. *Qararat al-Muʾtamar al-Thani, 1967*, pp. 121–122.

17. ʿAbd al-Rahman, p. 5.

18. Interview with ʿAbd al-Raʾuf al-ʿAlami, president of the Kuwait branch of the GUPW, February 26, 1984.

19. Interview with Jibril Zaydiyyah, member of GUPW executive committee, September 27, 1986.
20. ʿAbd al-Rahman, p. 8.
21. Zaydiyyah interview.
22. ʿAlami interview.
23. *Ibid.*
24. Interview with journalist Layla Ahmad, member of the women's committee of the Federation of Kuwaiti Workers, October 12, 1986.
25. Zaydiyyah interview.
26. Interview with Salwa Abu Khadra, former president of the Kuwait GUPWom, March 8, 1984.
27. Interview with Siham Abu Ghazalah, member of the cultural committee of the Kuwait GUPWom, March 5, 1984.
28. Abu Khadra, "Taqrir ʿan ʿAmal al-Ittihad al-ʿAmm l-il-Marʾah al-Filastiniyyah f-il-Fatrah al-Waqiʿah ma bayna 6/2/72–8/1/79."
29. Interview with Abu Khadra, March 14, 1984.
30. Abu Ghazalah interview.
31. Layla Ahmad, "The Winds of Illiteracy Blow on the Palestinians in Kuwait," *al-Watan*, April 12, 1984.
32. Basim Sirhan, "Taʿlim Fuqaraʾ al-Filastiniyyin Daribah ʿala Athriyaʾihim" [Educating the Palestinian Poor Is a Tax on the Palestinian Rich], *al-Watan*, April 19, 1984.
33. Interview with Siham al-Dabbagh, vice-president of the Kuwait branch of the GUPWom, March 5, 1984.
34. Interview with Siham al-Dabbagh, president of the Kuwait GUPWom, October 4, 1986.
35. Dabbagh interview, March 5, 1984.
36. Dabbagh interview, October 4, 1986.
37. Interview with Siham al-Sukkar, president of the Kuwait branch of the GUPWom, March 8, 1984.

8. Changing Organizational Horizons: The GUPS, GUPT and PRCS

1. Habib, *Al-Kuwayt*, p. 117.
2. This entire discussion is taken from an interview with Muhammad ʿAbd al-Qadir, a former member of the Kuwait branch of the GUPS (Progressive Bloc), March 10, 1984. Sari al-Dajani, another former member of the Kuwait branch of the GUPS (Fateh) was present for the interview.
3. ʿAbd al-Qadir interview.
4. From a discussion with Shafeeq Ghabra, whose wife, Taghreed al-Qudsi, was among the activist women, February 8, 1987.
5. Interview with Salih al-Kiswani, president of the Kuwait branch of the GUPS, September 27, 1986.
6. ʿAbd al-Rahman, "Al-Ittihadat w-al-Jamʿiyyat al-Shaʿbiyyah al-Filastiniyyah f-il-Kuwayt," p. 24.
7. "Khilafatuna maʿa Ittihad Talabat Filastin Jidhriyyah wa lakinnanah Mustaʿidduna li-Hiwar Mubashir" [Our Differences with the GUPS are Fundamental, but We Are Ready for Direct Dialogue], *al-Qabas*, November 16, 1981.
8. Interview with Dr. Ahmad al-Rabaʿi, professor of Islamic philosophy at

Kuwait University and member of the dissolved Kuwaiti National Assembly, October 11, 1986.

9. Kiswani interview.

10. Interview with Sari al-Dajani, March 1, 1984.

11. Kiswani interview.

12. Dajani interview.

13. *Ibid.*

14. *Ibid.*

15. ʿAbd al-Qadir and Kiswani interviews.

16. Kiswani and Dajani interviews.

17. Interview with Ahmad Shihab al-Din, a member of the first delegation of Palestinian teachers to go to Kuwait, October 9, 1986; and "Al-ʿAlaqat al-Kuwaytiyyah al-Filastiniyyah, 2" [Kuwaiti-Palestinian Relations, part 2], *Al-Qabas*, March 15, 1986.

18. Shihab al-Din interview.

19. "Kuwaiti-Palestinian Relations, part 2."

20. Interview with Hind al-Husayni, president of the Kuwait branch of the GUPT, April 8, 1984.

21. Asʿad ʿAbd al-Rahman, "Palestinians in Kuwait: Educational Attainments and Institutions." Unpublished paper prepared by TEAM International Engineering and Management Consultants, for the United Nations Economic Commission on Western Asia, January 1983, table 5.

22. Interview with Rafiq Qiblawi, former president of the Kuwait branch of the GUPT, March 10, 1984.

23. Qiblawi interview.

24. Husayni interview.

25. ʿAbd al-Rahman, "Palestinians in Kuwait," tables 6, 10, and 11.

26. ʿAbd al-Rahman, "Al-Ittihadat w-al-Jamʿiyyat," p. 16.

27. This section is based on two interviews with the director of the PRCS office in Kuwait, Shakib al-Ansari, on March 21 and April 4, 1984.

9. Identity Suppressed, Identity Denied

1. Aruri, *Jordan: A Study in Political Development, 1921–1965*, p. 50.

2. Konikoff, *Transjordan: An Economic Survey*, p. 17. The figure 340,000 is for 1943 and is an estimate based on World War II ration registration statistics.

3. These figures are from Vatikiotis, *Politics and the Military in Jordan: A Study of the Arab Legion, 1921–1957*, p. 9, and Gubser, *Jordan: Crossroads of Middle Eastern Events* p. 12. The variation in both refugee and population figures is endemic to the study of Palestinians. In Aruri, p. 49, the number is only 850,000. In "Palestine's Arab Population," pp. 53–54, Hagopian and Zahlan state that according to their calculations, the number of Palestinians that came to the West Bank was 363,689, making the total population of the districts of Jerusalem, Hebron, and Nablus approximately 775,000. In addition, 100,981 refugees went to Transjordan. Combined, their figures put the total Palestinian population of the West Bank and Transjordan in 1949 at 875,981. Another study, "The Summary of the Final Report on the Economic and Social Situation and

Potential of the Palestinian Arab People in the Region of Western Asia," takes a total Palestinian population in 1951 of 1.5 million and estimates that 48 percent (720,000) were in the West Bank and 7 percent (105,000) in the East Bank. This would mean a total Palestinian population in Jordan in 1951 of 825,000. The authors of the study admit, however, that the estimate of 1.5 million is not accepted by all students of Palestinian demography.

4. A Brief History of UNRWA 1950–62, UNRWA Reviews, Information Paper 1 (Beirut: UNRWA, September 1982), pp. 1–2.

5. According to the agency's classification system, a refugee was defined as one whose normal residence had been Palestine for a minimum of two years immediately before the outbreak of the conflict in 1948 and who, as a result of that conflict, lost both his home and means of livelihood. To be eligible for UNRWA assistance, one had to register with the agency, demonstrate need, and have taken refuge in the areas adjacent to 1948 Israel. Descendants of registered refugees who fulfilled the need requirement were also eligible for assistance. This definition of refugee served only to determine relief eligibility. For repatriation or compensation, according to General Assembly Resolution 194 (III) of December 11, 1948, the term "Palestine refugee" carries a less restrictive meaning.

6. Qurih, Ta῾lim al-Filastiniyyin: Al-Waqi῾ w-al-Mushkilat, pp. 33–34. Qurih discusses several of the proposed resettlement plans.

7. Report of the Commissioner General of the UNRWA for Palestine Refugees in the Near East, 1 July 1963–30 June 1964, UN Document A/5813 (New York, 1964), p. 5, paragraph 21.

8. Hadawi, Bitter Harvest, p. 174.

9. Gubser, p. 15.

10. Aruri, p. 37.

11. Gubser, p. 16.

12. See Vatikiotis.

13. Hurewitz, Middle East Politics: The Military Dimension, p. 319.

14. Ibid., p. 316.

15. Aruri, pp. 62–63.

16. Smith, Palestine and the Palestinians 1876–1983, p. 102.

17. For details of recent developments in the Jordanian army see Jureidini and McLaurin, Jordan: The Impact of Social Change on the Role of the Tribes; and Satloff, Troubles on the East Bank: Challenges to the Domestic Stability of Jordan, ch. 3.

18. Konikoff, p. 94.

19. Gubser, p. 51.

20. Fakhoury, An Analytical Study of Jordan's Balance of Payments, 1950–1958, p. 64.

21. Odeh, Economic Development of Jordan 1954–1971, pp. 37–38.

22. Mazur, Economic Growth and Development in Jordan, pp. 212–213.

23. Odeh, p. 42.

24. Shu῾aybi, Al-Kiyaniyyah al-Filastiniyyah, 1947–1977, p. 22.

25. See Smith, ch. 4, "The Decline of the Ruling Families, 1948–1967," pp. 75–111.

26. Mishal, West Bank/East Bank: The Palestinians in Jordan, 1949–1967, p. 107.

27. Smith, p. 100.

28. *Ibid.*, p. 96.

29. Mishal p. 10.

30. Interview with ʿAli Qubʿah, a Palestinian from the West Bank town of Qalqiliyyah, close to the 1948 Jordanian-Israeli armistice lines, April 28, 1984.

31. Plascov, *The Palestinian Refugees in Jordan, 1948–1957*, pp. 18–20.

32. *Ibid.*, pp. 18–20, 55.

33. Interview with Dr. Alfred Tubasi, July 10, 1984. Member of the Ramallah Municipal Council, 1962–1974; PNC member since 1964.

34. Tubasi interview.

35. For the most detailed description of political party activity during the pre-1967 period see Cohen, *Political Parties in the West Bank under the Jordanian Regime, 1949–1967*.

36. Smith, p. 103.

37. Aruri and Farsoun, "Palestinian Communities in Arab Host Countries," in Nakhleh and Zureik, eds., *The Sociology of the Palestinians*, p. 120.

38. Smith, p. 96.

39. Gubser, p. 93.

40. This was a policy stated by President Eisenhower in a June 5, 1957 message to Congress. According to it, the United States would provide economic or military assistance to any Middle Eastern country that required such assistance to maintain its national independence. The assistance would include the possible deployment of U.S. armed forces to protect the territorial integrity and independence of any country requesting aid against overt armed aggression by any nation controlled by international communism.

41. Smith, pp. 110–111.

42. This view is often expressed by Arab analysts.

43. Shuqayri, *Min al-Qimmah ila al-Hazimah*, p. 104.

44. Hawrani, *Al-Fikrah al-Siyasiyyah al-Filastiniyyah, 1964–1974*, p. 30; and Shuʿaybi, p. 104.

45. Qatarah, "ʿAlaqat al-Urdun bi-Filastin, 1921–1967,", p. 65.

46. *Al-Kitab al-Sanawi l-il-Qadiyyah al-Filastiniyyah, 1966* (1968), pp. 133–134.

47. Shuʿaybi, p. 127.

48. Gubser, p. 12.

49. Aruri and Farsoun, p. 123.

50. *Ibid.*, p. 125.

51. Gresh, *The PLO: The Struggle Within*, pp. 104–110.

52. Day, *East Bank/West Bank: Jordan and the Prospects for Peace*, pp. 61–62.

53. For a detailed discussion of the law see Hani Hawrani, "Mashruʿ Qanun al-Intikhabat al-Jadid li-Majlis al-Nuwwab," [The Plan for the New Parliamentary Election Law], *al-Urdun al-Jadid* (Spring 1986) 7: 27–50.

54. For the text of the speech by ʿUbaydat see *Journal of Palestine Studies* (Autumn 1986), 61: 214–219.

55. Interview with Salim al-Nahhas, member of the Jordanian Writers Union, August 26, 1986. Nahhas ran unsuccessfully for a seat in his hometown of Salt in the 1984 elections.

56. *Al-Ra' i al-'Amm*, November 19, 1984.

57. Interview with Nayif al-Sabti, distribution manager for *al-Watan*, October 12, 1986. Sabti attended both the 1985 and 1986 emigré conference.

58. Sabti interview.

59. *Al-Qabas*, October 10, 1986.

60. *Al-Watan*, January 19, 1985.

61. One example is Bakr al-Sadiq, once a strong 'Arafat supporter, who now describes himself as a leader of the *Jordanian* community in Kuwait.

62. *Al-Yawm al-Sabi'*, December 29, 1986.

63. Most of the following discussion of the professional unions is taken from an interview with Ibrahim Abu 'Ayyash, president of the Jordanian Engineers Union, August 27, 1986.

64. Gubser, pp. 16–17.

65. The discussion that follows is taken from an interview with Nimr Sirhan, August 27, 1986.

66. This is a common punishment for involvement in any political activities disapproved of by the regime, inside or outside Jordan. The *mukhabarat* confiscates the passport indefinitely, and without it, the person cannot leave the country. Passports may be taken away without warning upon a person's arrival in the country or at the airport as one prepares to depart. No official statistics are available; the estimate that this researcher heard most often is that as many as 40,000 Jordanians—Palestinians and Transjordanians alike—are thus "imprisoned" in Jordan.

67. Interview with 'Abd al-Jabir al-Tayyim, former president of al-Wahdat Youth Center, August 20, 1986.

68. I am indebted to Muwaffaq al-Muhadin, Jordan specialist and researcher at the Palestinian Studies Center, Damascus, for first suggesting this alternative explanation.

69. Gubser, p. 110.

10. Addressing Community Need: The FTUJ, GUPWom, and PRCS

1. *Mudhakkirat Husni Salih al-Khuffash*, p. 58. (Hereafter cited as *Khuffash Memoirs*.)

2. *Khuffash Memoirs*, pp. 59–60.

3. *Ibid.*, p. 60.

4. Interview with Musa Quwaydir, longtime Palestinian labor activist and member of the Jordanian Communist party, July 16, 1984.

5. *Khuffash Memoirs*, pp. 63–64.

6. Interview with Yusuf Hawrani, longtime labor activist associated with the Democratic Front and president of the Union of Bank Employees (1984–86), August 31, 1986.

7. Qaymari, *Al-Harakah al-'Ummaliyyah al-Niqabiyyah f-il-Urdun, 1950–1970*, pp. 9–12.

8. *Al-Jaridah al-Rasmiyyah*, no. 1134, April 16, 1953.

9. Quwaydir interview.

10. Yunis headed the union from 1954 until 1957, when he was expelled to Syria. From there he went to Cairo and then to Kuwait.

11. Hawrani, "Simmat al-Harakah al-ʿUmmaliyyah al-Urduniyyah wa-Tarkibiha al-Dakhiliyyah, 1950–1957," p. 99.

12. Hawrani interview.

13. Quwaydir interview.

14. Khurays and Safadi, Al-Harakah al-Niqabiyyah f-il-Urdun, p. 57.

15. Ibid., p. 86.

16. Jawhar, Al-Harakah al-ʿUmmaliyyah f-il-Urdun, Appendix 19, pp. 254–255.

17. Quwaydir interview.

18. Ibid.

19. Interview with Sami ʿAnabtawi, former West Bank trade union activist, July 12, 1984.

20. Khurays and Safadi, pp. 62–63.

21. Qaymari, pp. 50–51.

22. The written sources do not discuss the reasons for the dispute and those interviewed—Musa Quwaydir and Yusuf Hawrani—uniformly attribute it to personal clashes. Quwaydir also mentioned an unwillingness on the part of the GUPW to share power. Qaymari, p. 197, quotes Muhammad Jawhar, then president of the Jordanian federation, August 22, 1968, as saying that the dispute between the two unions created problems for the Jordanian federation in its relations with the IFATU. It seems likely that the Cairo-based IFATU would have taken Khuffash's side in any dispute.

23. Hawrani interview.

24. Khuffash Memoirs, p. 86.

25. Hawrani interview.

26. Quwaydir interview.

27. Khuffash Memoirs, p. 86.

28. Al-Mutamar al-Awwal l-il-Ittihad al-ʿAmm li-Ummal Filastin p. 40.

29. Qararat al-Muʾtamar al-Thani, 1967, p. 224.

30. Al-Muʾtamar al-Thalith, p. 73.

31. For full text, see Qaymari, pp. 190–194.

32. Hawrani interview.

33. Quwaydir interview.

34. The discussion that follows is taken from the Hawrani interview.

35. If the regime wants someone dismissed, the Ministry of the Interior sends a letter asking the employer to do without (yistaghna ʿan) the services of the employee. The company may refuse, or plead the employee's case, but given the economic downturn of the 1980s, an employer is unlikely to risk the wrath of the regime for someone it can replace at a lower salary.

36. See Khurays and Safadi, pp. 80–86; and Hawrani, pp. 107–108.

37. Interview with ʾIsam ʿAbd al-Hadi, a founding member of the GUPWom, May 1, 1984.

38. For short interviews with a variety of women, in which they discuss their political and social activity as well as the constraints they face, see Antonius, "Fighting on Two Fronts."

39. For a discussion of the sources and problems in studying the Palestinian women's movement see Rosemary Sayigh, "Femmes Palestiniennes en quête d'historiens," Revue d'études Palestiniennes (spring 1987), no. 23, pp. 13–34.

40. For more information on the pre-1948 period see Mogannam, *The Arab Woman and the Palestine Problem;* and *Kifah al-Mar'ah al-Filastiniyyah fi-Zill Thawratiha.*

41. Interview with 'Isam 'Abd al-Hadi, April 28, 1984.

42. Giacaman, "History of the Palestinian Women's Movement" (part 1).

43. Giacaman, "History of the Palestinian Women's Movement" (part 2).

44. *Al-Kitab al-Sanawi l-il-Qadiyah al-Filastiniyyah, 1965* (1967), p. 102.

45. *Ibid.,* pp. 103–106. Officers chosen for the new union were Zulaykha al-Shihabi, president; Wadi 'ah Khartabil and Yusra al-Barbari, vice-presidents; Zaynat 'Abd al-Majid, secretary; and Nuhayl 'Uwaydah, deputy secretary.

46. *Ibid.,* p. 107.

47. Yusuf, *Al-Waqi' al-Filastini w-al-Harakah al-Niqabiyyah,* p. 81.

48. 'Abd al-Hadi interview, May 1, 1984.

49. Giacaman (part 1).

50. Interview with Mayy Sayigh, member of the GUPWom General Secretariat, July 5, 1984.

51. Yusuf, p. 83.

52. In subsequent conferences of the GUPWom, Palestinian women in Jordan have been represented by well-known activists like 'Isam 'Abd al-Hadi, who distinguished themselves in the pre-1970 period.

53. Da 'd Muradh, "Tajribat al-Ittihad al-Nisa'i, 1974–1981" [The Experience of the Women's Union], *Al-Urdun al-Jadid* (spring 1986), 7:61.

54. *Ibid.,* p. 64.

55. *Ibid.,* pp. 63–64.

56. Interview with 'Abla Abu al-'Ulabi, former member of the GUPWom and the Women's Union in Jordan, August 30, 1986.

57. Majidah al-Masri, "Al-Azmah al-Rahinah l-il-Harakah al-Nisa'iyyah f-il-Urdun" [The Current Crisis of the Women's Movement in Jordan], *Al-Urdun al-Jadid* (spring 1986), 7:66–67.

58. Abu al-'Ulabi interview.

59. *Ibid.*

60. The concept of departicipation, the process of reducing popular involvement, is discussed in detail by N. Kasfir in "Departicipation and Political Development in Black African Politics," *Studies in Comparative International Development* (1974), 9(3):3–25.

61. 'Arafat, *Al-Sihhah w-al-Harb,* pp. 9, 11.

62. Interview with Fayizah Hammami, a PRCS founder (Jordan), May 29, 1984.

63. Interview with Fathi 'Arafat, current head of the PRCS, October 8, 1983.

64. 'Arafat, p. 31.

65. Hammami interview.

66. 'Arafat, p. 42.

67. Hammami interview.

68. *Ibid.*

69. *Ibid.*

70. For a full accounting of the losses, facility by facility, see Hamuri, "Al-Hilal al-Ahmar al-Filastini," pp. 544–545.

11. Mobilizing in Education

1. Khurays and Safadi, *Al-Harakah al-Niqabiyyah f-il-Urdun*, pp. 66, 68.
2. Interview with Muhammad al-ʿAyyash, a leading member of the UNRWA teachers' committee (Jordan), May 22, 1984.
3. Interview with Husayn al-Ajrab, a founding member of the GUPT, April 28, 1984.
4. Ajrab interview.
5. Musa, "Mulahazat Hawla Tajribat al-Ittihad al-ʿAmm l-il-Muʿallimin al-Filastiniyyin," p. 158.
6. Ajrab interview.
7. Interview with Husayn al-Ajrab, May 8, 1984.
8. Ajrab interview, April 28, 1984.
9. *Ibid.*
10. Musa, pp. 158–159.
11. As of 1970–71, the GUPT estimated that some 48,000 Palestinians served as teachers in the Middle East and North Africa: 10,000 in the occupied territories; 9,000 on the East Bank; 4,000 in Syria; 3,000 in Lebanon; 3,000 in Egypt: 7,000 in Saudi Arabia; 6,000 in Kuwait; 1,000 in the rest of the Gulf; 2,000 in Libya; and 3,000 in Algeria. As for those employed by UNRWA, the distribution was the following: 2,211 on the East Bank; 929 on the West Bank; 1,603 in Gaza; 949 in Syria; and 1,004 in Lebanon. Musa, p. 151.
12. *Ibid.*
13. ʿAyyash interview.
14. The information in the remainder of this section is taken from an interview with Muhammad al-ʿAyyash, August 20, 1986.
15. The following discussion of the student movement is taken in large part from the only publication that I have been able to find on the topic, "Al-Harakah al-Tullabiyyah al-Urduniyyah." Some of the points were confirmed in an interview with ʿAzzam al-Ahmad (Fateh), former member of the USTB and the GUPS (Iraq), May 8, 1984.
16. From a discussion with Muwaffaq al-Muhadin, a former Jordan University student activist and current Jordan specialist at the Palestinian Studies Center, Damascus, October 21, 1986.
17. Ahmad interview.
18. *Al-Harakah al-Tullabiyyah al-Filastiniyyah*, p. 20.
19. Interview with Nidal Abu Hayja, former head of the USTB, northern district (Irbid), July 5, 1984.
20. Abu Hayja interview.
21. Information in the following section, through 1977, is based on "Al-Harakah al-Tullabiyyah al-Urduniyyah," pp. 28–40.
22. A full discussion of the events leading up to the student sit-in (May 11–15, 1986), as well as how it developed, may be found in an underground publication, "Intifadat Jamiʿat al-Yarmuk."

12. Diversity in Diaspora

1. Shihadah Yusuf, *Al-Waqiʿ al-Filastini w-al-Harakah al-Niqabiyyah* [The Palestinian Reality and the Union Movement], Palestine Monographs No. 94 (Beirut: PLO Research Center, 1973), p. 68.

2. Badran and ʿAbd al-Rahim, "Waqiʿ wa-Afaq al-Munazzamat al-Jamahi-riyyah al-Filastiniyyah," p. 464.

3. A general picture of the history and development of the Palestinian popular organizations in Lebanon and Syria was gained from a series of interviews with members of the organizations conducted in Damascus, September 5–17, 1986; and Tunis, October 23–31, 1986.

A Note on Sources

Written material on the development of the Palestinian popular organizations examined in this book is scant at best. To compound the problem of the paucity of published sources, conditions of recurrent displacement, turmoil, and political repression have led to the loss, confiscation, or destruction of many materials that might have greatly enriched this study. Moreover, the contents of the single greatest repository of Palestinian historical materials, the Palestine Research Center in Beirut, were removed by the Israeli Defense Forces in the wake of their 1982 invasion of the Lebanese capital. Although the materials were finally returned to the PLO in November 1983, they were not available during the course of my fieldwork.

For these reasons, as the bibliography indicates, the single most important resource for this study was personal interviews with Palestinians who participated in the popular organizations. Their memories remain a most valuable, yet largely untapped, historical resource. The paucity of written documentary material meant that a great deal of interview time had to be spent simply putting together structural details and a very basic outline of historical developments in the institutions and the communities. More important, however, is that access to human experience requires far more than permission from a bureaucrat to use archival material. Sharing historical memory demands trust, a commodity which, given the displacement and repression of the last forty years, is often in short supply among Palestinians.

As an non-Arab American researcher I found myself in a strange position. The protection my passport afforded me vis-à-vis the countries in which I worked was equaled by the suspicion my interest in the Palestinian communities and their organizations raised. My fluency in Arabic, which after a while began to sound Palestinian even though my training was in Egypt, both increased initial concern while at the same time serving as my most effective and disarming research tool. People's curiosity quickly overcame their suspicion and generally turned to genuine and often aggressive support for me and my project once they were convinced of my honest interest in learning about their community and *qadiyyah*. Networks of contacts that I developed in one

country inevitably led to contacts in the next, largely thanks to the transnational nature of Palestinian society.

I sometimes wonder if my questions were at times too benign, if I should have pushed harder for additional information. Perhaps. But I was keenly aware of the value of the trust people had placed in me: preserving that trust was ultimately more important than asking for more sensitive information, however it might have strengthened the study. Nor did I use a tape recorder. My interview information is from handwritten notes taken during each session. Again, perhaps wrongly, I feared the use of a recorder might intimidate the interviewee.

It is worth noting here that of all the people I sought to interview, only two declined to see me. Some recounted stories that they asked not be used and I have honored their requests, although the experiences they related certainly helped shape my understanding of events. In one case, an interviewee agreed to talk only after first checking to see that no one was standing outside the window; his wife then insisted that a radio remain on throughout our conversation. Others agreed to be interviewed, but then dodged certain questions, for which one may imagine a myriad of explanations. However, it would seem that the most likely explanation of a hesitancy to share personal experiences is that in conditions where jobs, residence, children's futures, and personal security may depend upon silence, many prefer to leave certain stories untold. I am greatful to all those who, to whatever degree, chose to break the silence.

Bibliography

Arabic Sources

ʿAbd al-Rahman, Asʿ ad. "Al-Awdaʿ al-Taʿlimiyyah l-il-Jaliyah al-Filastiniyyah f-il-Kuwayt" [The Educational Conditions of Palestinians in Kuwait]. Beirut: TEAM International Consultants, 1982. Xerox.

——"Al-Ittihadat w-al-Jamʿiyyat al-Shaʿbiyyah al-Filastiniyyah f-il-Kuwayt" [The Palestinian Unions and Popular Societies in Kuwait]. N.p., n.d. Xerox.

——"Muqaddimah Awaliyyah Nahwa Tartib wa-Tathwir al-Bayt al-Filastini f-il-Kuwayt" [A Preliminary Introduction to the Organization and Awakening of the Palestinian Community in Kuwait]. N.p., n.d. Xerox.

——"Al-Nashat al-Siyasi al-Filastini f-il-Kuwayt" [Palestinian Political Activity in Kuwait]. N.p., n.d. Xerox.

Abu Kashif, ʿAbdallah. "Al-Hawiyyah al-Wataniyyah l-il-Filastiniyyin fi Misr" [The National Identity of Palestinians in Egypt]. Master's thesis, Faculty of Economics and Political Science, Cairo University, 1984.

Abu Khadra, Salwa. "Taqrir ʿan Aʿmal al-Ittihad al-ʿAmm l-il-Marʾah al-Filastiniyyah f-il-Fatrah al-Waqiʿah ma bayna 6/2/72–8/1/79" [Report on the Work of the General Union of Palestinian Women During the Period 6/2/72 Through 8/1/79]. Kuwait: GUPWom, 1979. Xerox.

Abu-Niml, Husayn. Qitaʿ Ghazzah 1948–1967: Tatawwurat Iqtisadiyyah wa-Siyasiyyah wa-Ijtimaʿiyyah wa-ʿAskariyyah [The Gaza Strip 1948–1967: Economic, Political, Social, and Military Developments]. Beirut: PLO Research Center, 1979.

ʿAjami, Muhammad Masʿud al-. Al-Harakah al-ʿUmmaliyyah w-al-Niqabiyyah f-il-Kuwayt [The Worker and Trade Union Movement in Kuwait]. Kuwait: al-Rabiʿan Publishing and Distributing Co., 1982.

ʿArafat, Fathi. Al-Sihhah w-al-Harb [Health and War]. PRCS, Central Education and Information Bureau, 1984.

Astal, ʿAwwad al-. "Al-Wadʿ al-Qanuni li-Qitaʿ Ghazzah tahta al-Idarah al-Misriyyah" [The Legal Situation in Gaza Under the Egyptian Administration]. Shuʾun Filastiniyyah (March–April 1987), 168–69: 3–27.

ʿAtiyyah, Jamal al-Din. Qanun f-il-Qitaʿ al-Ahli: Majmuʿat al-Qawanin al-Kuwaytiyyah [Law in the Public Sector: A Compendium of Kuwaiti Law]. Beirut: Dar al-Buhuth al-ʿIlmiyyah, 1969.

Badran, Nabil and ʿAdnan ʿAbd al-Rahim. "Waqiʿ wa-Afaq al-Munazzamat al-Jamahiriyyah al-Filastiniyyah" [The Reality and the Horizons of Palestinian Popular Organizations]. Shuʾun Filastiniyyah (January–February 1975), 41–42:451–467.

Bishri, Tariq al-. Al-Harakah al-Siyasiyyah fi Misr, 1945–1952 [Political Activity in Egypt, 1945–1952]. Cairo: al-Hayʾah al-Misriyyah al-ʿAmmah l-il-Kitab, 1972.

Dalil al-Jam'iyyat al-Khayriyyah f-il-Diffatayn al-Sharqiyyah w-al-Ghar-biyyah [A Guide to the Charitable Societies on the East and West Banks]. Jordan: Al-Ittihad al-'Amm l-il-Jam'iyyat al-Khayriyyah f-il-Urdun, 1980.

Al-Filastiniyyun f-il-Watan al-'Arabi: Dirasat fi Awda'ihim al-Dimughra-fiyyah w-al-Ijtima'iyyah w-al-Iqtisadiyyah w-al-Siyasiyyah [Palestinians in the Arab Homeland: Studies in their Demographic, Social, Economic, and Political Situation]. Cairo: Ma'had al-Buhuth w-al-Dirasat al-'Arabiyyah, 1978.

Habib, 'Aziz Muhammad. *Al-Kuwayt.* Cairo: Anglo-Egyptian Books, 1971.

Hadawi, Hasan al-. *Al-Jinsiyyah wa-Markaz al-Ajanib wa-Ahkamihim f-il-Qanun al-Kuwayti* [Nationality and the Place of Foreigners and Their Regulations in Kuwaiti Law]. Kuwait: Kuwait University, 1975.

Hamid, Rashid. *Muqarrarat al-Majlis al-Watani al-Filastini* [Decisions of the Palestine National Council]. Beirut: PLO Research Center, 1975.

Hamuri, Asad. "Al-Hilal al-Ahmar al-Filastini: Nazrah fi Nashatiha" [The PRCS: A Look at Its Activity]. *Shu'un Filastiniyyah* (January–February 1975), 41–42: 539–545.

Al-Harakah al-Tullabiyyah al-Filastiniyyah [The Palestinian Student Movement]. Kuwait: GUPS, 1983.

"Al-Harakah al-Tullabiyyah al-Urduniyyah" [The Jordanian Student Movement]. *Al-Thawri* (October 1981), no. 21.

Hasan, Bilal al-. *Al-Filastiniyyun f-il-Kuwayt* [The Palestinians in Kuwait]. Beirut: PLO Research Center, 1974.

Hawrani, Faysal. *Al-Fikrah al-Siyasiyyah al-Filastiniyyah, 1964–1974* [Palestinian Political Thought, 1964–1974]. Beirut: PLO Research Center, 1980.

Hawrani, Hani. "Simmat al-Harakah al-'Ummaliyyah al-Urduniyyah wa-Tarkibuha al-Dakhiliyyah, 1950–1957" [Characteristics of the Jordanian Labor Movement and Its Internal Structure, 1950–1957]. *Shu'un Filastiniyyah* (December 1979), 97:99–110.

Hindi, Khalil, Fu'ad Bawarshi, and Shihadah Musa, under the supervision of Dr. Nabil 'Ali Sha'th. *Al-Muqawimah al-Filastiniyyah w-al-Nizam al-Urduni: Dirasah Tahliliyyah li-Hajmat Aylul* [The Palestinian Resistance and the Jordanian Regime: An Analytical Study of the September Assault]. Beirut: PLO Research Center, 1971.

Husayni, Sharif al-. "Al-Mu'tamar al-Watani al-Sadis l-il-Ittihad al-'Amm li-Talabat Filastin" [The Sixth National Conference of the GUPS]. *Shu'un Filastiniyyah* (November 1971), 5:307–310.

——*Muwajahat al-Nashat al-Sahyuni 'ala al-Sa'id al-Tullabi* [Countering Zionist Activity on the Educational Front]. Facts and Figures Series No. 14. Beirut: PLO Research Center, 1968.

Hut, Bayan al-. *Al-Qiyadat w-al-Mu'assasat al-Siyasiyyah fi Filastin, 1917–1948* [Political Institutions and Leadership in Palestine, 1917–1948]. Beirut: Institute for Palestine Studies, 1981.

"Intifadat Jami'at al-Yarmuk: Al-Khamis al-Damawi, 15 Ayar 1986" [The Yarmuk University Uprising: Bloody Thursday, 15 May 1986]. Amman: The Jordanian Patriotic Political Parties and Organizations, June 1986. Xerox.

Jawhar, Muhammad. *Al-Harakah al-'Ummaliyyah f-il-Urdun* [The Labor Movement in Jordan]. Cairo: Matabi' Mu'assasat al-Ahram, n.d.

Kanafani, Ghassan. *Al-Athar al-Kamilah* [Complete Works], vol. 1: *Riwayat*

[Novels]. Beirut: Dar al-Tali'ah, 1972; vol. 2: *Qisas Qasirah* [Short Stories]. Beirut: Dar al-Tali'ah, 1973.

Khulusi, Muhammad 'Ali. *Al-Tanmiyah al-Iqtisadiyyah fi Qita' Ghazzah-Filastin, 1948–1961* [Economic Growth in the Gaza Strip–Palestine, 1948–1961]. Cairo: United Commercial Press, 1967.

Khurays, 'Ali and Salah 'Abd al-Karim al-Safadi. *Al-Harakah al-Niqabiyyah f-il-Urdun* [The Trade Union Movement in Jordan]. Jordan: n.p., n.d.

Khuri, Ilyas. *Ihsa'at Filastiniyyah* [Palestinian Statistics]. Beirut: PLO Research Center, 1974.

Khususi, Badr al-Din 'Abbas al-. *Dirasat fi Tarikh al-Kuwayt al-Ijtima'i w-al-Iqtisadi f-il-'Asr al-Hadith* [Studies in Kuwait's Economic and Social History in the Modern Period]. Kuwait: Manshurat Dhat Salasil, 1983.

Kifah al-Mar'ah al-Filastiniyyah fi-Zill Thawratiha [The Palestinian Woman's Struggle Under the Auspices of her Revolution]. Cairo: GUPWom, n.d.

Labadi, 'Abd al-'Aziz al-. "Al-Hilal al-Ahmar al-Filastini" [The PRCS]. *Shu'un Filastiniyyah* (January 1979), 86:144–150.

Al-Lajnah al-'Ulya li-Shu'un al-Muhajirin al-Filastiniyyin: A'maluha munthu Takwiniha ila Nihayat 'Am 1966 [The Higher Committee for Palestinian Immigrant Affairs: Its Work from Its Formation Until the End of 1966]. Cairo: Ministry of Social Affairs, n.d.

Al-Majlis al-Watani al-Filastini. *Nidal al-Mar'ah al-Filastiniyyah* [The Struggle of the Palestinian Woman]. Beirut: PLO Research Center, 1975.

Mudhakkirat Husni Salih al-Khuffash [The Memoirs of Husni Salih al-Khuffash]. Palestinian Books Series No. 42. Beirut: PLO Research Center, 1973.

Al-Mu'tamar al-Awwal l-il-Ittihad al-'Amm li-'Ummal Filastin [The First Conference of the GUPW, Gaza, April 14–17, 1965]. GUPW, n.p., n.d.

Al-Mu'tamar al-Thalith: Taqrir al-Amin al-'Amm, al-Qahirah 1969, al-Juz' al-Awwal: Watha'iq [The Third Conference (of the GUPW): The Report of the General Secretary, Cairo, July 1969, Part 1: Documents]. GUPW, n.p., n.d.

Musa, Shihadah. "Hawla Tajribat al-Ittihad al-'Amm li-Talabat Filastin" [On the Experience of the GUPS]. *Shu'un Filastiniyyah* (November 1971), 5:178–193.

——"Mulahazat Hawla Tajribat al-Ittihad al-'Amm l-il-Mu'allimin al-Filastiniyyin" [Observations on the Experience of the GUPT]. *Shu'un Filastiniyyah* (December 1972): 16:150–162.

Al-Nashrah al-Ihsa'iyyah al-Sanawiyyah [Annual Statistical Publication]. Jordan: Da'irat al-Ihsa' al-'Amm, selected years.

Al-Nizam al-Asasi [The PRCS Constitution]. PRCS Central Education and Information Bureau, 1981. N.p. Xerox.

Al-Nizam al-Asasi l-il-Ittihad al-'Amm l-il-Mar'ah al-Filastiniyyah [The Constitution of the GUPWom], 1974; revised 1980. N.p. Xerox.

Al-Nizam al-Asasi l-il-Ittihad al-'Amm li-Talabat Filastin [The Constitution of the GUPS]. N.d. Xerox.

Al-Nizam al-Asasi li-Rabitat al-Mar'ah al-Filastiniyyah [The Constitution of the League of Palestinian Women]. Egypt: n.d. Xerox.

Al-Nizam al-Asasi w-al-Dakhili [The Constitution and Bylaws of the GUPT]. Damascus: GUPT, 1979.

Al-Nizam al-Dakhili l-il-Ittihad al-ʿAmm li-ʿUmmal Filastin [The Constitution of the GUPW]. N.p., n.d. Xerox.

Qararat Majlis Jamiʿat al-Duwal al-ʿArabiyyah al-Khassah bi-Qadiyyat Filastin [Decisions of the Arab League Council on the Palestine Issue]. Cairo: Jamiʿat al-Duwal al-ʿArabiyyah, al-Imanah al-ʿAmmah, Idarat Shuʾun Filastin, 1961.

Qararat al-Muʾtamar al-Thani, 1967 [Decisions of the Second Conference (of the GUPW), 1967]. Cairo: GUPW, n.d.

Qatarah, ʿAdhfil al-. "ʿAlaqat al-Urdun bi-Filastin, 1921–1967" [Jordan's Relations with Palestine, 1921–1967]. Bachelor's thesis, Jordan University, 1977.

Qaymari, Muhammed Sulayman al-. *Al-Harakah al-ʿUmmaliyyah al-Niqabiyyah f-il-Urdun, 1950–1970* [The Labor and Trade Union Movement in Jordan, 1950–1970]. Amman: Jamʿiyyat ʿUmmal al-Matabiʿ al-Taʿawwuniyyah, 1982.

Qitaʿ Ghazzah [The Gaza Strip]. Cairo: UAR Ministry of Information, n.d.

Qurih, Nazih. *Taʿlim al-Filastiniyyin: Al-Waqiʿ w-al-Mushkilat* [The Education of Palestinians: The Reality and the Problems]. Beirut: PLO Research Center, 1975.

Sabah, Amal Yusif al-ʿAdhabi al-. *Al-Hijrah ila al-Kuwayt min ʿAm 1957 ila 1975* [Immigration to Kuwait from 1957 to 1975]. Kuwait: Kuwait University, 1978.

Sayigh, Mayy. *Al-Marʾah al-ʿArabiyyah w-al-Filastiniyyah* [The Arab and Palestinian Woman]. GUPWom, n.p., n.d.

Shuʿaybi, ʿIsa al-. *Al-Kiyaniyyah al-Filastiniyyah: Al-Waʿi al-Dhati w-al-Tatawwur al-Muʾassasati, 1947–1977* [Palestinian Statism: Entity Consciousness and Institutional Development]. Beirut: PLO Research Center, 1979.

Shuqayri, Ahmad al-. *Min al-Qimmah ila al-Hazimah* [From the Summit to the Defeat]. Beirut: Dar al-ʿAwdah, 1980.

"Taqrir: Al-Muʾtamar al-Sanawi al-Awwal l-il-Munazzamat al-Shaʿbiyyah al-Filastiniyyah" [Report: The First Annual Conference of Palestinian Popular Organizations]. December 18, 1977–January 29, 1978. Kuwait. Xerox.

Tarikh al-Harakah al-Tullabiyyah al-Filastiniyyah [The History of the Palestinian Student Movement]. GUPS executive committee, n.p., n.d.

ʿUmar, Mahjub. "Aylul fi Janub al-Urdun" [September in South Jordan]. *Shuʾun Filastiniyyah* (October 1977), 71:121–145.

Wathaʾiq al-Muʾtamar al-Khamis, 8–10 Junyu 1974 [Documents of the Fifth (GUPW) Conference, 8–10 June 1974]. Cairo: GUPW, n.d.

Yasin, Muwaffaq. *Taʿlim Abnaʾ Filastin f-il-Kuwayt* [The Education of Palestinian Children in Kuwait]. Beirut: PLO Planning Center, 1976.

Yusuf, Shihadah. *Al-Waqiʿ al-Filastini w-al-Harakah al-Niqabiyyah* [The Palestinian Reality and the Trade Union Movement]. Beirut: PLO Research Center, 1973.

Newspapers and Periodicals

Al-Anbaʾ. Kuwait.

Balsam. Nicosia. Monthly publication of the RCS.

Al-Jaridah al-Rasmiyyah [The Official Newspaper]. Cairo weekly.

Al-Kitab al-Sanawi l-il-Qadiyyah al-Filastiniyyah [The Palestine Year Book].
  Beirut: Institute for Palestine Studies, annual.
Al-Kuwayt al-Yawm [Kuwait Today]. Kuwait, weekly.
Al-Qabas. Kuwait.
Al-Ra'i al-'Amm. Kuwait.
Al-Urdun al-Jadid [New Jordan]. Nicosia, quarterly.
Al-Waqa'i' al-Misriyyah [Eyptian Events]. Egypt, weekly.
Al-Watan. Kuwait.
Al-Yawm al-Sabi'. Paris, weekly.
Al-Yawmiyyat al-Filastiniyyah [Palestine Diary]. Beirut: PLO Research Center.

English and French Sources

'Abd al-Nasir, Gamal. *Nasir Speaks: Basic Documents*. Tr. E. S. Farag. London:
  Morsett Press, 1972.
Abdallah, Ahmad. *The Student Movement and National Politics in Egypt*. Lon-
  don: Al-Saqi Books, 1985.
Abu Iyad with Eric Rouleau. *My Home, My Land*. New York: Times Book,
  1981.
Antonius, Soraya. "Fighting on Two Fronts: Conversations with Palestinian
  Women." *Journal of Palestine Studies* (spring 1979), 31:266–45.
Aruri, Naseer H. *Jordan: A Study in Political Development, 1921–1965*. The
  Hague: Martinus Nijhoff, 1972.
Badran, Nabil A. "The Means of Survival: Education and the Palestinian Com-
  munity, 1948–1967." *Journal of Palestine Studies* (summer 1980), 36:48–74.
Baker, Raymond. *Egypt's Uncertain Revolution Under Nasser and Sadat*. Cam-
  bridge, Mass.: Harvard University Press, 1978.
Baron, Xavier. *Les Palestiniens Un Peuple*. Paris: Le Sycomore, 1978.
Bell, J. Boyer. *The Long War: Israel and the Arabs Since 1946*. Englewood Cliffs,
  N.J.: Prentice Hall, 1969.
Bertelsen, Judy S., ed. *Nonstate Nations in International Politics: Comparative
  Systems Analyses*. New York: Praeger, 1972.
Brass, Paul. "Ethnicity and Nationality Formation." *Ethnicity* (1976), vol. 3,
  no. 3.
"Briefing Notes" for the refugee camps of al-Husayn, Irbid, Zarqa', al-Wahdat,
  al-Karamah, Marka, al-Biqa'ah, Talbiyyah, al-Suf, al-Husn, and Jarash.
  Amman: UNRWA Field Office, 1984.
Buehrig, Edward H. *The UN and the Palestine Refugees*. Bloomington: Indiana
  University Press, 1971.
Cobban, Helena. *The Palestinian Liberation Organization: People, Power and
  Politics*. New York: Cambridge University Press, 1984.
Cohen, Amnon. *Political Parties in the West Bank Under the Jordanian Re-
  gime, 1949–1967*. Ithaca: Cornell University Press, 1982.
Dajani, Maha Ahmad. *The Institutionalization of Palestinian Identity in Egypt*.
  Cairo Papers in Social Sciences Vol. 9, Monograph 3. Cairo: American Uni-
  versity in Cairo Press, 1986.
Day, Arthur R. *East Bank/West Bank: Jordan and the Prospects for Peace*. New
  York: Council on Foreign Relations, 1986.

Dodd, Peter and Halim Barakat. *River Without Bridges.* Beirut: Institute for Palestine Studies, 1969.

Elmessiri, A. M., tr. *The Palestinian Wedding: A Bilingual Anthology of Contemporary Palestinian Resistance Poetry.* Washington, D.C.: Three Continents Press, 1982.

El-Rayyes, Riad and Dunia Nahas. *Guerrillas for Palestine.* London: Croom Helm, 1976.

Fahmy, Ismail. *Negotiating for Peace in the Middle East.* Baltimore: Johns Hopkins University Press, 1983.

Fakhoury, Naʿman Issa. *An Analytical Study of Jordan's Balance of Payments, 1950–1968.* Amman: Central Bank of Jordan, 1974.

Farah, Tawfic. "Political Socialization of Palestinian Children in Kuwait." *Journal of Palestine Studies* (summer 1977) 24:90–102.

Geertz, Clifford, ed. *Old Societies and New States: The Quest for Modernity in Asia and Africa.* New York: Free Press of Glencoe, 1963.

Germani, Gino. *Marginality.* New Brunswick, N.J.: Transaction Books, 1980.

Ghabra, Shafeeq. *Palestinians in Kuwait: The Family and the Politics of Survival.* Boulder, Colo.: Westview Press, 1987.

Giacaman, Rita. "History of the Palestinian Women's Movement," in three parts. *The Jordan Times,* June 18, 19, and 20, 1984.

Gresh, Alain. *The PLO: The Struggle Within.* London: Zed Press, 1983.

Gubser, Peter. *Jordan: Crossroads of Middle Eastern Events.* Boulder, Colo.: Westview Press, 1983.

Hadawi, Sami. *Bitter Harvest: Palestine Between 1914–1967.* New York: New World Press, 1967.

Hagopian, Edward and A. B. Zahlan. "Palestine's Arab Population." *Journal of Palestine Studies* (summer 1974), 12:32–73.

Hamid, Rashid. "What Is the PLO?" *Journal of Palestine Studies* (summer 1975): 16:90–109.

Hart, Alan. *Arafat: Terrorist or Peacemaker?* London: Sidgwick and Jackson, 1984.

Hinnebusch, Raymond A. *Egyptian Politics Under Sadat: The Post-Populist Development of an Authoritarian-Modernizing State.* New York: Cambridge University Press, 1985.

Hirst, David and Irene Beeson. *Sadat.* London: Faber and Faber, 1981.

Hudson, Michael. *Arab Politics: The Search for Legitimacy.* New Haven, Conn.: Yale University Press, 1977.

Hurewitz, J. C. *The Middle East and North Africa in World Politics.* Vol. 2. New Haven, Conn.: Yale University Press, 1979.

——*Middle East Politics: The Military Dimension.* New York: Praeger, 1969.

——*The Struggle for Palestine.* New York: Schocken Books, 1976.

Ismael, Jacqueline S. *Kuwait: Social Change in Historical Perspective.* Syracuse, N.Y.: Syracuse University Press, 1982.

Issawi, Charles. *Egypt in Revolution: An Economic Analysis.* London: Oxford University Press, 1963.

Jackson, Elmore. *Middle East Mission: The Story of a Major Bid for Peace in the Time of Nasser and Ben Gurion.* New York: Norton, 1983.

Jureidini, Paul A. and William E. Hazem. *The Palestinian Movement in Politics.* Lexington, Mass.: Lexington Books, 1976.

Jureidini, Paul A. and R. D. McLaurin. *Jordan: The Impact of Social Change on the Role of the Tribes*. Washington, D.C.: Praeger and the Center for Strategic and International Studies, 1984.

Kadi, Leila. *Basic Political Documents of the Armed Palestinian Resistance Movement*. Beirut: PLO Research Center, 1969.

Kayyali, A. W. *Palestine: A Modern History*. London: Third World Center, n.d.

Kazziha, Walid W. *Palestine in the Arab Dilemma*. New York: Barnes and Noble, 1979.

——*Revolutionary Transformation in the Arab World: Habash and His Comrades from Nationalism to Marxism*. London: Charles Knight, 1975.

Kiernan, Thomas. *Arafat: The Man and the Myth*. New York: Norton, 1976.

Kerr, Malcolm H. *The Arab Cold War 1958–1967*. New York: Foreign Policy Association, 1967.

Khoury, Philip S. *Urban Notables and Arab Nationalism: The Politics of Damascus, 1860–1920*. Cambridge: Cambridge University Press, 1983.

Konikoff, A. *Transjordan: An Economic Survey*. Jerusalem: Economic Research Institute for the Jewish Agency for Palestine, 1946.

Mallakh, Ragaei el-. *Economic Development and Regional Cooperation: Kuwait*. Chicago, Ill.: University of Chicago Press, 1968.

Mazur, Michael P. *Economic Growth and Development in Jordan*. London: Croom Helm, 1979.

Mishal, Shaul. *West Bank/East Bank: The Palestinians in Jordan 1949–1967*. New Haven, Conn.: Yale University Press, 1978.

Mitchell, Richard P. *The Society of the Muslim Brothers*. London: Oxford University Press, 1969.

Mogannam, Matiel E. T. *The Arab Woman and the Palestine Problem*. Westport, Conn.: Hyperion Press, reprint edition, 1976.

Muslih, Muhammad Y. *The Origins of Palestinian Nationalism*. New York: Columbia University Press and the Institute for Palestine Studies, 1988.

Nakhleh, Khalil and Elia Zureik, eds. *The Sociology of the Palestinians*. London: Croom Helm, 1980.

Nutting, Anthony. *Nasser*. New York: Dutton, 1972.

Odeh, Hanna S. *Economic Development of Jordan 1954–1971*. Hashemite Kingdom of Jordan: Ministry of Culture and Information/Jordan Press Foundation, 1972.

Peretz, Don. "Palestinian Social Stratification: The Political Implications." *Journal of Palestine Studies* (autumn 1977), 25:48–74.

Petran, Tabitha. *Syria*. London: Ernest Bevin, 1972.

Plascov, Avi. *The Palestinian Refugees in Jordan, 1948–1957*. London: Frank Cass, 1981.

Quandt, William B., Fuad Jabber, and Ann Mosely Lesch. *The Politics of Palestinian Nationalism*. Berkeley: University of California Press, 1973.

Ro'i, Yaacov. *From Encroachment to Involvement: A Documentary Study of Soviet Policy in the Middle East, 1945–1977*. New Brunswick, N.J.: Transaction Books, 1974.

Ronen, Dov. *The Quest for Self-Determination*. New Haven, Conn.: Yale University Press, 1979.

Ross, Jeffrey A. and Ann Baker Cottrell, eds. *Mobilization of Collective Identity*. Lanham, Md.: University Press of America, 1980.

Rothschild, Joseph. *Ethnopolitics: A Conceptual Framework*. New York: Columbia University Press, 1981.
Rubenberg, Cheryl. *The Palestine Liberation Organization: Its Institutional Infrastructure*. Institute of Arab Studies Monograph Series, Palestine Studies No. 1. Belmont, Mass.: Institute of Arab Studies, 1983.
Satloff, Robert B. *Troubles on the East Bank: Challenges to the Domestic Stability of Jordan*. The Washington Papers, 123. New York: Praeger and the Center for Strategic and International Studies, 1986.
Sayigh, Anis. *Palestine and Arab Nationalism*. Palestine Essays No. 3. Beirut: PLO Research Center, 1970.
Sayigh, Rosemary. *Palestinians: From Peasants to Revolutionaries*. London: Zed Press, 1979.
Sha'th, Nabil. "High-Level Palestinian Manpower." *Journal of Palestine Studies* (winter 1972), 2:80–95.
Shoukri, Ghali. *Egypt: Portrait of a President, 1971–1981: Sadat's Road to Jerusalem*. London: Zed Press, 1981.
Smith, Pamela Ann. *Palestine and the Palestinians 1876–1983*. New York: St. Martins, 1984.
"Summary of the Final Report on the Economic and Social Situation and Potential of the Palestinian Arab People in the Region of Western Asia." Beirut: TEAM International Consultants, for the UN Economic Commission for Western Asia (ECWA), Doc. Ref. No. TEAM/F.R./SUM, 1983.
Tilly, Charles. *From Mobilization to Revolution*. Reading, Mass.: Addison Wesley, 1978.
Touval, Saadia. *The Peace Brokers: Mediators in the Arab-Israeli Conflict, 1948–1979*. Princeton, N.J.: Princeton University Press, 1982.
Turki, Fawaz. *The Disinherited: Journal of a Palestine Exile*. New York: Monthly Review Press, 1974.
UN Economic Commission for Western Asia (ECWA). "Social and Economic Conditions of Palestinian Women Inside and Outside the Occupied Territories." E/ECWA/SDHS/CONF. 4/6/Rev., Damascus, 1979.
UN General Assembly Official Records:

Session 10, Supplement 15, A/2978.
Session 11, Supplement 14, A/3212.
Session 13, Supplement 14, A/3931.
Session 14, Supplement 14, A/4213.
Session 18, Supplement 13, A/5513.
Session 19, Supplement 13, A/5813.
Session 20, Supplement 13, A/6013.
Session 21, Supplement 13, A/6313.
Session 23, Supplement 13, A/7213.
Session 24, Supplement 14, A/7614.
Session 25, Supplement 13, A/8013.
Session 27, Supplement 13, A/8713.

UNRWA. *A Brief History of UNRWA 1960–1982*. UNRWA Reviews, Information Paper 1. Beirut: UNRWA, 1982.
UNRWA. *UNRWA: A Brief History 1950–1982*. Vienna: UNRWA Headquarters, 1983.

Vatikiotis, P. J. *Politics and the Military in Jordan: A Study of the Arab Legion, 1921–1957*. New York: Praeger, 1967.

Ward, Richard, Don Peretz, and Evan M. Wilson . *The Palestine State: A Rational Approach*. Port Washington, New York: Kennikat Press, 1977.

Yehya, Karem. "The Image of the Palestinians in Egypt, 1982–1985." *Journal of Palestine Studies* (winter 1986), 16:45–63.

Interviews

With only a few exceptions, all interviews and discussions were conducted in Arabic.

Abu al-ʿAmrayn, Musa. Assistant general secretary of the Egypt branch of the GUPT. In Cairo, August 4, 1986.

Abu ʿAyyash, Ibrahim. President of the Jordanian Engineers Union. In Amman, August 27, 1986.

Abu al-ʿUlabi, ʿAblah. Former member of the Jordan branch of the GUPWom. In Amman, August 30, 1986.

Abu Ghazalah, Samirah. President of the Egypt branch of the GUPWom; founding member of the GUPWom. In Cairo, October 17 and November 28, 1983; January 12, 1984.

Abu Ghazalah, Siham. Member of the Kuwait branch of the GUPWom. In Kuwait, March 5, 1984.

Abu Hayja, Nidal. Former head of the USTB, northern district (Irbid). In Damascus, July 5, 1984.

Abu Kashif, ʿAbdallah. Palestinian student involved in extensive field research on the Palestinian community in Egypt. Numerous discussions. In Cairo, October, November, and December 1983.

Abu Khadra, Salwa. Former president of the Kuwait branch of the GUPWom and founder of the Dar al-Hanan School. In Kuwait, March 8 and 14, 1984.

Abu Khalid, Khalid. Palestinian poet and member of the Syria branch of the General Union of Palestinian Writers and Journalists. In Damascus, September 9, 1986.

Abu Mayzir, ʿAbd al-Muhsin. Official spokesman of the Palestine National Salvation Front and former member of the PSU, Cairo. In Damascus, September 11, 1986.

Abu Saʿud, Hind. Founding member of the Egypt branch of the PRCS. In Cairo, December 22, 1983.

Abu Shirar, Inʿam. Member of the General Union of Palestinian Lawyers and Jurists. In Amman, April 28, 1984.

Ahmad, ʿAzzam al-. Former member of the USTB and the Iraq branch of the GUPS. Currently PLO representative, Baghdad. In Amman, May 8, 1984.

Ahmad, Layla. Member of the women's committee of the Federation of Kuwaiti Workers. In Kuwait, October 12, 1986.

Ajrab, Husayn al-. Founding member of the GUPT. In Amman, April 28 and May 8, 1984.

Amirkani, Amal al-. PRCS Public Relations Division, Cairo. In Cairo, July 30, 1986.

Ansari, Shakib al-. Director of the PRCS office, Kuwait. In Kuwait, March 21 and April 4, 1984.

Arnus, ʿAbd al-Majid. Former director of the UNRWA office, Cairo. In Cairo, December 3, 1983.

ʿAbbas, Fuʾad Ibrahim. Member of the Egypt branch of the General Union of Palestinian Writers and Journalists and longtime resident of Egypt. In Cairo, December 20, 1983.

ʿAbd al-Hadi, Arab. Former member of the Egypt branch of the GUPWom. In Cairo, January 11, 1984.

ʿAbd al-Hadi, Fayhaʾ. Member of the Egypt branch of the GUPWom. In Cairo, July 31, 1986.

ʿAbd al-Hadi, ʿIsam. Founding member of the GUPWom. In Amman, April 28 and May 1, 1984.

ʿAbd al-Qadir, Muhammad. Former member of the Kuwait branch of the GUPS. In Kuwait, March 10, 1984.

ʿAbd al-Rahim, ʿAdnan. Director of the Palestine Studies Center, Damascus. In Damascus, July 4, 1984.

ʿAbd al-Rahman, Asʿad. Former member of the Lebanon branch of the GUPS and professor of political science, Kuwait University. Several discussions in Kuwait, February and March 1984.

ʿAbd al-Rahim, ʿAdnan. Director of the Palestinian Studies Center, Damascus. In Damascus, July 4, 1984.

ʿAlami, ʿAbd al-Raʾuf al-. President of the Kuwait branch of the GUPW. In Kuwait, February 26, 1984.

ʿAli, Faʾiqah Muhammad. Former member of the Palestinian Women's League, Alexandria. In Alexandria, February 9, 1984.

ʿAnabtawi, Marwan. Former member of the Aleppo chapter of the Syria branch of the GUPS. In Damascus, July 6, 1984.

ʿAnabtawi, Sami. Former West Bank trade union activist. In Irbid, July 12, 1984.

ʿArafat, Fathi. Founding member and current head of the PRCS. In Cairo, October 8, 1983.

ʿArafat, Inʿam. Longtime member of the Egypt branch of the PRCS. In Cairo, December 10, 1983.

ʿArafat, Khadijah. Head of Social Affairs Section of the Egypt branch of the PRCS. In Cairo, December 28, 1983.

ʿAtiyyah, ʿAdil Husayn. Secretary of the GUPW. In Cairo, September 25 and December 24, 1983.

ʿAyyash, Muhammad al-. Member of UNRWA teachers' committee, Jordan. In Amman, May 22, 1984; August 20, 1986.

ʿAzzah, Jalal al-. UNRWA public affairs officer. In Amman, July 1984.

Battash, ʿAwni. Former general secretary of the Kuwait branch of the GUPW. Current director of the PLO office, Kuwait. In Kuwait, March 7, 1984.

Bibi, Ghanim. Former member of Palestinian student group, Lebanon. Several discussions, in Cairo, October 1983.

Dabbagh, Siham al-. Vice-president of the Kuwait branch of the GUPWom. In Kuwait, March 5, 1984; October 4, 1986.

Dajani, ʿAblah al-. Member of the Egypt branch of the GUPWom. In Cairo, October 30, 1983.

Dajani, Ahmad Sidqi al-. Member of the PNC and head of the PLO Department of Education. Longtime resident of Egypt. In Cairo, November 15, 1983.

Dajani, Sari al-. Former member of the Kuwait branch of the GUPS. In Kuwait, March 1, 1984.

Fahmawi, Kamal Ahmad. Education field supervisor, UNRWA, Amman. In Amman, May 14 and 28, 1984.

Farra, Colonel 'Abdallah al-. Office of the Military Governor-General of Gaza in Cairo. In Cairo, December 1, 1983.

Ghawshih, Subhi al-. Member of the PNC and of the Kuwait branch of the General Union of Palestinian Doctors and Pharmacists. In Kuwait, March 20, 1984.

Ghunaymi, Zaynab al-. Former member of the Egypt branch of the GUPS, and member of the GUPWom administrative council. In Damascus, September 13, 1986.

Hammami, Fayizah. Founding member of the PRCS, Jordan. In Amman, April 19 and May 29, 1984.

Harb, Nadiyah. Teacher in the Center for Arabic Studies, American University in Cairo. In Cairo, October 10, 1983.

Hasan, Hanan al-. President, Society of Family Care, Amman. In Amman, May 1984.

Hawrani, Yusuf. Jordanian labor activist and president of the Union of Bank Employees, 1984–86. In Amman, August 31, 1986.

Hijazi, Sa'dallah. Palestinian businessman and longtime resident of Kuwait. In Kuwait, October 10, 1986.

Husayni, Hind al-. President of the Kuwait branch of the GUPT. In Kuwait, April 8, 1984.

Husayni, Nahidah al-. Founding member of the Egypt branch of the PRCS. In Cairo, January 10, 1984.

Kamal, Sa'id. Former member of the Palestinian student chapter in Iraq, and the GUPS, Egypt. In Cairo, November 28, 1983.

Katari, Yunis al-. Member of the PLO Department of the Occupied Homeland and the Egypt branch of the GUPW. In Cairo, November 21 and December 6, 1983.

Kawni, Naji al-. Founding member of the GUPW. In Cairo, August 4, 1986.

Kayyali, Yusra al-. Member of the Egypt branch of the GUPWom and 1948 Palestinian refugee to Egypt. In Cairo, November 19, 1983.

Kazziha, Walid. Professor of political science, American University in Cairo. In Cairo, November 22, 1983.

Khatib, Zuhayr al-. Former president of the GUPS and current member of the Kuwait branch of the General Union of Palestinian Lawyers and Jurists. In Kuwait, March 10 and 11, 1984.

Kiswani, Salih al-. President of the Kuwait branch of the GUPS. In Kuwait, September 27, 1986.

Mahmud, General 'Adil Muhammad. Egyptian military governor-general of Gaza in Cairo. In Cairo, December 1, 1983.

Mandas, Hani. Palestinian scholar and researcher at the Palestinian Studies Center, Damascus. In Damascus, July 4, 1984.

Muhadin, Muwaffaq al-. Former student activist in Jordan. Jordan specialist at the Palestinian Studies Center, Damascus. Several discussions between October 7 and 19, 1986.

Murar, Ghazi Fakhri. Former member of the Egypt branch of the GUPS. Member of the PLO Department of Education. In Cairo, January 10, 1984.

Naffaʿ, Imili. Member of the Arab Women's Society, Jordan. In Amman, July 12, 1984.

Nahhas, Salim al-. Founding member of Jordanian Writers Union. In Amman, August 26, 1986.

Nijim, Sulayman. Longtime UNRWA employee in Lebanon and Jordan. In Amman, May 17, 1984.

Qaddumi, Hani al-. First director of the Kuwaiti Bureau of Passports and Residence. In Kuwait, October 6 and 8, 1986.

Qasim, Anis. Palestinian lawyer, Kuwait. In Kuwait, February 21, 1984.

Qiblawi, Rafiq. Former president of the Kuwait branch of the GUPT. In Kuwait, March 10, 1984.

Qiddis, Raghib. Employee in the World Council of Churches' refugee relief program, Egypt. In Cairo, December 27, 1983.

Qubʿah, ʿAli. Former member of the ANM and the Kuwait branch of the GUPW. In Amman, April 28 and June 7, 1984.

Qubʿah, Ibrahim. PNC member. In Amman, several discussions, July 1984.

Qudrah, Zuhdi al-. Former member of the Egypt branch of the GUPS. In Cairo, January 22, 1984.

Quwaydir, Musa. Longtime labor activist and member of the Jordanian Communist party. In Amman, July 10 and 16, 1984.

Rabaʿi, Ahmad al-. Professor of philosophy, Kuwait University and former member of the National Assembly. In Kuwait, October 11, 1986.

Sabti, Nayif al-. Director of the circulation department, al-Watan. In Kuwait, October 12, 1986.

Saʿdi, Ibrahim. Longtime UNRWA employee in Lebanon and Jordan. Several discussions in Amman, May 1984.

Sarafi, Muyassir. Member of the Egypt branches of the PRCS and the GUPWom. In Cairo, December 28, 1983.

Sarraj, Fakhri. Director of PLO office, Cairo. In Cairo, November 21 and December 27, 1983; January 24, 1984; as well as numerous informal discussions.

Sayigh, Mayy. Member of the GUPWom's general secretariat. In Damascus, July 5, 1984.

Sharif, ʿAbd al-Fattah. Former employee of the APG and longtime resident of Egypt. In Cairo, February 15, 1984.

Sharif, Samir Muhammad. Member of the Kuwait branch of the General Union of Palestinian Engineers. In Kuwait, February 26, 1984.

Shaʿth, Maysun. Member of the Egypt branch of the GUPWom. In Cairo, December 14, 1983.

Shihab al-Din, Ahmad. Member of the first delegation of Palestinian teachers to Kuwait. In Kuwait, October 9, 1986.

Shihab al-Din, Yusra. Former member of the Egypt branch of the GUPWom. In Cairo, February 5, 1984.

Sirhan, Basim. Professor of sociology, Kuwait University. In Kuwait, February 23 and 26, 1984; October 6, 1986.

Sirhan, Nimr. Head of the Committee for the Annual Celebration of Palestinian Folklore. In Amman, August 27, 1986.

Subayh, Muhammad. Former president of the GUPS. In Cairo, November 26, 1983.

Sukkar, Siham al-. President of the Kuwait branch of the GUPWom. In Kuwait, March 8, 1984.

Tayyim, 'Abd al-Jabir al-. Former president of the Youth Center at al-Wahdat camp, Amman. In Amman, August 20, 1986.

Tayyim, 'Abd al-Salam al-. Cultural officer, PLO office, Amman. In Amman, April 1984.

Tubasi, Alfred. PNC member since 1964 and former member of the Ramallah Municipal Council (1962–1974). In Amman, July 10, 1984.

Yaghmur, 'Abd al-Khaliq. President of the Federation of Charitable Societies in Jordan. In Amman, April 27, 1984.

Yasin, 'Abd al-Qadir. Palestinian writer and historian. In Cairo, December 24, 1983; in Amman, September 4, 1986.

Zaydiyyah, Jibril. Member of the executive committee of the GUPW. In Kuwait, September 27, 1986.

First names only:

Alexandra. Former member of the Palestinian Women's League in Alexandria. In Alexandria, February 9, 1984.

Jabir. Former member of the Asyut chapter of the Egypt branch of the GUPS. In Damascus, July 5, 1984.

Index